Praise for Masterpiece in Progress

"Intensely positive and upbeat, Sean DeLaney crafts a master class in personal development. This book is about the art of AMPing up your life." – Frank Slootman, CEO, Snowflake and author of *Amp It Up*

"Operating in some of the world's most challenging environments, I've seen first-hand the importance of grit, resilience, and relentless pursuit of excellence. *Masterpiece in Progress* embodies these principles, offering a roadmap to all who aim to conquer their personal and professional battles."— Michael Burns, US Navy SEAL (Retired), Bronze Star Medal with Valor

"Sean DeLaney's *Masterpiece in Progress* is a playbook for life. Dive in, train hard, and see results." – Monica Seles, former World No. 1 Tennis Player and Nine-Time Grand Slam Champion

"Sean's insights light your path as he delves deep, providing not just inspiration but tangible tools to help you craft the life you envision. A master class in self-growth and a must read." – Scott O'Neil, CEO Merlin Entertainments and former CEO of Philadelphia 76ers and New Jersey Devils

"Sean's beautiful, thoughtful writing reminds you what's important and calls your attention to a perspective that lifts your spirit each day. Highly recommended." – Derek Sivers, author, sive.rs

"In *Masterpiece in Progress*, Sean DeLaney invites us to become the architects of our own lives. Reading it is like undergoing a transformation, and it offers sustainable inspiration. Sean's words resonate deeply, urging one to craft a life that is your masterpiece." – Dr. Tara Swart, neuroscientist, Senior Lecturer at MIT Sloan and author of the bestseller *The Source*

"Sean masterfully weaves personal stories, evidence-backed solutions, and practical application so well that you're sure to get better if you put in the work to implement all that he's teaching you. Read this book and then take action. You'll be better for it." – Ryan Hawk, Host of The Learning Leader Show, Author of *Welcome to Management* and *The Pursuit of Excellence*

Masterpiece in Progress

A Daily Guide to a Life Well Crafted

Sean DeLaney

Excelsior LLC

Excelsior LLC

ISBN 979-8-9889531-0-4 (ebook)

ISBN 979-8-9889531-1-1 (paperback)

ISBN 979-8-9889531-2-8 (hardback)

ISBN 979-8-9889531-3-5 (audiobook)

Mom and Dad, you gave me the three greatest things I could ever ask for: roots to ground me, wings to fly, and love to hold me.

Kelsey, may the threads of our love echo into eternity...

Introduction

These pages don't claim to be final truths, but merely thoughts — powerful ones that have reshaped my life. These are concepts that have left an indelible mark on me. Not all of these reflections may ring true to you; they're snippets of my journey, not certainties. Some might resonate, and a handful might strike that buried chord that unlocks you. Lean into what speaks to you. Leave behind what doesn't. Each entry is an opportunity to dig deeper, expand your view, or simply ponder. They're gateways to reimagining and creating your life. Jump in at any page and let inspiration find you where you stand. Not every page will resonate with you today, but I'm optimistic you'll find catalysts here.

Now let your journey begin.

Day 1

Your Year, Your Masterpiece

Isn't it intriguing? An entire year stretches before us: a vast canvas filled with possibility and opportunity. Think of it as a timeline of stories yet to be told.

Seize this year. Not merely the days that seem bright and promising, but also those shrouded in doubts and difficulties. Every challenge, every surprise twist, the highs, the lows — they all stitch together the intricate tapestry of your life.

But here's the beautiful part: In every stumble, there's a lesson. In every triumph, a reward. Every moment you face, no matter how trivial or monumental, carries the potential for growth. They can either point you backward, keep you stagnant, or propel you forward. The direction largely depends on how you choose to perceive and act upon each moment.

Realize that your life, with its undulating rhythms and varied experiences, is uniquely yours. A singular, unparalleled masterpiece. And deep within, you possess every tool, every ounce of resilience, and every bit of wisdom needed to navigate it.

So as you stand at the precipice of this year, remember: Your life isn't just happening to you. It's a reflection of you. A dance between circumstance and choice.

Grab the reins. Take charge. Sculpt it.

After all, why wouldn't you? It's your narrative, your legacy.

And this year? It's yet another chapter waiting to be written.

Day 2

The Most Important Conversation of Your Life

T he conversation you have with yourself is the most important conversation in your life. That's it. The entire essence of self-awareness and personal growth is contained in that one statement.

Your inner dialogue is not just a passing thought or an occasional self-reminder. It's the constant, ongoing narrative that shapes your perception, your decisions, your actions, and your entire life.

This inner conversation can be your greatest ally or your most formidable adversary.

Imagine two voices inside your head. One is empowering, positive, and encouraging. It tells you, "You've got this. You're capable. You can do it." It pushes you towards growth, boldness, dreams, and fulfillment.

The other voice is limiting, negative, and discouraging. It tells you, "You can't. You're not good enough. You'll fail." It pulls you towards fear, doubt, hesitation, and mediocrity.

Now, here's the empowering realization: You are in control of these voices. You decide which one gets the microphone.

If you let the negative voice dominate, you'll find yourself trapped in a self-fulfilling prophecy of limitation and failure. You'll hold yourself back, doubt your abilities, and sabotage your own success.

But if you let the positive voice take center stage, you unlock the potential for greatness. You empower yourself to strive, to overcome, to accomplish.

The power of this inner conversation cannot be overstated. It's not a trivial or superficial thing. It's the core of who you are and what you become.

So how do you master this dialogue? How do you make sure that the empowering voice wins?

- **It starts with awareness.** Recognize the conversation. Hear the voices. Understand the impact.

- **It continues with choice.** Decide which voice you'll listen to. Make a conscious, deliberate effort to focus on the positive, empowering narrative.

- **It requires practice.** Cultivate the empowering voice. Feed it, nurture it, strengthen it. Make it a habit, a part of who you are.

This is not a one-time thing. It's a continuous, lifelong practice. It's a commitment to yourself, your growth, and your success.

And it's worth it. Because the conversation you have with yourself doesn't just shape your day or your week or your year. It shapes your life.

The conversation is happening right now. What will you say?

Day 3

Embracing Responsibility for Your Life

Here's something I've noticed: The ones who really make changes in their lives are those who take full responsibility. They're not pointing fingers or laying blame. They're claiming their own role in their future.

You are the only one in charge of your journey. You. Nobody else. Not the weather, not luck, not other people. This isn't just a phrase or a nice idea. It's a radical way of living. It's a commitment to yourself.

Being the architect of your life means understanding that every decision, action, and thought is a brick in the building of your existence. If something's not going the way you want, who's going to fix it? Not some external force. Not luck. You.

This doesn't mean it's all about hard control. It's about conscious control: knowing what you can and cannot change and having the wisdom to know the difference. It's about embracing failure, learning from it, and adjusting the sails as you go.

And here's something you might not expect: Taking responsibility gives you more empathy and compassion for others. When you realize how hard it is to steer your own ship, you can appreciate the efforts of others doing the same. You start to see how we're all trying to navigate this complex world.

So next time you find yourself pointing at something outside of you, turn that finger around and point it back at yourself. Ask, "What can I do?"

Day 4

Sculpting Life One Day at a Time

L ife can feel overwhelming when you look at it in its entirety — the grand plans, the big dreams, and the lifelong goals. Yet, when you zoom in, life is just a series of days, a string of single moments. Every day, you wake up with a blank canvas, and you paint it with your actions, thoughts, and emotions. The patterns that emerge become the artwork of your life.

The beauty of this realization is that you don't have to wait for some monumental shift to start changing your life. You don't have to put off happiness, success, or fulfillment until "someday." It starts today. And then it continues tomorrow. And the next day. If something feels off, don't wait for a new year or a big event to change it. Start this very moment.

If something feels right, don't just celebrate it as a one-time win; make it a new standard. The little things you do every day add up to the big picture of your life. Every day is a chance to experiment, learn, and adjust. Every day is a new opportunity to live the life you want to live.

It doesn't matter if you messed up yesterday. Today is new.

You have a say in how you spend your time, who you spend it with, what you focus on, and what you ignore. These are the building blocks of your life. Put them together with care, thoughtfulness, and joy, and see what a beautiful structure you can build over time.

How you act today, how you feel, how you think — they aren't just for today. They're a small-scale version of your entire life. Make it count. Make it yours. It's your masterpiece in the making.

Day 5

Someone is Going to Accomplish Your Dreams, Why Not Make It You?

Dreams. We all have them: those wild, beautiful visions of what we could create, who we could become, or the impact we could have. They dance in our minds, inspiring us, taunting us, and daring us to make them real.

But here's a thought: Someone is going to accomplish those dreams. Someone somewhere will do those very things you're dreaming about. Why not make it you?

It's a simple question, but it cuts to the core of what holds so many of us back: doubt, fear, and the nagging voice that whispers, "*Who am I to do this?*"

Who are you not to?

Your dreams are not random. They are not accidents or indulgences. They are expressions of your unique combination of talents, passions, experiences, and desires. They are a call to action, a challenge to step into your power and create something extraordinary.

Of course, it's not easy. Dreams require work, risk, failure, and persistence. They demand that you stretch beyond your comfort zone; that you learn and grow and become more than you were before.

But here's the thing: All of that effort and struggle is what makes the dream worth pursuing. It's what shapes you into the person capable of making it real. It's what gives the dream its depth, substance, and meaning.

So don't let your dreams remain just dreams. Don't leave them for someone else to fulfill. Take them up, embrace them, and make them your own.

Start small if you need to, but start. Take one step, then another, then another.

Your dreams are waiting for you, and they are worth every ounce of effort, every drop of sweat, every tear, and every laugh.

Someone is going to accomplish those dreams.

Why not make it you?

Day 6

The Myth of Time Management

Time is one of those elusive things we all grapple with. Many of us complain about never having enough of it. We say we struggle with time management, and we read books or take courses to get better at controlling this seemingly uncontrollable force.

But here's something I've come to realize, something that may surprise you: No one ever has a time-management problem. They have a priority-management problem.

Time itself is neutral. It ticks away second by second, completely indifferent to our desires or needs. It doesn't care if we're busy or bored, fulfilled or frustrated. It simply is.

What we do with that time, however, is entirely up to us. And that's where priorities come into play.

Think about it: When we say we don't have enough time for something, what we're really saying is that it's not a priority. We make time for what matters most to us. We find a way to fit in the things we value. And the things we ignore or push aside? Well, they're simply lower on the priority list.

Here's a simple but powerful exercise I like to do. Grab a piece of paper and list all the things you wish you had more time for. Maybe it's spending quality time with family, writing that novel, learning a new skill, or volunteering for a cause you believe in.

Now, next to each item, write down the last time you did something to make that wish a reality. If it's been a while or never, ask yourself why.

Are you truly unable to find the time, or is it just not a priority?

It's a tough question, and it may sting a little. But it's also liberating because it puts you in control.

You see, managing priorities is about making conscious choices. It's about aligning your actions with your values, desires, and goals. It's about saying "yes" to what truly matters and "no" to what doesn't.

Time itself doesn't bend to our will, but we have complete control over our priorities. Once you understand that, you're not managing time; you're managing life. And that's a far more empowering perspective.

Next time you catch yourself saying, "I don't have time for that," stop and reflect. Is it really a lack of time or is it a lack of priority? The answer might change how you approach not just your days, but your entire life.

Day 7

Unlock Your Cage

The mind is a powerful tool. It's our greatest ally, but it can also be our biggest barrier. Often it is our own mind that crafts the cages we find ourselves locked in. Our prison is made solid by the bars of doubts, fears, insecurities, and limiting beliefs. These barriers are not of the world but of the mind. They're what's known in Hinduism as *mayas*, or illusions of the mind.

But here's the empowering twist: Just as our mind can build these cages, it holds the key to unlock them. Every cage formed by the mind can be dismantled by the mind.

Your mind holds the power to challenge and change its own constructs. It can question its doubts, face its fears, overcome its insecurities, and shatter its limiting beliefs. This is the beauty of the human mind: Its potential for growth and change is limitless.

Unlocking the cage is not a one-time act; it's a continuous process. It requires awareness, courage, and persistence. It's about recognizing when you're standing in your own way and then daring to step aside.

So let's begin the process of stepping aside. Here's how.

- **Recognize your cage.** Start by acknowledging the bars of your cage. Are you held back by self-doubt, fear of failure, or a need for perfection?

- **Understand your cage.** Investigate your thoughts and beliefs. Where do they come from? Are they serving you?

- **Unlock your cage.** Challenge the thoughts and beliefs that limit you.

Embrace a growth mindset. Believe in your ability to change and grow.

- **Step out of your cage.** Take action. Even small steps matter. It's the accumulation of many small steps that leads to significant change.

Remember, your mind can be your cage, but it is also the key. You have the power to unlock the cages you've built, free yourself from self-imposed limitations, and step into the vast potential of your life.

The key is in your hand. Will you use it?

Day 8

The Unbreakable Triad of Transformation

Focus + Effort + Time. It sounds so simple, doesn't it? Yet these three elements combine to form a powerful formula that leads to transformative change.

Let's start with focus. It's like a laser beam that concentrates all your energy on a single point. You can have all the dreams, ambitions, and resources in the world, but without focus, they become diluted, scattered, and ineffective. What is it that you truly want? Narrow it down. Hone in on it. Concentrate all your attention on that one thing. It's not just about seeing the goal; it's about feeling it, living it, breathing it.

Next, effort. Focus alone isn't enough. You can zero in on your goal, but without the sweat, without the work, without the persistent push, that goal remains a distant dream. Effort is the fuel that drives you forward. It's the muscle behind the dream. It's rolling up your sleeves and diving into the work even when it's hard, even when you're tired, even when you'd rather do anything else — because you know that's what it takes.

And then there's time. Real transformation doesn't happen overnight. It's a slow burn. It's a gradual build. It's the accumulation of days, weeks, months, even years of focused effort. Time is the secret ingredient that allows the magic to unfold. It's not about rushing; it's about persisting. It's about giving your dream the space and time it needs to grow.

Now combine these three together: Focus to know where you're going, effort to drive you there, and time to let it unfold. That's the unbreakable triad of transformation.

But here's the thing: It's not easy.

It's not easy to maintain focus when distractions abound. It's not easy to exert effort when you're faced with obstacles and setbacks. It's not easy to give it time when you want results now.

And yet that's where the transformation happens.

It's in the moments when you choose to focus even when you're being pulled in a hundred different directions. It's in the moments when you choose to put in the effort even when you don't feel like it. It's in the moments when you choose to be patient and give it time even when you're impatient for results.

Focus + Effort + Time. It's a triad, a trinity, a trifecta. It's unbreakable because it requires all three. One without the others falls short. All three together create transformation.

So what is it that you want to transform? What's your focus? What effort are you willing to put in? How will you give it the time it needs?

Engage with this unbreakable triad and watch how it changes you.

Day 9

You Haven't Met All of You Yet

How fascinating it is that we can live with ourselves every day, be with ourselves every moment, and yet still not fully know who we are. There's a profound truth to embrace here: You haven't met all of you yet.

Within you lie uncharted territories, untrodden paths, and hidden dimensions of self waiting to be explored. You are a labyrinth of thoughts, emotions, beliefs, and potential that has no end. This is not something to fear or shy away from. It's something to embrace with curiosity and excitement.

Imagine adopting a mindset where each new day offers a chance to meet a more profound, more courageous, and more authentic version of yourself.

It's not about changing who you are, but uncovering who you truly are. It's a continuous process of self-discovery and self-realization, of peeling back layers to reveal the essence of your being. You'll realize that you are never stuck, never stagnant, and never confined to being one thing. You are fluid, evolving, and ever-growing.

So take a moment today to meet yourself anew. Ask yourself questions that provoke thought and inspire reflection. Engage in activities that challenge and stretch you. Be willing to stand before the mirror and look beyond the surface, deep into your own eyes, recognizing the vast unknown that lies within.

Remember, you haven't met all of you yet. What a beautiful adventure awaits in getting to know yourself a little more.

Day 10

By Running, We Become Trapped

We all have things in life we don't want to face. It could be a past mistake, a difficult conversation, feelings of guilt, or perhaps a problem that seems too big to handle. It's natural to want to run away from what brings us pain or discomfort. We want to avoid the confrontation, the struggle, and the uncertainty.

But here's where the paradox lies: In running away from these challenges, we're not only avoiding the pain but also running away from our own freedom.

Freedom is not just the ability to choose or the absence of constraints. True freedom includes the capacity to face ourselves honestly, engage with our lives fully, and confront what holds us back. When we run away from our problems, we're also running away from the opportunity to grow, learn, and expand our horizons.

Think about the last time you avoided something that scared you. Maybe it was a conversation you didn't want to have or a task you felt overwhelmed by. What happened when you ran away from it? The problem didn't disappear. It likely lingered in the back of your mind, creating anxiety, stress, or a nagging sense of incompleteness.

Now imagine what might have happened if you had faced it head-on. It would have been uncomfortable, yes. It might have even been painful. But through that process, you would have learned something about yourself. You would have grown stronger. And you would have moved closer to a sense of freedom that comes from knowing you can handle life's challenges.

Confront it, and you'll dismantle the walls of the cage it built around you.

Running away from ourselves is a temporary solution to a permanent reality. We can't escape who we are or what we need to face in our lives. The more we run, the more entangled we become in a web of avoidance, fear, and limitation.

The beautiful thing is that we have the choice to stop running. We have the power to turn around and face what we've been avoiding. It takes courage, resilience, and a willingness to be vulnerable. But in doing so, we open the door to true freedom.

Remember, running away from yourself is also running away from your freedom.

Stop running.

Day 11

This Is Not a Rehearsal

We've all watched those practice matches, right? The ones where players are testing the waters, saving their energy, keeping their best strategies tucked away for the 'real' match. It's as if they're waiting for something more important, something bigger.

But imagine this: What if we've misunderstood the concept of life and started treating it like one of those practice sessions? Here's a wake-up call: This is not a rehearsal. This is not a practice match. This is the championship for all the marbles.

This is your life. It's live, and it's happening right now. You only get one shot at it. There's no second chances. This is it. Each moment you live is unique; it will never come around again in quite the same way.

What does it feel like to know you're in the middle of your one and only shot?

Now here's the million-dollar question: If life is this championship match, why do we sometimes play as if we're in a rehearsal? Why the hesitation? The apprehension?

It's time to flip the switch in our minds. Stop saving your best moves for someday. Put on those metaphorical cleats, step out onto the field, and play like there's no tomorrow — because quite frankly, the promise of tomorrow is an illusion.

Dive into opportunities, take calculated risks, love deeply, and embrace each challenge. There's no 'next time' where you can rectify the things you wish you had done differently. What are you waiting for? You're in the championship. This is it. No repeats, no rewinds. Play with all you've got.

Day 12

One Final Call

If the sands of time were to trickle down to their last ten minutes for you, and the universe granted you a final call to make, who would you dial?

It's an unsettling thought, isn't it? But within its discomfort lies a profound revelation. It's about those cherished connections, the ones that transcend time and circumstance. The ones that give our lives meaning, depth, and texture.

Don't wait for that theoretical ticking clock to appreciate these relationships. Don't wait for fate to corner you into making that call. Instead, seize the moment now.

Reach out to that person. Not because the end is near, but because life is here, vibrant and pulsing, and it's these connections that make it worth living.

Your actions today are your memories of tomorrow. Let one of those actions be a phone call that you won't regret: a call that brings warmth, connection, and perhaps even closure.

Every conversation could be a last conversation.

Make them count.

Day 13

The Five Balls We All Juggle

I once read a story that went something like this. Imagine you're juggling five balls, and each one represents an essential part of your life: work, family, health, friends, integrity. Now imagine you realize that one of those balls is made of rubber while the other four are made of glass. That rubber ball is work. If you drop it, it will bounce back. But the other four balls—family, health, friends, integrity—are delicate and fragile. If you drop one of those, the damage may be irreparable.

We often prioritize work over everything else, treating it as if it were as fragile as glass. But in reality, work is more forgiving. We can recover from career setbacks. We can find new jobs or reinvent ourselves professionally. But what about those glass balls? How often do we take for granted the people who love us, our friends who support us, our health that sustains us, and our integrity, which defines us?

Think about family. Those precious relationships need to be nurtured. They can't be put on hold or neglected without causing harm. Consider your health. How many times have you sacrificed sleep, good nutrition, or exercise for work? Your body and mind are your most valuable assets. Reflect on friends. True friendship requires time and attention. You can't expect to maintain meaningful connections if you're always too busy to reach out. And integrity? This is the core of who you are. Compromise your values, and you compromise yourself. You may not notice the cracks at first, but over time, they will grow, and the damage may be irreversible.

I'm not suggesting that work isn't essential or that ambition is a bad thing. I'm just reminding you to keep perspective. Know what bounces back and what doesn't.

Day 14

Your Guiding Habit

What if you had one practice, one ritual, one guiding habit that if done every day set a positive domino effect in motion for the rest of your tasks? A single habit that kickstarts your day, sets the tone, and propels you forward with energy, focus, and determination.

This guiding habit is different for everyone. It could be a morning run, meditation, journaling, or even something as simple as making your bed. It's about finding that one thing that resonates with you and gives you a sense of momentum.

This habit is not just about routine or discipline. It's a habit that empowers you, invigorates your spirit, and clears your mind to tackle the tasks ahead.

So how do you find this guiding habit? It's a journey of exploration. It might take some trial and error. You might need to experiment with different habits until you find the one that clicks.

Start with something you enjoy that aligns with your values and gives you a sense of accomplishment. Observe how it makes you feel. Does it energize you? Does it clear your mind? Does it set a positive tone for the rest of your day? If the answer is yes, you're on the right track.

Find what works for you and what resonates with your unique self. Once you find that habit, embrace it. Honor it. Make it a non-negotiable part of your day.

The Classroom of Anxiety

Anxiety. It's like a buzzing in your ear, a shadow lurking just out of sight, or an uninvited guest that overstays its welcome. We've all felt it. The temptation is to push it away, run from it, or let it paralyze us. But what if there's another way?

What if instead of treating anxiety as an enemy, you invited it in for a conversation?

Imagine sitting down with your anxiety not as a hostile force but as a teacher with lessons to impart. Instead of asking, "Why are you doing this to me?" ask, "What are you trying to tell me?"

When you engage with your anxiety in this way, something fascinating happens: It loses some of its power over you. By treating it as something to understand rather than something to fear, you turn the spotlight on it and take control of the narrative.

Perhaps your anxiety is signaling a boundary being crossed or a value being compromised. Maybe it's a sign you need to focus more on saving than spending.

The lessons are unique to each of us, but the process is the same: pause, engage, inquire.

It's not about making the anxiety go away. That's a battle you're unlikely to win. But you can learn to move with it, to understand its rhythms and patterns, and to find the wisdom hidden within its unsettling embrace.

So the next time you feel anxiety's grip, remember that it doesn't have to be your enemy. Invite it in, have a conversation, and see what it has to teach you.

Day 16

The Little Devil

Here it is, the little saboteur that lives in each of us, perched ever so conveniently on your shoulder. You know the one. It's that voice that speaks up just when you're about to take a leap, make a change, or push yourself out of your comfort zone. It's crafty, cunning, and always prepared with a well-crafted excuse.

This devilish presence thrives in our tired moments and our moments of doubt and fear. "Too tired." "Not now." "Maybe tomorrow." The excuses are endless, but they all serve the same purpose: to hold you back.

Next time you find yourself succumbing to the whispers of this tiny trickster, pause. Recognize it for what it is. It's not your friend. It's not your ally. It's a manifestation of your fears, doubts, and insecurities.

Then, in that very moment, call upon the image of your future self. What choice would they want you to make right now? What action would they thank you for in the years to come? How would they want you to respond to this saboteur?

Then, physically flick that pesky devil away from your shoulder. It may sound silly, but it's a powerful symbol, a conscious choice to reject the negativity and embrace the strength and tenacity of the person you are becoming.

Choose the action that propels you closer to that ideal self. Embrace the discomfort. Embrace the challenge. Embrace the growth. Don't let that little voice on your shoulder define your path. Don't let it limit your potential.

You are in control. You are powerful. You are on a path to becoming your best self. And nothing, not even the craftiest of saboteurs, can stand in your way.

Michelangelo's Insight

There's a captivating story in the marble of Michelangelo's sculpture of David, and it's not necessarily the tale of David's triumph over Goliath. Instead, the genius of Michelangelo captured something more elusive: the precise moment when David decided to face his giant adversary.

Consider the anatomy of a decision. The word *decide* itself traces its origins to the Latin *decidere*, which translates to "to cut off." To decide is to sever: to eliminate other avenues and dedicate oneself to a singular path with unwavering focus.

David stands not in post-battle glory but in contemplative determination. His gaze is neither one of triumph nor one of fear. It's a look of resolution, capturing the essence of that profound moment of decision. Michelangelo understood that it's not just the act of confronting our challenges that matters, but the conscious, deliberate choice to do so.

The true metamorphosis of our character and fate emerges from these moments of choice. Before the slingshot, before the duel, before the accolades, there is the internal pledge to act. Michelangelo's David is not just a tribute to a hero but a testament to the power of the human spirit in that split second when we commit to a path.

In David's chiseled features and determined eyes, Michelangelo offers a timeless reminder: Our greatest victories start long before the battle in the quiet, introspective moments when we decide to rise to the challenge.

Day 18

Uncovering Your Why

Your "why" in life is the driving force that gives meaning to your actions, decisions, and aspirations. It's the underlying motivation that fuels your choices and directs your path.

Uncovering your "why" is a deeply personal and often reflective process. Asking yourself probing and sometimes challenging questions can help you get to the core of your beliefs, values, and passions. Here are some questions that may guide you on this journey.

What am I passionate about? What activities, causes, or ideas make you lose track of time and feel most alive?

What are my core values? What principles guide your decisions, actions, and thoughts?

What impact do I want to make? How do you want to be remembered? To what positive change in your community or world do you want to contribute?

What am I willing to sacrifice for? What goals or ideals are you willing to put significant effort into and perhaps even endure hardship for?

What inspires me? Are there any role models, quotes, books, or philosophies that resonate with you and align with your vision for yourself?

When do I feel most authentic and fulfilled? Reflect on moments in your life when you feel most true to yourself, and consider what elements contributed to those feelings.

What are my strengths and talents? How can you align your natural abilities with your purpose?

If money and time were no obstacle, what would I do? This can help you see past societal and personal constraints to what truly motivates you.

What are the common themes in my happiest memories? Looking back on your happiest moments, what were you doing? With whom? What seems to be the recurring theme?

What frustrates or angers me about the world? Sometimes our "why" is tied to wanting to make significant changes in areas we feel deeply about.

What do I want to learn or master? Is there a skill or subject that intrigues you and aligns with your life's purpose?

How do I define success and happiness for myself? Your personal definitions of success and happiness can reveal what drives you at your core.

What fears or barriers could be holding me back? Understanding what might be preventing you from pursuing your "why" is just as critical as knowing what it is.

These questions are by no means exhaustive, and not every question will resonate with everyone. It's a process that might take time, reflection, and perhaps even guidance from a coach or mentor who can facilitate this exploration. But the effort to uncover your "why" could be a transformative experience that aligns your life with purpose and intention.

Day 19

Don't Let Your Mind Limit You

Discomfort. We've all felt it. Whether it's a new project at work, a strenuous physical workout, or a difficult conversation, it's that nagging feeling that starts whispering, "Stop! This is too hard. Let's go back to what's comfortable."

But here's an intriguing truth: Often our mind gives up before our body or our abilities. The mind loves comfort. It loves the familiar and the easy. So when we step into new territory, it's the first to raise a white flag. Your body is far more resilient than the mind often gives it credit for.

Think about those times you've pushed through a workout and found a reserve of strength you didn't know you had, or when you've immersed yourself in a challenging project and found innovative solutions to problems you initially thought were insurmountable.

It's not that the task changed. It's that you silenced the mind's initial resistance and tapped into your real capabilities.

This mental surrender to discomfort is a defense mechanism. It's a way of protecting ourselves from potential failure or pain. But it's also a barrier. It's what keeps us from growing, learning, and achieving more.

So what's the solution?

It's about practice. The more you stretch your comfort zone, the more resilient your mind becomes. The more you recognize that you can handle discomfort, the less likely your mind is to panic at the first sign of it.

Next time you feel discomfort, take a moment to pause. Is this your mind or your body talking? Are you truly at your limit, or is this a chance to push through and discover a new level of capability?

Remember, discomfort is often growth in disguise. Don't let your mind rob you of that opportunity.

Day 20

Owning Your Authenticity

Authenticity. It's a word that's often tossed around, but what does it truly mean? Is it a license to expose everything about ourselves without consideration for others? No, it's more nuanced than that.

Being authentic means embracing what makes you unique, but it also means recognizing that your actions, your words, and your being all affect those around you. We're all interwoven into this vast tapestry of human existence, where the push and pull of individual threads can be felt across the whole.

Authenticity is not about selfishly proclaiming your individual identity but about integrating your unique self into a wider community with grace. Our differences don't divide us; they make us richer.

Being authentic isn't just about you; it's about how you fit into the world, how you bring value to others, and how you contribute to the shared humanity that binds us all.

Walking the tightrope of authenticity is a delicate balance. On one side is the temptation to lose oneself in the collective, becoming a mere echo of others. On the other side is the risk of isolating oneself heedless of the impact on those around us.

The mindful path lies in the middle, where we embrace our unique selves while recognizing our responsibility to others. Your authenticity is a gift not just to you but to the world. Cherish it, cultivate it, and share it with a compassionate heart. That's how we build bridges, foster understanding, and create a world where everyone has a space to shine.

Day 21

Regret As Your Guide

Pause for a moment and truly consider this: If life in all its unpredictable glory ceased to be yours tomorrow, what would be your greatest regret? What experiences did you miss? What words were left unsaid? What opportunities were never seized?

That regret is your compass. It's your cue to action. It's your soul whispering to you, urging you to not let another day slip by unfulfilled.

This isn't a gloomy reminder of mortality but rather a clarion call to vitality.

It's about acknowledging those unfulfilled dreams and unspoken words and taking steps today to ensure they become reality, not just possibilities. Transform the seed of regret into the bloom of fulfillment.

Today — this moment — is all we truly possess. Let's not squander it living someone else's life.

Let's not allow the noise of others' opinions to drown out our inner voice. Have the courage to follow your heart and intuition.

Make sure that when your tomorrow comes, you're not laden with regrets but instead filled with the satisfaction of a life fully lived.

Day 22

The Five Pillars of Purpose

P urpose. It's a word that can feel heavy — even intimidating — because it's wrapped up in big existential questions. But if you distill it down to its core, it's simple and beautifully human.

Purpose is a direction. It's the path you carve in the world through the accumulation of your choices, passions, and values. It's a personal North Star that guides your decisions and shapes your actions.

Purpose is what infuses your days with meaning. It's what gets you up in the morning, fuels your drive, and sustains your energy. It's what makes the tough times bearable and the good times even more joyous.

But purpose is also fluid, evolving with you as you journey through life. It's okay if your purpose shifts, grows, or changes entirely as you learn, grow, and change too.

So don't put pressure on yourself to find your purpose as if it's a treasure hidden away. Instead, cultivate your purpose by pursuing what matters to you, what sparks joy and passion in you, and what aligns with your values.

Purpose is not about a destination; it's about direction. It's not about finding; it's about creating. It's not an answer to life's big questions; it's a guide for your daily actions. So lean into what lights you up, and let that guide your way.

I've found that purpose can often be found at the intersection of five key elements.

Let's explore them.

What brings you the deepest joy? What lights you up? What activities or ideas make you lose track of time? These joyful experiences are clues to your purpose. They reveal what resonates with your core.

Your talents. Your unique skills and abilities are not random; they're part of your purpose. Your talents are tools that enable you to accomplish something significant in the world.

It must positively impact others. Purpose is not just about personal satisfaction. It's about contributing to something larger than yourself. What can you do that will make a positive difference in others' lives?

It's in alignment with your deepest values. Your values are the principles that guide your life. When your actions align with your values, you're living with integrity, and this alignment fuels a sense of purpose.

It is in service to something greater than yourself. Purpose often involves a sense of mission or calling that goes beyond personal gain. It connects you to a larger community or even to humanity as a whole.

Each of these elements is like a piece of a puzzle. Alone, they may not reveal much, but together, they form a picture of what your purpose might be.

Remember, purpose is not something you have; it's something you discover and cultivate. It's a guiding light that can illuminate your path, infuse your life with meaning, and propel you toward your true calling.

Day 23

The Only One Who Can Stop You

B ob Turco was more than just my lacrosse coach. He was a mentor and a guide, and his influence reached far beyond the field. He had this ability to see through you into the core of your potential.

One day, he looked me in the eye and said something that has stuck with me ever since: "The only person who can stop Sean DeLaney is Sean DeLaney."

It wasn't until years later that the profound depth of those words truly sank in. We all have dreams, ambitions, and goals; we also have fears, doubts, and insecurities. These internal barriers often feel insurmountable. They loom large, casting shadows on our path, making us question our abilities and worth. But here's the thing: those barriers are self-made. They're constructs of our own mind. And if we created them, we can dismantle them.

That's the insight I gained from Coach Turco's words. The only person who can hold me back is me. The only person who can unleash my potential is also me. It isn't about external factors, opponents, circumstances, or luck. It is about self-belief, self-awareness, and self-empowerment.

We all have the ability to liberate ourselves from the shackles of self-doubt and move past the fears that have kept us stuck. Realize that your greatest obstacle and your greatest ally is the same person: yourself.

Day 24

The Art of Unlearning

There's something alluring about the collecting of insights, skills, and wisdom like precious gems. But as time marches on, I've come to realize that unlearning can be just as vital as learning.

Unlearning isn't a process of forgetting but a deliberate act of letting go of outdated beliefs, misconceptions, or habits that no longer resonate with who we are or who we're becoming.

Unlearning is about recognizing that sometimes the things we cling to can become chains rather than wings.

We're often so fixated on accumulating, adding, or enhancing that we overlook the beauty of decluttering, simplifying, and releasing.

There's an extraordinary kind of wisdom and courage in admitting that some things we've been taught, some principles we've clung to, are in fact shackles hindering our growth.

Our lives are as much about the erasing as they are about the writing.

So as we grow older, let's honor this process of unlearning, surrendering, and allowing old constructs to fall away.

It's in these spaces that our authentic selves flourish, unburdened and unchained.

Day 25

Turning Ruins into New Beginnings

We all find ourselves in situations where it feels like we're lying in the rubble of our own creation, surrounded by the ruins of failed endeavors or broken dreams. It's an image that's too easy to dwell on.

But remember, life is never about the rubble. It's about the reconstruction.

These moments, as painful and challenging as they may be, are not endpoints; they are the beginning of something new.

Your next great adventure, project, or personal transformation is waiting to be born from these very ruins.

Let go of the rubble. Stop staring at it. Stop identifying with it.

You are not the ruins. You are the rebuilder. Every day is a chance to start anew, to create something beautiful from the broken pieces.

Embrace the reconstruction.

See the potential in the debris, and realize that every moment is an opportunity to shape the future you desire. The same energy and passion that you once put into lamenting what went wrong can be refocused on creating something new and exciting.

Your story isn't over. It's just waiting for you to write the next chapter— and you have all the tools you need. Now go build.

Day 26

Head Down, Heart Lost

L ast night, I found myself at a dinner scene that was all too familiar and yet increasingly disconcerting: people with their heads down, shrouded in the phosphorescent glow of their devices, completely oblivious to the living, breathing person who sat across from them. An entire ecosystem of emotion, connection, and human interaction was being eclipsed by the pull of the digital world.

Every tap and swipe seemed to be another stitch in the fabric of their disconnection.

The more their eyes were fixed on their screens, the less they saw of the people they presumably care about, who were just an arm's reach away.

This is not an indictment of technology but a call to wake up from the sleepwalking state we so often find ourselves in.

It is an invitation to be present, to cherish the fleeting, irreplaceable moments of authentic human connection.

It's a reminder that life is not lived in pixels and data but in smiles and laughter, in shared stories and communal silence, in the love and warmth we give and receive from the very people we choose to break bread with.

So how about today, instead of looking down, we look up and connect?

Day 27

Playing the Long Game

There's an alluring trap most of us fall into: the siren call of instant reward. It's human to crave that immediate hit of dopamine, the rush that comes from short-term pleasures. But let's pull back the curtain on the true magic of life: it unfolds not in the impulsive moments but in the dedicated stretches of patience and perseverance. It's a long game.

Ever watched a seasoned surfer? Surfers know something that many of us often forget in our fast-paced lives. They watch, they wait, and they choose their waves wisely based on a longer game. Imagine if they paddled for every ripple or fleeting splash. They'd wear themselves out and miss the truly magnificent waves — the ones that offer a ride of a lifetime.

Similarly, in life the landscape is dotted with shiny objects, distractions, and momentary attractions. If we lunge at every new thing, we're drained before the real opportunities arise. It's those deep, meaningful pursuits — the ones we waited and prepared for — that bring genuine fulfillment. The little distractions? They're like the small waves that come and go. It's the big ones, the ones we've patiently observed and chosen, that provide the richest experiences.

So next time you're enticed by the newest or loudest thing around, pause and consider: Is this a fleeting ripple or the wave of a lifetime? Because by waiting, observing, and choosing intentionally, you align with the opportunities that resonate most deeply with your soul's purpose.

Play the long game.

Day 28

It's All a Story

Did they ever mention this in school? Among the myriad of tales — from sweeping epics to romance novels — the most compelling story is the one you're weaving every day. It's the story of your life, and you're writing it now.

Each day is a new page. Each decision, a sentence. Now here's where it gets really interesting: If the current narrative feels stifling or negative, you're entirely in charge of changing the storyline.

Caught in a torrential downpour in the middle of your story? Encountering villains at every turn? Well, here's a writer's trick: If the story you're narrating is dominated by thoughts like "This is unbearable," consider a rewrite. Perhaps it's time to shift the narrative to "This is the chapter where I face my dragons and emerge stronger."

What if the challenges, heartbreaks, and hiccups aren't setbacks but rather the very cruxes of your story where your character grows the most? Each obstacle can be the stepping stone to your next big arc.

Question the stories you tell yourself, especially during challenging phases. Are they limiting or empowering? Stories have the power to shape perceptions. If you're the hero of your story (and you most certainly are), why not frame every challenge as an adventure? A point of growth? Craft narratives that empower you and remind yourself of your strength, tenacity, and the endless possibilities that lie ahead.

Life is less about the events that happen to us and more about the stories we tell about those events. So next time you pick up that metaphorical pen, write a tale that uplifts, transforms, and champions you. You're the author of your own epic journey.

Day 29

A Guide from the Future

Picture yourself five years from now. Imagine where you'll be, what you'll be doing, and who you'll be with. Now ask yourself what you'll wish you had done sooner.

It's a jarring question, isn't it? It's filled with insight into your deepest desires and unmet yearnings. It reveals the path not yet taken, the courage not yet summoned, the dreams so far left unexplored. It's a mirror reflecting what could be, what might be, and what should be.

But rather than wallowing in what could have been or sinking into the mire of missed opportunities, let's make this insight a call to action.

That dream project you've been pondering? Launch it.

That truth you've been longing to speak? Say it.

That leap of faith you've been hesitating to take? Jump.

These aren't just whispers of future regret. They are signposts pointing the way to a richer existence. They are markers leading you to a more meaningful journey.

The future is being crafted in the current moment. It's an accumulation of 'todays,' each filled with the potential to shape your destiny, mold your fate, and influence your legacy.

Let foresight be your guide. Don't wait for regret to become your prompt. Don't let hesitation become your anchor. Don't allow indecision to become your chain. Act today.

Day 30

Embracing Tough Conversations

In the vastness of human interaction, few things seem as daunting as tough conversations. We avoid them, sometimes choosing superficial peace over confronting uncomfortable truths. Yet the very discussions so charged with potential conflict can lead to profound personal growth and deeper connections.

Consider tough conversations as gateways. What lies beyond them? A stronger self, more authentic relationships, and clarified values. But to reach that destination, one must pass through the gate. This journey is not about winning or being right, but about understanding and growth.

Evading challenging dialogues can bring temporary relief, but it leaves behind lingering shadows of unresolved issues. These shadows grow darker over time, often resulting in bigger conflicts. However, when approached with an open heart and mind, these very conversations can illuminate misunderstandings, align expectations, and forge tighter bonds.

While the process might feel grueling, the outcome often justifies the effort. After the storm, there's clarity. After the fire, there's rejuvenation. The conversation itself is a crucible where raw emotions and thoughts are refined into clearer perspectives.

Here's a proposition: The next time you're tempted to avoid a tough conversation, view it as an opportunity. Remember, it's a chance to grow, learn, and strengthen your bonds. Equip yourself with empathy, patience, and the willingness to listen, and watch how these conversations transform you.

Day 31

The Symbiotic Dance

Too often we see ourselves as passive observers, waiting for the universe to bestow kindness, understanding, and love.

But here's the profound truth: We're not just part of the audience; we're dancers in this grand performance.

If you desire kindness, be kind.

If you crave understanding, extend it willingly to others.

Paint your every action with the things you want, and you'll find these same energies reflected to you. This is not mere philosophy; it's the foundational principle of life.

The world isn't something happening to you; it's something happening with you. You are an active, contributing member of this beautiful dance, and every step you take influences the entire performance.

In offering the energies you wish to receive to the world, you become a vibrant part of the universal exchange.

The more you give, the more you receive, because in this dance, you and the world are not separate entities but partners, shaping each other with every beat.

So be generous with the qualities you seek.

Embrace your role in this cosmic exchange and realize you're not just receiving from the world but actively shaping it even as it shapes you. It's a beautiful, symbiotic dance, and it's one you've been part of all along.

Day 32

Seeking Permanent Peace

W e've all encountered bits of wisdom, those unexpected flashes of insight that resonate so deeply they become embedded in our psyche. For me, it was the simple but profound axiom: "Always study to secure your permanent peace."

On the surface, the world today is fixated on the hustle and the relentless pursuit of more. More achievements, more possessions, more of everything. In the middle of this frenzied chase, we sometimes find ourselves trapped in a spiral where every achievement only leads to more desires and more stress.

The phrase "Always study to secure your permanent peace" is a profound reminder that our primary focus should be on seeking inner tranquility. It's not about avoiding ambition or aspirations; it's about aligning them with what brings genuine peace to our hearts.

I've come to realize that this 'study' isn't just about books or formal education. It's a lifelong process of discovery, understanding, and deliberate choices. It's about questioning. "Will this choice add to my peace or detract from it?" Sometimes it might mean walking away from seemingly golden opportunities because they don't align with our core desire for tranquility.

Remember: Not every good opportunity is a good opportunity. Sometimes what looks tempting might be the very thing that pulls you away from your quest for permanent peace.

By adopting this mindset, we can declutter, prioritize, and shift our perspective. It allows us to see the difference between what is genuinely fulfilling and what is merely distracting.

In a world that often measures success by external yardsticks, let's dare to be different. Let's measure our success by the peace we feel when we lie down at night, the contentment in our hearts, and the tranquility on the inside.

To secure your permanent peace is to live deliberately, choose wisely, and align actions with the heart's truest desires. It's the guide I recommend for all of us navigating through the beautiful maze called life.

Day 33

The Quiet Whisper of Dreams

D reams. They start as gentle whispers, tender calls to action that resonate deep within us, hinting at the life we yearn to lead.

Yet they're easily drowned out by the cacophony of our day-to-day lives. Ignoring them, however, decays our soul.

Listening to these subtle voices requires more than just hearing. It requires a deep kind of listening that tunes out the noise, distractions, and endless clamor of our busy lives.

This listening isn't passive; it's an active engagement with the very core of who we are.

So how do we do it? How do we tune into the soft whispers of our dreams?

- **Create space.** In our rush, we often forget to pause, to breathe, to be still. Yet it's in the stillness that we find clarity. Carve out time in your day for reflection, for contemplation, for simply being. It doesn't have to be much; even a few minutes can make a difference. Sit quietly, breathe deeply, and listen.

- **Be present.** Mindfulness isn't just a buzzword; it's a way of being. By being fully present in the moment and focusing our attention on the here and now, we open ourselves up to the subtler signals that guide us. We allow ourselves to connect with our inner wisdom.

- **Trust yourself.** Sometimes the whispers of our dreams may seem outrageous, unattainable, or even silly. Trust them anyway. Believe in them. They're a part of you, and they know something important.

- **Act on your insights.** Listening is just the first step. It's the beginning of a journey, not the end. Take those whispers, those dreams, and turn them into something tangible. They're pointing you in a direction. Follow it.

- **Keep listening**. The whispers of our dreams are not one-off messages. They continue to guide us, to evolve with us, to shape our journey. Keep listening, and they'll keep speaking.

Dreams are not just flights of fancy. They're profound insights, deep longings, and unfulfilled potential. They're the blueprints to a life that resonates with who we truly are and who we could be if we dare to listen.

Our dreams are not loud. They're not brash. They don't shout at us or demand our attention. They whisper gently, patiently, and persistently. It's up to us to tune in, hear what they're saying, and let them guide us.

The whispers may be soft, but their message is powerful. Don't miss out on what they have to say. Listen closely, and they just may change your life.

Day 34

The Warning Signs of Misalignment

We all have moments where we catch ourselves blaming others, complaining about circumstances, or getting defensive. I've learned to see these as warning signs, signals that I'm not aligned with my best self.

Why? Because my best self knows that I have control over my reactions, my attitude, and my choices. My best self knows that complaining and blaming are fruitless, and getting defensive often means I'm not open to growth or change.

So when I find myself slipping into those patterns, I try to stop, breathe, and ask myself: "What's really going on here?" The answer usually lies in fear, insecurity, or lack of taking responsibility. Acknowledging that is the first step towards realignment.

Blaming someone else? That's often a refusal to take responsibility for my part in a situation. Complaining about something is often a way to avoid taking action to change it. Getting defensive may be a sign that I'm protecting a fragile ego, unwilling to admit that I might be wrong.

Recognizing these patterns is not about beating myself up; it's about understanding myself better. It's a sign that I need to take a step back and reevaluate. If I'm not being my best self, I ask myself, "What would my best self do in this situation?" The answer is usually clear, and it guides me back on track.

Life is too short to spend it blaming, complaining, or getting defensive. These are not the paths to happiness or success. They're distractions, barriers, and roadblocks.

Day 35

Discovering Your Non-Negotiables

L ife has a way of testing us. Sometimes it's a gentle nudge; other times it's a storm that shakes us to our core. That's why understanding our non-negotiables is so crucial. They are our anchor and our lighthouse, guiding us through the roughest seas.

Think of these non-negotiables as the principles that stand firm even when the tides of popular opinion shift or the winds of circumstance blow with ferocity. They are your bedrock, your roots — elements of your character that you refuse to barter away for short-term gains.

Your non-negotiables are your personal constitution. They define the essence of who you are and what you stand for. They're your roots, holding you steady when the world is shifting around you.

They're the boundaries you will not cross no matter the pressure or the temptation.

Here's how you can discern and embrace your non-negotiables.

- **Identify your principles.** What principles do you live by no matter what? Your values are the building blocks of your non-negotiables.

- **Reflect on past decisions.** Look at the choices you've made, especially the hard ones. What lines did you refuse to cross? These are clues to your non-negotiables.

- **Visualize different scenarios.** Imagine situations that would challenge your integrity. What would you absolutely refuse to do? The answers will help you identify your non-negotiables.

- **Write them down.** Put your non-negotiables in writing. Make them tangible. They're not just ideas; they're commitments.

- **Live them every day.** Your non-negotiables aren't just for the stormy times; they're your daily guide. Practice them, reinforce them, and make them a part of who you are.

- **Guard them vigilantly.** Once you've identified your non-negotiables, don't let them erode. Stand firm. Defend them against the pressures that will inevitably come.

Understanding your non-negotiables is more than an intellectual exercise. It's a deep, personal exploration that can guide you through life's most challenging moments.

Take the time to explore your non-negotiables. Embrace them, live them, and let them guide you. They will keep you true to yourself no matter the storms you face. They're the foundation upon which you build a life of integrity and meaning.

They're the unshakeable core that defines you.

Day 36

Enrich Every Moment

The highest form of living is when every moment that unfolds before you is enriched and elevated by your presence.

Marinate on that today. It's a beautiful goal to work towards.

To truly live at the summit of life, dedicate yourself to serving the present moment with unwavering devotion. Pour your total being into the here and now, infusing each second with presence, energy, and mindfulness.

Let the earth feel your gravity.

Embrace the privilege of shaping each moment with your light, and watch how your life becomes an exquisite masterpiece of your own making.

Live not as a solitary entity but as part of a beautiful interconnected web of life where our actions resonate far beyond ourselves. And most of all, this is about the profound realization that every moment is a precious opportunity to create something meaningful, to make a difference, to leave a mark.

That's not just living; that's living at its highest form. Go enrich life.

Day 37

Shaping Who We Become

Here's an illuminating thought: We hold the immense power to shape the person we become. Have you ever really thought about that?

The most profound and transformative journey we can embark upon is the one within ourselves.

We hold the pen, the brush, and the palette to create the masterpiece of our existence. You're the artist of your life. Your thoughts, your actions, your dreams — these are the colors you use to paint your world.

Where to begin? It all begins with a captivating vision — a vivid image of the person we wish to become. What's your vision? What's the ultimate version of yourself that you aspire to be?

This vision becomes our guiding star lighting the path toward our aspirations. It's the beacon in the night, the guide that leads us forward.

But vision alone isn't enough. As we align ourselves with the version of ourselves we desire, we must also heed the call to take courageous and deliberate actions in the present moment.

It's about action, intention, and movement. It's about bridging the gap between where we are and where we aspire to be.

Here's how to do it.

- Ask yourself, "What is the ultimate version of myself I want to be someday?" Get clear on your vision. Paint a vivid picture in your mind. Feel it, see it, taste it.

- "What is the action I could take right now that the ultimate version of myself would do?" What's the next step? What's the immediate action you can take to move toward your vision?

- Take the action that the future version of yourself would take. Do it now. Take the step. Move forward.

Keep doing that, and you become that person! Repeat these steps. Keep moving, keep growing, keep evolving.

This is not a passive process. It's a conscious commitment. It's an intentional choice. It's the art of self-envisioning and the craft of self-creation.

Isn't that an extraordinary way to live?

Your life is your masterpiece. Your vision is your guiding star. Your actions are your brush strokes.

Now go paint your world. Create your masterpiece. Become the person you aspire to be.

Isn't that something worth striving for?

Day 38

Effort Transcends

We live in a world that loves to point fingers. It's the economy, it's our boss, it's the lack of opportunity, it's everything and everyone but ourselves. We blame the lack of resources or other people for holding us back in life. But what if the real obstacle is not the absence of resources but the lack of effort? Effort is the noble currency that measures the true essence of a person's character and potential.

It's easy to overlook effort in a world obsessed with talent and circumstance. But talent alone won't get you very far. Circumstances can change in an instant. Effort, though, is something that's entirely within your control.

Effort transcends mere talent or circumstance; it is the driving force that propels individuals towards their zenith. In the crucible of effort, dreams are forged into reality and aspirations become attainable milestones. Effort is the silent architect of success, shaping destinies and overcoming obstacles that have knocked others down.

Effort is the little voice inside you that says "Keep going" when everything else is telling you to give up. It's the fire in your belly that refuses to be extinguished. Effort is the cornerstone of success and the pillar on which empires of achievement are built.

Don't let the lack of resources hold you back. Don't blame others for your failures. Look within yourself and ask, "Am I really giving it my all? Am I really putting in the effort?" Effort is the key. And it's right there inside you waiting to be unleashed.

Day 39

We Are Never Done

Growth. It's an intriguing concept, isn't it? We strive for it, work towards it, and yet it always seems just slightly out of reach. But that's the magic of growth and what makes it so endlessly fascinating. We think we've arrived or reached the pinnacle only to discover that there's always more to learn, more to explore, more to become.

Reaching "infinity" in personal growth is an illusion because there is no final destination. Instead it's an ongoing journey filled with surprises and revelations that lead us down new paths and into new understandings.

When we embrace this journey, every day becomes an opportunity for progress. We discover that the things we thought we knew were just the tip of the iceberg. Our understanding deepens, our skills sharpen, and our perspective widens.

Even when we think we've "made it" and reached some arbitrary point of perfection, there's always room to grow. It's not about reaching a finite goal but about embracing the endless possibilities for self-discovery and transformation.

So let's not be discouraged if we think we haven't reached "infinity." Let's celebrate the progress we've made no matter how big or small. Let's continue to strive, continue to learn, and continue to grow. Because in the end, it's not about reaching a destination but about embracing the beautiful, messy, exhilarating journey of becoming.

Day 40

You Never Know What Bad Luck Can Save You From

Life has an interesting way of presenting us with surprises, doesn't it? Sometimes what appears to be bad luck at first glance might be something quite different.

Too often our immediate judgments are narrow. We tend to label events as "good" or "bad" based on our immediate reactions and limited perspectives. But we rarely have the full picture in the present moment.

It's tempting to wallow in self-pity when things don't go our way. But consider holding off on making that judgment. Embrace a broader, longer-term perspective. Recognize that today's bad luck might be tomorrow's blessing in disguise.

This doesn't mean we should become passive or fatalistic. On the contrary, it's about maintaining an open and curious mindset, recognizing that life's twists and turns are often beyond our control and understanding.

So the next time you find yourself facing what seems like bad luck, take a deep breath and remember that you never really know what worse luck it might be saving you from.

Who knows? What seems like a setback today may turn out to be the very thing that sets you on a more meaningful path tomorrow.

Day 41

Impossible or Inconvenient?

How many times have you heard someone say, "That's impossible," or "There's no way to do that"? I've heard it plenty, and sometimes I've even said it myself.

But you know what? Often, these statements aren't really about impossibility; they're about inconvenience. When we label something as impossible, we're sometimes shielding ourselves from a truth we don't want to face.

Maybe it's something that requires hard work, challenges a belief we hold, or is just downright uncomfortable. We label it as "impossible" because that's easier than facing the inconvenient reality.

But here's a thought: What if we stopped doing that? What if instead of dismissing things as impossible, we started asking, "How could this be possible?" or "What would it take to make this happen?"

It's a subtle shift in thinking, but it can lead to profound changes. Suddenly the impossible becomes a puzzle to be solved, not a wall blocking our way.

It doesn't mean everything becomes easy. In fact, some things are genuinely difficult, and the truth can be very inconvenient. But facing, acknowledging, and working with it instead of hiding behind the label of impossibility opens up a world of potential.

This isn't about being optimistic or naive. It's about being honest with ourselves and recognizing that many of our "impossibilities" are self-imposed limitations.

So the next time you're faced with something that seems impossible, take a moment to ask yourself if it's truly impossible or just inconvenient. Challenge yourself to look beyond the discomfort and explore the possibilities.

You might be surprised by what you find. Life is full of opportunities, but we often miss them because we're too busy telling ourselves what can't be done.

Remember, impossible is often just a code word for inconvenient. Break the code, and you'll discover paths you never knew existed.

Day 42

Roundtable of Mentors

When faced with a difficult decision or complex problem, it's easy to feel overwhelmed, uncertain, or stuck. It's in these moments that I turn to a thought experiment I call "My Roundtable of Mentors."

Picture it: a large, sturdy table set in a room filled with soft, contemplative light. Seated around this table are some of the greatest minds in history — those brilliant thinkers, creators, leaders, and visionaries who have inspired, challenged, and shaped me.

Marcus Aurelius, the embodiment of Stoic wisdom, joins this council alongside Brunello Cucinelli, the beacon of humanistic capitalism, and Charlie Munger, the paragon of investment prudence.

These mentors are not just figments of my imagination. They are real. They are alive in the works they've left behind, the ideas they've shared, and the lives they've touched.

I've read their books, studied their lives, and absorbed their philosophies. They are my trusted guides, intellectual companions, and metaphorical mentors.

When I sit down at this roundtable, I present my dilemma, question, or challenge. I listen as each mentor offers their perspective, advice, and wisdom.

The great part about this roundtable is that you can select anyone to be your trusted mentor. You can choose those who resonate with you, who speak to your soul, who challenge and inspire you. You can invite them into your mind, heart, and life, and let their wisdom guide you.

By doing this, you step outside of your own thinking. You tap into the greatest minds, the timeless truths, the universal principles that transcend cultures, eras, and industries.

You may never meet these mentors in person, but you can know them, learn from them, and grow with them. You can carry them with you in the way you live and work and move in the world.

So next time you find yourself stuck or uncertain, pull up a chair, gather your mentors, and listen. Let their wisdom illuminate your path, their insights spark your creativity, and their examples embolden your spirit.

You have access to the greatest minds, the deepest wisdom, and the most profound insights. All you have to do is invite them in and let them guide you.

Day 43

You Are a Masterpiece

G et this: You're the result of an incredible cosmic journey that's been going on for 13.8 billion years. You, right here, right now, are made from stardust and shaped by time and space, a unique combination that's never been and will never be again.

You're truly one of a kind.

That's not just some fancy science fact or poetic whimsy. It means something. It means you are unique. You're a rare gem in this vast universe. And that's not something to keep hidden. You are here to shine.

You don't have to pretend to be someone else, fit into some mold, or meet someone else's expectations. Just be you. Fully and completely you.

The universe didn't go on a 13.8-billion-year adventure just for you to hide away. So be brave, step out, and be yourself. Let the world see your brilliance.

You are a cosmic masterpiece, a marvel of the universe. Let your unique light shine. After all, that's what you're here for.

Day 44

Go First

In a world that often waits, hesitates, and looks for the perfect moment, these two words stand out as a call to action: Go first.

Be the one to break the mold. Be the pioneer, the trailblazer. Be the one who steps out from the shadows of hesitation into the radiant light of action.

Why? Because the world needs leaders. Not just those who hold titles and positions but those who lead by example. Those who shatter the barriers of complacency and inertia.

It's easy to wait. It's comfortable to stay in the familiar. It's tempting to hold back until the conditions are just right. But that's not where change happens. Change is not a spectator sport. It requires participation, engagement, and courage. It requires someone to go first. *That someone could be you.*

Think about what you want to see in the world: the impact you wish to have and the difference you aim to make. Now ask yourself, what's stopping you from being the catalyst for that change?

You don't have to wait for permission. You don't have to wait for the perfect moment. You can step into the forefront of change right now, today, in this very moment. And when you do, you're not just paving the way for yourself. You're creating ripples, sending out waves of positive change that can reach far beyond your own sphere of influence.

So heed the call. Embrace the challenge. After all, someone has to go first. Why not you?

Day 45

It's About Making a Life

It's so easy to get caught up in *doing*. We set targets, make timelines, and chase them down. It's like a never-ending to-do list, each item marked with its own deadline.

But is that all there is? A sequence of targets, a series of deadlines? I don't think so.

Life is a symphony, a beautiful artwork. It's an intricate blend of moments, experiences, and emotions. It's more about being than doing. And while goals are important, they shouldn't be our only compass. They shouldn't become a rigid framework that restricts our movements, limiting us to predetermined paths.

We need to step back and look at the bigger picture: the kind of life we wish to lead. The impact we want to make. The person we aspire to become.

This goes beyond our work. It transcends our job titles and paychecks. It's about aligning our profession with our passion. It's about finding a vocation, a calling, something that resonates with our deepest values and aspirations. This isn't just about making a living. It's about making a life.

Ask yourself: What kind of life do I want to live? How can my work contribute to that vision? How can I make my days not just productive but also fulfilling?

As you move forward, strive not just for goals but for a way of life. Don't just focus on the what; delve into the why and the how. Because at the end of the day, the targets and timelines will fade, but the memories you've crafted and relationships you cultivated will be your legacy. That will be your life.

Day 46

Inner Wealth

When you're young and ambitious, the world seems to be a treasure chest waiting to be unlocked. You dream of riches, fame, and glittering accolades. You strive, hustle, and grind. It all feels so important.

But here's what everyone who has reached that status says: No amount of money is ever worth trading for your peace of mind, your joy, or your inner light.

You might dismiss this as a joke from the rich. It's a lesson you think you'll get to later, after you've made your mark. The truth is, the richness of our inner world far outweighs any accumulation of material possessions. That inner world is our real home, the place we live, the place that shapes our every thought and action.

You might be nodding along now but shrug this off as soon as the next shiny opportunity comes along. That's okay. We're wired to chase and conquer. It's only later, often when the damage is done, that these words might ring true.

But why wait for devastation? Why learn the hard way? We can make conscious choices now to prioritize what truly matters. That's not just peace and joy, but the richness of connections, love, curiosity, and purpose.

I've often said that what you say no to defines you more than what you say yes to. Subtract the obsession with winning at all costs, and you make room for what adds up to a life well-lived.

I'm not saying to not chase wealth; money is great and can be extremely helpful. But don't do it at the expense of your peace of mind.

Day 47

Racing Blindly Through Life

Each moment arrives cloaked in the ordinary, a precious gift awaiting our recognition. Life, in its infinite wisdom and elegance, showers us with tiny gifts every moment.

Yet in our relentless pursuit of the next big thing, of more, of validation, we often overlook these packages of wonder. We sprint through the corridors of life, eyes fixated on some distant goal, unaware of the beauty that blooms in our periphery.

Each sunrise, each moment of shared laughter, each act of kindness, every breath we take — these are the humble gifts life offers us.

These moments, however fleeting, hold the power to infuse our lives with joy, meaning, and fulfillment. When we attune ourselves to the present moment, we start unwrapping these little gifts that life has to offer.

So let's not race blindly through our days chasing after more and bigger and better. Let's not forget the magic in the simplest things, the deepest connections that come from the smallest gestures, or the joy that can be found in the most ordinary places.

Day 48

An Internal Locus of Control

There's this idea woven through many layers of research and real-world observations that points to one of the underlying factors behind a person's success. It's called an internal locus of control. It might sound complex, but it's grounded in something simple and profound.

Having an internal locus of control means believing that you have control over your own actions and the outcomes they produce. You're not a ship aimlessly adrift on a stormy sea; you're the captain, steering your vessel, responsible for its direction.

Now contrast that with an external locus of control. This is where you think outside forces, like luck or fate or other people, have ultimate control over your life. It's like saying, "I'm at the mercy of the wind, and there's nothing I can do."

The difference between these two perspectives is massive. With an internal locus of control, you're empowered. You believe you can shape your destiny. You see challenges as opportunities to learn and grow. With an external locus, you may feel helpless, a spectator in your own life.

So how do we nurture this internal locus of control?

- **Understand responsibility.** Recognize that you are responsible for your choices, actions, and reactions. This doesn't mean you control everything that happens to you, but you do control how you respond.

- **Set goals and plan.** Having clear goals gives you a roadmap. By creating a plan and following it, you affirm your ability to shape your path.

- **Embrace failure as feedback.** Instead of fearing failure, see it as valuable information. What can it teach you? How can it guide your next steps? This approach reinforces the belief that you're in charge of your learning and growth.

- **Avoid victim mentality.** Resist the temptation to blame others or circumstances for your problems or failures. It's a trap that pulls you into an external locus of control.

- **Build on small successes.** Start with manageable challenges and build from there. Each success, no matter how small, reinforces the belief that you have control.

- **Reflect and adjust.** Regularly reflect on your actions and their outcomes. What's working? What's not? What can you change? This reflective practice keeps you engaged in your own growth and development.

The shift from an external to an internal locus of control isn't an overnight transformation. It's a gradual process of understanding, practice, reflection, and growth. It's about building a relationship with yourself grounded in the belief that you have the power to shape your life.

By cultivating an internal locus of control, you're not just improving your chances of success in a specific endeavor; you're embracing a way of being that can enrich your entire life.

Day 49

Stress Is... Enhancing?

For much of my life, I saw stress as an enemy, a harmful force to be avoided at all costs. I built walls, designed strategies, and invested energy in protecting myself from the perceived negative impacts of stress. And yet in my pursuit of a stress-free life, I missed something essential.

I began to notice that stress wasn't just a villain. It was more complex, nuanced, and even valuable in certain contexts. Not all stress is created equal, and I realized that certain types of stress could be a gift, an amplifier of my potential.

This shift in perspective didn't come overnight. It required a new understanding of and, a different relationship with stress. I had to distinguish between chronic stress, that relentless, grinding pressure that wears us down, and acute stress, those short bursts of tension that challenge us and push us to grow.

Chronic stress is indeed something to be managed and mitigated. It's unhealthy and can lead to a host of physical and mental health problems. But acute stress, I discovered, can be harnessed — even embraced — as a catalyst for growth.

I began to see acute stress as a signal that I care about something, that it matters to me. Whether it's a new project, a speech, or a personal challenge, the presence of stress indicates that I am engaged, invested, and alive to the opportunity.

I started to adopt what I call a stress-is-enhancing mindset. Rather than fearing or avoiding stress, I sought to understand it, work with it, and use it as a tool. This doesn't mean that I sought out stress for its own sake, but rather I learned to recognize its potential value in the right context.

The stress of a looming deadline became a motivator, focusing my energy and sharpening my thinking. The stress of a new challenge became an opportunity for growth, pushing me out of my comfort zone and into a space of learning and development.

This shift in perspective was liberating. It allowed me to see stress not as something to be feared or escaped but as a complex and multifaceted part of the human experience.

It's important to note that this approach to stress isn't about glorifying or romanticizing struggle. It's about recognizing that not all stress is harmful and that in the right context, with the right mindset, it can be a powerful ally.

By adopting a stress-is-enhancing mindset, I've been able to transform what was once a source of fear and avoidance into a force for growth and positive change.

What I've learned is that stress, like so many aspects of life, is not just something that happens to us. It's something we can engage with, learn from, and harness. It's not just a threat; it's an opportunity. And like so many opportunities, it's what we make of it that truly matters.

Day 50

Be So Good They Can't Ignore You

Steve Martin, a master of comedy and a prolific writer, actor, and musician, has a way of simplifying things down to their essence. When asked what advice he'd give to a young comedian trying to make it in the cutthroat world of stand-up, his answer was disarmingly simple: "Be so good they can't ignore you."

That's it. Seven words. But within them is an entire philosophy of pursuit, excellence, and differentiation.

His advice isn't about following trends or trying to fit into what's popular. It's not about hustling harder, networking more, or self-promoting louder. It's about focusing on your craft. It's about becoming undeniably good.

When you're that good, you transcend competition. You become the standard, not just a contender. When you're that good, doors open. Opportunities seek you out. You're no longer knocking on doors; doors are knocking on you.

When you focus on being genuinely outstanding, recognition will follow. It's not about chasing validation but about committing to excellence so deeply and profoundly that the world can't help but notice.

So take Steve's advice to heart. In a world trying to be louder, just be better. Be so good they can't ignore you.

Day 51

Gnawing Regret of Unrealized Potential

L et me share with you something life has taught me: The discomfort of growth is far less painful than the gnawing regret of unrealized potential and opportunities missed.

Imagine getting to the end of your life and looking back only to realize that you never truly lived. Imagine the torment of knowing that you could have been so much more — that you had dreams and potential and opportunities, but you let them slip through your fingers.

Imagine hearing the echoes of dreams you didn't dare to chase haunting you, taunting you, reminding you of what could have been. That, to me, is a fate worse than any struggle we could face in pursuit of our dreams.

For in the grand narrative of your life, it's not the challenges that will haunt you. It's not the failures, the mistakes, the obstacles, or the setbacks; it's the dreams you didn't chase. It's the risks you didn't take. It's the opportunities you didn't seize. It's the life you didn't live.

In the marketplace of life, our unrealized potential is the most expensive item left unpurchased.

So embrace the discomfort of growth. Embrace the struggle, uncertainty, and risk. Embrace the possibility of failure. Because the alternative — the regret of unrealized potential — is far more painful and far more tragic.

Day 52

Resisting Change

Change is an eternal constant in life. It's not just something that happens to us; it's something that's always happening, always flowing, always moving. And yet how often do we resist it? How often do we dig in our heels, clench our fists, and try to push against the current?

It's a natural human tendency, this resistance to change. We find comfort in the familiar, in the known. We like things to stay the way they are because they feel safe and controlled. But here's the truth: The resistance to change is often what causes the most discomfort, not the change itself.

Imagine standing in a river trying to hold back the water with your bare hands. It's a futile effort, and all it does is create tension, strain, and fatigue. Now imagine that instead, you relax your arms, let go of the resistance, and allow the river to carry you forward. It might be scary at first, letting go of control, trusting the flow. But it's also liberating, exhilarating, and freeing.

When we stop resisting change and start embracing it, we open ourselves up to new possibilities, new horizons, and new growth. We recognize that change is not something to be feared or fought against but something to be understood, accepted, and harnessed. Because change is not just a force of destruction; it's a force of creation. It's not just a bringer of endings; it's a bringer of beginnings. It's a chance to let go of what's no longer serving us and embrace what's waiting for us.

So let's stop pushing against the current. Let's stop trying to hold back the river. Let's learn to flow with it, to ride its waves and harness its energy.

The river is flowing. The question is, are we willing to flow with it?

Day 53

External Bandages Can Never Heal an Internal Wound

L et's face it. We're great at collecting. Collecting praise, possessions, experiences. Each one like a shiny bandage hoping to cover up something raw and throbbing inside. We're in a relentless pursuit: maybe the next thing, the next compliment, the next thrill will finally mend that gnawing ache.

But here's a subtle truth I've come to respect: Real wounds aren't on the surface. They're deep, and they need more than surface solutions. An external fix can't patch up an internal rift. It's like trying to fix a leaky boat with duct tape. It might hold for a while, but soon enough water finds its way in.

You see, genuine healing, the kind that lasts, is an inside job. It begins with sitting quietly with our pain, understanding its origins, and gently addressing the root, not just the symptom. It's not about the noise from the outside, but the stillness from within.

The world's remedies are abundant and loud, but real tranquility? That comes from a quieter place, from confronting our own vulnerabilities, understanding them, and nurturing them back to health.

So next time you feel that instinctual pull toward another external solution, pause. Ask yourself: What's truly going on inside? What wound am I trying to cover? Because often the healing you seek is not in the world outside but in the universe within. External bandages can provide temporary relief, but it's the inner work that heals.

Day 54

Sawubona

Hailing from the Zulu tribe of South Africa, the word *sawubona* is a greeting that carries a profound message. It's more than a simple "hello." It's a declaration, an affirmation, and a connection.

When someone says *sawubona*, they are essentially saying, "I see you. I see your humanity. I see your dignity. I see your soul." This is not a casual greeting but a powerful acknowledgment of the other person's essence.

In our fast-paced, digitally-driven world, where so many of our interactions are fleeting and transactional, the spirit of *sawubona* is a refreshing reminder of what it means to truly connect with one another. It's about seeing beyond external appearances, labels, and judgments. It's about recognizing the shared humanity that binds us all together; the universal spark that resides in each of us.

Sawubona encourages us to slow down, to really look at one another and honor the inherent dignity and worth of each individual. It's an invitation to empathy, compassion, and understanding.

In the spirit of *ubuntu*, which means "I am because we are," *sawubona* teaches us the interconnectedness of all beings. It's not just about me, you, or them. It's about us together, woven into a tapestry of humanity that is rich, diverse, and beautiful.

Sawubona is more than a word; it's a philosophy, a way of being. It's a gentle call to each of us to acknowledge the worth and dignity of every person we encounter regardless of their background or circumstances.

By embracing *sawubona*, we can break down barriers, dissolve prejudices, and build a world that celebrates the beauty of our shared humanity.

Imagine if we all greeted each other in this way, with open hearts, open minds, and open souls. Imagine the kindness, the understanding, and the connections that would blossom.

Let's carry the spirit of *sawubona* with us in our interactions, relationships, and communities. Let's see each other, truly, deeply, soulfully. Let's honor the humanity in one another and create a world where compassion and acceptance prevail.

It starts with a simple greeting, a look, a recognition. It starts with *sawubona*.

Day 55

Preventing the Fire

In life's multifaceted expedition, a valuable lesson emerges: Preventing fires is far easier than extinguishing them. By cultivating an acute awareness of our surroundings and the early signs of potential challenges, we equip ourselves to intercept and address them before they escalate into overwhelming predicaments.

This principle holds true across all aspects of life, be it in business, relationships, or personal growth.

You can't control every little thing that comes up in life, but you can reduce the risk of a fire. In your relationships, this might mean noticing a friend's subtle signs of distress and reaching out with support before a crisis occurs. In business, it might mean identifying a minor inefficiency and rectifying it before it becomes a substantial problem.

The essence of this approach is not about control or fear but about attentive care. It's a mindset that encourages us to be present, observant, and engaged with our surroundings and the people in our lives. It prompts us to ask ourselves, "What am I noticing here? What small actions can I take now to prevent future problems?"

Rather than being reactive, we adopt a proactive stance, tuning in to the initial sparks of discord or inefficiencies to nip them in the bud. In doing so, we save precious time, energy, and resources that would otherwise be spent battling larger infernos.

So let us remain vigilant to the subtle cues of change and growth and take timely action to foster a harmonious and thriving existence. Prevention paves the way for smoother journeys.

Day 56

Skill Stacking

We often hear that specialization is key to success. Become the best at one thing and the world is yours, they say. But what if you're interested in many things? What if you don't want to choose just one? That's where skill stacking comes into play.

Skill stacking is a term that might sound intricate but is beautifully simple at its core. It's like weaving together threads of different colors to create a unique and stunning piece of fabric. Each thread represents a skill you're good at, and when you intertwine them, they create something new and extraordinary.

Imagine you're a decent writer, a competent musician, and you have a knack for technology. Each of these skills is valuable on its own. But combine them, and you could be writing about music technology, creating tech tools for musicians, or producing innovative music using technology. Suddenly your unique combination of skills opens up a niche that might have been unreachable if you'd chosen only one path.

Skill stacking isn't about being the best in the world at one particular thing. It's about leveraging your unique combination of skills to carve out a space where you can be exceptional in your own way. You don't need to be in the top 1% of any particular field. You can be in the top 25% of three or four, and that intersection becomes a space where you are in the top 1%.

This approach promotes a more holistic view of growth and development. You're not a one-trick pony. You're a multifaceted human being with diverse interests and abilities. Why not use them all?

By embracing skill stacking, you open yourself to opportunities that might not be apparent if you're narrowly focused on one area. It's about forging your path, connecting the dots in your own way, and crafting a personal brand that truly reflects who you are.

In a world that's constantly evolving and where innovation is key, skill stacking might be more relevant than ever. It's about adaptability, creativity, and finding your unique place in the world. It's not about fitting into a box but about building your own.

So go ahead. Embrace your multiple skills. Stack them, weave them, play with them. Find that unique intersection that's just yours and become great at it.

The world doesn't just need more specialists. It needs more of you.

Day 57

Life's Not an Equation to Solve

I see people attempting to quantify life, trying to fit it into neat little boxes and calculations. They're looking for formulas, rules, and equations that can explain everything, predict the outcome, and guarantee success. But life doesn't work like that.

Life, like a work of art, can't be solved; it needs to be experienced. This world — your life — is a vibrant canvas, not a sterile spreadsheet.

Imagine if you approached a beautiful painting with a ruler and a calculator, attempting to break it down into numbers and equations. You would miss the essence of the art, the emotion, the story, the beauty. You can't capture the essence of a masterpiece by measuring its dimensions.

Life is like that painting. It's rich, complex, and nuanced. It's filled with color, texture, and depth. Life is to be lived, not solved. Our most cherished memories can't be quantified or explained through logic and reason. They are felt, lived, embraced.

When we approach life as a sterile spreadsheet, we risk losing touch with the beauty, mystery, and art of living. We become disconnected from the human experience and trapped in our heads, analyzing and calculating instead of feeling and experiencing.

So what if we approach life more like artists and less like accountants? See the colors, hear the music, taste the flavors. Tango with the uncertainty, play with the possibilities, and engage with the mystery. Life isn't an equation to be solved; it's a masterpiece to be experienced.

Day 58

Less But Better

Today's mantra, "less but better," offers a refreshing perspective on how to navigate the complexities of modern life. Instead of succumbing to the pressure of doing it all, this guiding principle invites us to pause and reflect on what truly matters to us. It prompts us to strip away the superfluous and focus our energies on a select few pursuits that align with our values and aspirations.

The disciplined pursuit of less but better is not about denying ourselves opportunities or settling for mediocrity. It is about discerning what truly brings us joy, fulfillment, and a sense of purpose.

By letting go of the excess, we free ourselves from the burdens of overcommitment and allow space for what really matters. As we devote ourselves wholeheartedly to these chosen paths, the quality of our efforts amplifies and the impact we create resonates on a deeper level.

So let us embrace the art of simplicity and the beauty of focus.

Let us have the courage to say no to the noise and distractions that threaten to pull us away from what matters.

By choosing to do fewer things but doing them exceptionally well, we embark on a life built on quality. In the disciplined pursuit of less but better, we uncover the essence of a life well-lived.

Day 59

Does This Path Have a Heart?

Every crossroad we encounter in life demands a decision from us. While pros and cons, rational calculations, empirical evidence, and well-intentioned advice all play their roles, there's one question that truly matters: "Does this path have a heart?"

Asking if a path has a heart is like asking if it aligns with your core values, passions, and purpose. It's about whether the choice resonates with the most profound part of who you are. It's that quiet voice that whispers, "Yeah, this feels right." Amidst all the noise and advice, it's that gentle reminder pointing us at what truly matters. More often than not, listening to it leads us down the right path.

It's not about easy or hard nor about safe or risky. Instead, it's about authenticity, meaning, and connection. A path with a heart is one that gives you a deep sense of belonging, even amidst challenges and uncertainty.

Navigating life through this heart-centered lens empowers us to live more authentically. It allows us to forge a path that may not be the easiest or the most conventional but is undeniably ours.

Ultimately, a path with a heart isn't just about what you do; it's about who you are and who you aspire to be.

Feel it. Trust it.

It knows the way.

Day 60

Stop Searching for Equilibrium

In our lives, we often strive for perfection: some imagined equilibrium where everything is just right. We look for that perfect job, the perfect relationship, or the perfect balance between work and life.

But there's no such thing.

Life is constantly changing. Just when you think you've found the perfect balance, something shifts. You change. The world changes. And suddenly, you're adjusting your sails again.

And that's not a bad thing.

If you were to find that mythical perfect balance, that stable equilibrium where everything was just right, what then? You would stagnate. You would stop growing, stop learning, stop living. You would be begging for change.

Embrace the wind and waves. Learn to ride the changes, to adapt and grow. Recognize that the pursuit of perfection is a false goal, a mirage on the horizon.

Life is not about finding some perfect balance where everything is constant. It's about learning to thrive in the constant ebb and flow and in the unpredictability and excitement of being alive.

There is no perfect situation, no arrival, no equilibrium. There is only the journey, and it's a beautiful one if you learn to see it that way.

So hoist your sails, embrace the wind, and enjoy the ride.

Day 61

Where We Suffer Most

Seneca nailed it when he said, "We suffer more in imagination than in reality." Our minds are impressively good at spinning out scenarios, predicting disasters, and imagining problems that hardly ever happen.

Imagine your mind as a movie director constantly writing scripts for worst-case scenarios. Now think about how often these scenes actually make it to the "reality" screen. Rarely, right?

I've noticed that I can spend hours, even days, worrying about something that never happens. A conversation that might go wrong. A decision that could have terrible consequences. A risk that seems too big to take. The mind spins intricate stories filled with catastrophe and failure.

Our minds have the power to turn a slight concern into a full-fledged drama. The stories we tell ourselves can trap us, make us anxious, even paralyze us. But they're just that — a story, a thought, a figment of our imagination.

What's cool is that we're not just the director; we're also the editor. We get to decide what stays in the final cut. We have the control to cut, mute, or totally trash these anxiety-inducing scenes.

Since we create these imaginary problems, we also have the power to let them go.

- First, recognize that your mind is doing this. It's natural. It's what minds do. But just because your mind thinks something doesn't mean it's true.

- Then bring yourself back to the present. What's actually happening right now? Not in your mind's projection of the future or its recreation of the past, but right now, in this very moment.

- Next, get practical. Is this something that needs real attention, or can you place your attention somewhere else?

- Lastly, practice. The mind's tendency to suffer in imagination is a habit, and habits can be changed. Practice noticing when you're suffering in your imagination and consciously choose to return to the present. Over time, it gets easier.

Most of our angst and worry is born in the imagination, not in reality. By acknowledging this, we get a little closer to understanding the power of our minds, the influence of our thoughts, and the liberation that comes from directing and editing our internal narrative.

Day 62

What's Your Definition of Success?

People often charge ahead, head down, working hard, aiming for success. But if you stop them and ask, "*What is your definition of success?*" you often get a blank stare or a vague, rehearsed answer that doesn't resonate deeply.

Success isn't a one-size-fits-all suit. Society may present a polished image of what success should be, but that doesn't mean it will fit you. It's a personal thing tailored to your values, desires, and vision.

If you're running a race you didn't choose, how satisfying will it be to cross that finish line?

Take the time to sit down and define what success really means to you. Be honest with yourself, and don't be swayed by what others think success should be.

Once you have that definition, everything changes. Every decision, every action, and every goal aligns with that vision. It's not about meeting someone else's expectations; it's about fulfilling your unique purpose.

This understanding eliminates the noise and distractions. It helps you say no to what doesn't align and yes to what does.

Defining success is not a one-time act. Life changes. You grow, and your needs and desires evolve. Regularly revisit your definition, refine it, and make sure it still resonates with who you are.

Define your success. Own it. Live it. Enjoy the journey.

Day 63

The Invisible Barriers

How many times have you held yourself back because you were afraid to fail? How often have you hesitated to take a bold step because you doubted your abilities?

These internal barriers are more powerful and more limiting than any external obstacle you'll ever face. They shape your thoughts, your actions, your entire life.

And the most challenging part? You created them.

That might sound harsh, but it's also empowering because if you've created these barriers, you can dismantle them. But how?

- **Recognize the barriers.** The first step in overcoming your internal obstacles is recognizing them. You have to identify the self-doubts, fears, and limiting beliefs that are holding you back.

- **Understand them.** Dive deep into these barriers. Understand where they come from. What experiences or influences have shaped them? Why do they have such a strong hold over you?

- **Challenge them.** Once you recognize and understand your internal obstacles, it's time to challenge them. Question them. Are they really true? Do they truly define you? Most of the time, you'll find that they don't.

- **Replace them.** Replace those limiting beliefs with empowering ones. If you've been telling yourself, "I can't," tell yourself "I can." If you've been held back by fear, replace it with courage.

- **Act on them.** Finally, take action. Break through those barriers with bold, decisive action. Step out of your comfort zone. Do the things you've been afraid to do.

Don't let yourself be the obstacle. Be the way forward.

The path is open. The journey is yours. What will you do with it?

Day 64

The Wisdom of Not Knowing

Age and experience bring many things: wisdom, maturity, and a sense of perspective. Perhaps one of the most profound lessons I've learned through the years is the realization of how little I actually know.

When we're young, the world seems clear and definite. We're taught facts and figures, equations and theories, and we're led to believe that there's a definitive answer to every question. Knowledge feels like a puzzle to be solved, and we strive to fill in all the pieces.

As we grow older and more experienced, we begin to see that life's complexities can't always be reduced to simple answers. We encounter paradoxes, ambiguities, and contradictions that defy our neatly constructed understanding. We learn that wisdom is not always a matter of collecting information; it's often the ability to navigate life without all the information.

This doesn't mean that the knowledge is meaningless. On the contrary, it's invaluable. But it's complemented by a growing appreciation for the gray areas, the unknown territories, and the mysteries that life still holds. The phrase "I don't know," does not signal defeat but rather demonstrates wisdom. It's an acknowledgment of life's boundless complexities. It's a starting point for learning, a door opening to new possibilities, and an invitation to others to share their perspectives and contribute to our understanding.

So appreciate the mystery, wonder, and infinite complexity of life. And rather than seeking to conquer all of life's questions, find joy in exploring, learning, growing, and recognizing that the more you know, the more there is to know.

Day 65

Speak Your Truth

How do we speak our truth, especially when that truth feels vulnerable, uncertain, or contrary to the prevailing winds? The answer is simple but not easy: We must have courage. Courage to speak when others are silent. Courage to stand when others sit. Courage to say what we believe even when our voice shakes with fear.

Speaking our truth is not about volume or bravado. It's not about being the loudest or the boldest. It's about being genuine, authentic, and true to ourselves.

When we speak our truth, we expose our hearts. We open ourselves to criticism, judgment, and rejection. That's scary. It's why so many of us choose to stay silent, keep our thoughts and feelings hidden, and conform to the expectations and demands of others. But when we hide our truth, we also hide our power. We suppress our potential.

When we share our truth, we share ourselves. We invite others to see us, know us, and understand us. And in that vulnerable, honest, naked space, we create the possibility for real connection, real change, and real impact.

Speaking our truth is a choice. It's a conscious decision to say, "This is me. This is what I believe. This is what I stand for." It's a commitment to be real, honest, and brave. It's also a gift. When we speak our truth, we give others permission to do the same.

So find your voice. Speak your truth. Do it with courage, passion, and love. Let your voice shake, your heart race, and your knees wobble. It's okay. It's real. It's powerful.

Day 66

All of Your Obligations Vanish

I magine a blank slate where all of your responsibilities and obligations have disappeared. There's no more pressure, no deadlines, no tasks demanding your attention. It's a momentary glimpse into complete freedom where you can breathe without any constraints.

But as you float in this liberated state, what do you miss? What are the things that even without obligation, you would reach out to grasp again? What are the activities, connections, or pursuits that light you up from within and that you would continue to embrace even if you didn't "have to"?

These are the core elements of your life, the pieces that resonate with your deepest values and desires. They are what make you feel alive, connected, and fulfilled.

Now think about intentionally adding back only these essential elements, crafting a life around what truly matters to you. Let go of the noise and distractions, the "shoulds" and "have tos," and focus on what fuels your soul.

It's an empowering exercise — a way to get back to the core of who you are and what you want. By letting your mind wander into this world, you have a chance to see your life from a fresh perspective, recognize what really matters, and build your life around those fundamental truths.

Day 67

Will I?

Have you ever found yourself pondering a task, project, or personal goal and asking, "Can I do this?" Maybe it's a new job, a creative project, or even a relationship commitment. "Can I?" echoes through our minds.

But I think we're asking the wrong question.

The real question is not "Can I?" It's "Will I?"

The difference between these two questions is subtle yet profound.

"Can I?" is about ability. It's a question filled with doubt, uncertainty, even fear. It's looking for reasons to say, "Well, maybe this isn't for me."

"Will I?" is about commitment. It's a question filled with determination, clarity, and personal responsibility. It's asking, "Am I willing to put in the work, the effort, and the sacrifice needed to make this happen?"

When you shift your mindset from "Can I?" to "Will I?", you change the equation.

You stop looking for external validation or permission. You stop waiting for the right time, the right place, the right whatever. You start focusing on what you can control, what you can do, and what steps you can take.

The truth is that most of the time, the answer to "Can I?" is "Yes, I can." We live in an era filled with information, resources, and opportunities. If you want to learn something, achieve something, or be something, you can. The tools are there. The paths have been paved by those who've gone before you.

The real question, the important question, the question that determines your path is "Will I?"

Will you put in the time?

Will you face the fear?

Will you take the risk?

Will you make the sacrifice?

"Will I?" is a commitment. It's a pledge to yourself. It's a decision to act, to move, to do.

Next time you find yourself wondering if you can do something, stop. Shift the question. Ask yourself, "Will I do this?"

Then listen to the answer.

It might be a whisper, a tiny voice in the back of your mind, but it's there. It's your inner calling, your personal guide, pointing you in the direction that's true for you.

Follow it.

Day 68

Two Books You Should Always Carry

There are two types of books I try to carry with me at all times. These aren't just any books. One is filled with the thoughts, philosophies, and experiences of those who have come before me. The other is a blank canvas waiting to be filled with my reflections, questions, and insights.

Think of the first book as a mentor. It's filling your mind with wisdom and helping you grow. It could be about philosophy, business, or just something you're passionate about.

It's a bridge to the collective knowledge of humanity. It speaks to you, challenges you, and helps you see the world from a vantage point you might not have discovered on your own.

The other book, the blank one, is equally precious. It's a mirror reflecting your mind. Here, you don't just consume knowledge; you interact with it.

You question, ponder, and explore. You note down your thoughts, disagreements, and epiphanies. It's a dialogue between you and yourself; a space where you can be completely honest, vulnerable, and inquisitive.

These two books are like two sides of a coin, each complementing the other. The book you read fills your mind with ideas, stories, and perspectives. The book you write in helps you digest this information, personalize it, and integrate it into your unique worldview.

In an age where information is abundant but often shallow, this duo of books offers depth. It encourages you to slow down, to think, and to engage not just with the words on the page but with yourself. The book you read will enlighten your mind, and the book you write will illuminate your soul.

So find a book that resonates with you — something that makes you think, that inspires and challenges you. Pair it with a journal that becomes your personal space for exploration. Let these two become your trusted companions.

This isn't just about knowledge. It's about wisdom. Don't just absorb what's been thought before; contribute your voice to the conversation.

Day 69

Oasis of Calm

L ife is noisy. There's the literal noise of traffic, chatter, machines, media, and all the sounds of modern living. Then there's the noise inside our minds: thoughts, worries, plans, dreams, and endless internal dialogue.

The noise can be invigorating, stimulating, and even inspiring. But it can also be overwhelming. That's why it's essential to carve out a tranquil haven where you can retreat each day.

Think of it as your sacred space. It doesn't have to be a physical room. It can be a quiet corner of your mind, a brief moment with a cup of tea, a meditative practice, or even just a deep breath. In this pocket of stillness, you can pause. Breathe. Reflect. Realign.

It's a moment of solace for your restless mind, a place to collect your thoughts and find clarity amidst the noise. It's an opportunity to reset and refocus on becoming the person you aspire to be.

The world won't stop spinning. The noise won't magically disappear. But in this sanctuary of stillness, you can rise above it. It's in the quiet moments that we often find our loudest insights. The world's chaos fades away, and what's left is the pure, unfiltered essence of your thoughts, feelings, and intuition.

Allow the pocket of stillness to become your sacred practice. Whether it's five minutes or an hour, make it a part of your daily routine. Let it be a serene refuge to rejuvenate, reorient, and rekindle the profound reservoirs of your innate potential.

In the stillness, the noise fades away, and all that's left is you.

Hit the Reset Button

Here's an empowering idea that's too good not to share: What happened earlier today doesn't have to dictate how the rest of your day goes. Sounds simple, right? But boy, is it powerful.

Let's say you woke up late, skipped breakfast, got caught in traffic, and had a rough morning meeting. It's easy to let these early bumps color the rest of your day. You might find yourself thinking, "Well, today's a write-off." But it doesn't have to be that way.

In a single instant, with one bold spark of thought, you can change the entire tone of your day. You can choose to let go of the missteps, stress, worry, and frustration. You can choose to reset, restart, and reclaim your day.

It's like hitting the reset button on a video game. Sure, you might've messed up that last level, but here's a fresh start. Here's a chance to do it differently.

The power of this idea lies in its simplicity and immediacy. There's no need for complex rituals or long-winded mantras. It's just a decision, a choice not to let the past drag down the present.

So if you're having a rough day, remember it's not set in stone. You have the power to change it. In one bold moment, you can shift your thoughts and transform your day. And the beauty of it all? You can do this anytime, anywhere. It's a superpower we all have, and it's just waiting to be used.

So go ahead and hit that reset button. Let go of the past and embrace the new. Because every moment is a chance for a fresh start.

Day 71

Loss Is a Gateway

Loss. It's one of those words that can feel heavy. When we lose something — a job, a relationship, an opportunity — it's easy to feel a sense of setback or defeat. But I've come to see loss in a different light.

Think of loss as a gateway.

Imagine you're walking down a well-trodden path, and suddenly you come across a closed gate. At first, it may seem like an obstacle, a dead end. But take a closer look, and you'll find that there's a key in your pocket that opens this gate. This key is your perspective, your ability to see loss not as a barrier but as an aperture into something new.

You see, every ending is a beginning. Every loss is an invitation. Every setback is a beckoning toward a different path ripe with undiscovered possibilities.

When one door closes, another one opens. But we often look so long and so regretfully upon the closed door that we do not see the one that has opened for us.

What if, instead of mourning what's gone, we embrace the space it leaves behind? What if we look at loss as a clearing, a room to grow, a chance to pivot, and an opportunity to explore?

Sometimes, losing something is the universe's way of nudging us out of complacency, urging us to take a leap, and daring us to explore the unknown.

It's like the end of one chapter in a riveting book. You don't mourn the end of the chapter; you eagerly turn the page to see what happens next. What awaits you might be more beautiful, more enriching, and more aligned with who you are and who you're becoming.

So next time you face a loss, take a moment to pause. Feel what you feel, but then look beyond the immediate pain or disappointment. Look for the gateway, the open door, the invitation to something new.

Your path hasn't ended. It's just taken a beautiful turn leading you to new horizons, new lessons, and new growth.

Loss isn't a setback. It's a setup for something greater. Embrace it, explore it, and see where it leads you.

Day 72

Finding Your People

People often say that we become the average of the five people we spend the most time with. Whether that's statistically accurate or not, there's a powerful truth in the idea.

Consider this: If you're surrounded by those who are constantly complaining, finding fault, or remaining stuck in mediocrity, it's easy to fall into those patterns yourself. The opposite is equally true. Surround yourself with individuals who are driven, compassionate, creative, or whatever traits you aspire to, and those qualities start to rub off on you.

Think of it as a beautiful dance where the steps, rhythm, and energy of those around you become a part of your own dance. It's not about copying or losing your own identity; it's about enhancing and shaping yourself through the influence and inspiration of others.

This is why mentors are so influential, why mastermind groups are so effective, and why having friends who share your values is so comforting.

Finding these people — those who embody what you aspire to be — isn't always easy. But the effort to seek them out and include them in your life is worth every ounce of effort. They become mirrors reflecting your potential, lights guiding you on your path, and catalysts igniting the spark within you.

Engage with them. Learn from them. Let their actions, words, and beliefs inspire and challenge you. And most importantly, recognize the value they bring into your life.

This isn't a one-way street, either. As you grow and embody these qualities, you'll become that guiding light for others. You'll join the chain of growth and positivity, and in doing so, contribute to a cycle of mutual upliftment.

Your companions are the soundtrack of your life. Make sure they harmonize with the melody of your dreams.

So take a moment to reflect on the company you keep, and ask yourself if those people represent the person you want to become. If not, don't be afraid to seek out those who do. In their presence, your path to greatness becomes not just a possibility but a beautiful reality.

Day 73

Clean Out Your Mind

Our minds, like attics, can accumulate a lot of junk over time. Old thoughts, outdated beliefs, and worn-out perspectives often gather dust in the corners. They feel familiar, even comforting. But they're not necessarily useful. In fact, they can be downright burdensome.

Think of these outdated beliefs as heavy suitcases. Some are filled with "I can't," "I shouldn't," and "That's just the way it is." They weigh you down, slow your progress, and keep you stuck.

But here's the cool part: You're not a luggage carrier. You're a dynamic, evolving human being, constantly growing and changing. You're free to drop any piece of luggage that's too heavy and to lighten your load whenever you choose.

So go ahead. Unpack those suitcases. Sort through the contents. Keep what's still useful and discard what's not. Shed the weight of outdated beliefs, and watch how quickly you can move forward.

Remember, your mind is your playground, not your storage unit. Keep it clean, keep it fresh. Let go of the mental baggage that no longer serves you and enjoy the liberating feeling of a lightened load. You'll be amazed at how much faster and how much farther you can travel with a little less weight on your shoulders.

Day 74

Make Their Eyes Shine

A question anchors my thoughts today: How can I make the eyes of those I cherish shine with joy?

Take a moment to think about it and how you can do this in your life.

Recall a time when someone did something unanticipated for you. It might have been an encouraging note left on your table, a surprise lunch from a colleague, or even a warm smile on a challenging day. It's these moments that light up our world, making our souls feel seen and valued.

Now think of the power you hold: the magic you wield to be that beacon of light for someone else. It's not about grandiose actions or expensive gifts. It's about authenticity — showing up genuinely for someone and recognizing the spaces in their heart that could use a little sunshine.

It's an enlightening realization: Our capacity to enrich someone's day is often right at our fingertips. It could be as simple as genuinely listening when they speak, offering a helping hand, or sharing words of encouragement.

So today, as you navigate the corridors of your routines, take a deliberate pause. Look around and see where you can bring a touch of sparkle. Shift from a passive stance to one of purpose. Seek out those small, golden opportunities to light up a loved one's world.

For in making their eyes shine, you'll find your world becomes a little brighter too.

Day 75

No More Shoulds

"Should." It's a word filled with both promise and procrastination — a word that signifies intention but often lacks commitment. We all have our "shoulds" — those things we know we ought to do but somehow never make it to the forefront of our lives.

But today, something's different. Today, I'm reclaiming my power, and I'm turning one of those "shoulds" into an action.

No longer will it linger in the shadowy realm of wishful thinking. Today, it moves onto the Done list.

And you can do this too.

You have the power, the capability, and the wisdom to take your "shoulds" and make them real. Today, choose one that resonates deeply with you, one you've been longing to tackle.

Reclaim your power. Put it on the Done list.

Feel the exhilaration of moving from intention to action. Feel the satisfaction of taking control and making something meaningful happen.

With each step forward, feel the shackles of "shoulds" fall away, leaving behind a trail of empowered decisions and fulfilled aspirations. Today, break free from the confines of "should" and embrace the endless possibilities that await you.

Today is your day. Your "should" is waiting. Turn it into a "did."

Where My Talent and Deep Gladness Meet

F rederick Buechner's question, "At what point do my talents and deep gladness meet the world's deep need?" is more than just a passing thought. It's a calling, a beckoning towards something greater.

Most of us hustle through life neglecting to align our passions with a higher purpose. We get caught up in routines, responsibilities, and chasing after things we're told we should want.

But pause for a moment. Breathe. Reflect.

What are you uniquely good at? What brings you profound joy? Now, how can those unique gifts meet a need in the world?

This is where the magic happens.

This is where life becomes more than existence. It becomes a mission, a path filled with meaning and fulfillment.

The intersection of your talents and passions and the world's needs is where you'll find your calling.

It's where work becomes more than a means to an end. It's where you make a difference.

So carve out some time today to reflect on that. Tomorrow, say, "*Today is the day I give the world my gifts.*"

Day 77

It Holds No Power Over Us

One of life's most profound revelations is understanding that the moment in front of us holds no power over us; it is our reaction and perception that shape our experience.

The moment itself is neutral, yet we have the incredible ability to either embrace it with open arms or burden ourselves with frustration about the way things aren't.

The choice lies within us: to free ourselves from the self-inflicted troubles we create in our minds.

In this revelation lies the crux of liberation. The burdens we carry and the worries that weigh us down are self-imposed. The shackles of the mind are but illusions we create. Their essence remains neutral, waiting for our perception to shape their significance.

We have this incredible ability to choose our response to life. We can embrace it with curiosity, acceptance, and grace. Or we can fight against it, resist it, and burden ourselves with frustration.

That choice shapes our experience.

Choose wisely.

Day 78

The Discomfort Paradox

There's a notion we've been sold rather convincingly by the world around us. It whispers, "Life's aim? Make it easy. Make everything a fingertip away." It's tempting. I mean, who doesn't love the thrill of a gourmet meal at the door with a tap on a screen or diving into a vast sea of digital entertainment for less than ten bucks? And every time we find a shortcut or an app that saves us five minutes, we get this satisfying little nod, as if to say, "Yeah, I've nailed this modern life thing."

But let me throw a curveball at that narrative. What if that's a grand illusion?

When I look back on my life, every single moment that I'm proudest of or in which I grew the most was nowhere near these comfort zones. They weren't during Netflix binges or while munching on the sofa. Instead, they were wrapped in layers of unease, challenge, and, dare I say, struggle. Those moments of pushing through barriers — whether mental, physical, or emotional — that's where the magic truly unfurled.

Oddly enough, I've found that there's profound growth in deliberately seeking discomfort. It's in those uncertain waters that you discover what you're made of. It's there, amidst the grumbles of the mind and the hesitations, you realize a fantastic truth: "Oh, I can go further." Not in a masochistic way but in a way that reminds us of the infinite potential hidden beneath layers of self-imposed limitations.

You see, comfort, while seductive, can be deceptive. It can make us stagnant, letting us cruise in the familiar. But think of life as a muscle. For it to grow, it needs resistance. It's in the stretch and the strain that we really define ourselves. So every now and then, I've made it a point to look my comforts square in the eye and venture beyond them — to embrace a situation not for its ease but for its potential to challenge me.

Don't misinterpret me. There's a place for ease and there's value in relaxation. But if personal growth is the game, perpetual comfort can't be the name.

Next time you find yourself coasting, maybe, just maybe, it's a sign to shake things up a bit. Dive into the unfamiliar, wrestle with a new challenge, and savor the growth that inevitably follows. Because often, it's just beyond the comfort zone that we find our most authentic selves.

Day 79

Colliding with the Future

Imagine a line. At one end is the past, full of memories and lessons learned. At the other end is the future, a vast, open space filled with possibilities. And right in the middle is you at this very moment.

Life isn't a straight, predictable line from past to future. It's more like a meandering river colliding with the future at every twist and turn. That collision isn't something to be feared or avoided. It's an opportunity. It's a chance to redefine yourself, create something new, and grow in unexpected ways.

Sure, you can dwell in the past. You can get stuck in what you once were, what you once did, what once happened to you. The past has value, of course. It's where you've come from. It's what's shaped you. But it's not where you're going. That's the future, and it's an open canvas.

Each collision with the future is a chance to paint something new on that canvas. Each decision, each action, and each thought is a brushstroke. You can't predict exactly what the future will look like. Nobody can. But you can influence it. You can shape it. You can make it more like what you yearn for.

That means embracing change. It means being willing to evolve, try new things, make mistakes, and learn from them. It means letting go of old, limiting beliefs and embracing new, empowering ones. It means recognizing that you're not confined by what you once were. You're defined by what you long to be, and every day, every moment, is an opportunity to move in that direction.

Life is a magnificent journey, and you're right in the middle of it. Where will you go from here?

Day 80

It's Not Your Fault

When something isn't your fault, it can be tempting to throw up your hands and say, "Not my problem!" And in some cases, that might be the appropriate response. But other times, even when something isn't your fault it is still your responsibility.

Maybe it's a problem at work that lands in your lap. Maybe it's a friend or family member who needs help. Maybe it's a societal issue that you feel passionate about addressing.

In these moments, we have a choice. We can get caught up in blame and fairness, or we can step up and take responsibility.

Taking responsibility doesn't mean you accept fault. It means you recognize that for whatever reason, this is your challenge to face, your opportunity to grow, your chance to make a difference.

It means moving past questions of blame and fairness and asking instead, "What can I do? How can I help? What is the right thing for me to do in this situation?" It means recognizing that life isn't always fair, that things don't always go as planned, and that we still have the power to choose how we respond.

When we take responsibility for things that aren't our fault, we empower ourselves. We move from a place of victimhood to a place of agency. We become not just passive recipients of life's whims but active participants in shaping our destiny.

It's not always easy. It can be frustrating, exhausting, even infuriating. But it's also an opportunity for growth, leadership, and making a difference in the world.

So next time you find yourself faced with something that's not your fault, ask yourself: Is it still your responsibility? And if so, what will you choose to do about it?

Because things that aren't your fault can still be your opportunity to shine.

Day 81

Smile Through the Tears

"Even through my tears, I give my smile to the world." A simple statement, yet it's packed with profound resilience and grace.

Life is not always easy. It can throw curveballs that leave us feeling overwhelmed and broken. In those moments, the world may seem dark, and smiling might feel like the last thing we want to do.

But that smile, that act of choosing to express a glimmer of hope even in the midst of pain, is a powerful declaration. It's a reminder to ourselves that we're more than our current circumstances. It's a message to others that grace and resilience are possible even when life is tough.

This isn't about pretending everything's okay when it's not or about suppressing real emotions. It's about recognizing our capacity to endure and to find pockets of joy and gratitude even when things are tough.

We all have this ability. It's like a muscle that we can exercise and strengthen. And by doing so, we not only lift ourselves but also inspire those around us.

So if you find yourself amidst tears, remember your power to smile. Embrace it. Share it with the world. It may just be the beacon of hope that someone else needs to see. It's an act of courage and a testament to the human spirit that even in our most vulnerable moments, we have the power to uplift ourselves and others.

Day 82

Life Is Lived Moving Forward

Life is a fascinating paradox, isn't it?

You stand at the edge of a great vista, looking back at the winding path you've carved, and it all makes sense. The decisions, mistakes, successes, and failures all form a clear and coherent story. But turn your eyes forward to the path that awaits and it's shrouded in mist, uncertainty dancing with the unknown.

This concept is a timeless truth: We can only understand life when looking backward, but we must live it moving forward.

When you look back at the past, you see patterns and connections. You understand why one door led to another, why a failure was actually a lesson, why a certain encounter changed your direction.

But here's where it gets beautifully complex: You can't live life backward.

You can't stand gazing forever at what's already happened. Life is perpetual motion, and you're carried along facing forward into the mystery. You have to make decisions, take risks, and move without the luxury of understanding how it all fits together.

So what's the takeaway? How do we navigate this paradox?

Perhaps it's a reminder to embrace both the clarity of reflection and the thrill of uncertainty. It's a call to find peace in not knowing, to make peace with imperfect information, leaps of faith, and gut instincts.

It's about trusting that just as the past now makes sense, the future will one day too. It's about having the courage to move, to act, to live even when the path ahead is not clear.

Maybe it's also about forgiveness. Forgive yourself for not knowing earlier what you know now.

The wisdom you have today was earned through living, through moving forward without knowing, through embracing life's uncertainty.

And perhaps most beautifully of all, it's an invitation to dance with life's twists and turns, surprises and lessons. Life doesn't offer a roadmap, and that's what makes it so rich, so challenging, so infinitely interesting.

Trust yourself. Keep moving forward. Someday, it will all make sense.

You Have What So Many Desire

Imagine standing at the threshold of the world's vast library, a place filled with the knowledge and wisdom of countless generations. You have the key. You can open the door, step inside, and feast on the intellectual treasures within. You can read, learn, grow, and transform your life in ways that many can only dream of.

Now pause for a moment. Look over your shoulder. There, on the other side of that door, are billions of faces yearning for the very opportunity you hold in your hands. They long to learn but are restrained by circumstances. They hunger for knowledge but are starved by lack of access. They want to read but don't have access to books.

You are lucky. You have what so many desire.

It's easy to lose sight of this privilege. In the rush of daily life, in the maze of our busy routines, we often forget how fortunate we are. We overlook the power we possess, the possibilities in front of us, and the potential we hold.

But here's the thing: that realization of our advantage is not meant to weigh us down with guilt or shame. Instead, it's fuel. It's inspiration. It's a call to action.

Use what you have. Learn, grow, and never take it for granted. Don't let opportunities slip through your fingers like sand. Grasp them, embrace them, and make the most of them.

Read that book. Take that course. Pursue that dream. Not just for yourself, but for those who can't. Live with purpose knowing that your actions honor the unfulfilled desires of so many others.

And while you're at it, consider how you can extend that opportunity to others. Share a book. Teach a skill. Open a door. You never know whose life you might change.

Remember, life is not just about what you have; it's about what you do with what you have. It's about recognizing your privilege and using it as a springboard for growth not just for yourself but for the world around you.

So go on, seize the day. Make the most of your opportunities. Learn, grow, and never forget the faces on the other side of the door.

That's the fuel. That's the fire. Use it.

Day 84

The Lessons From Your Scars

O ur most painful experiences often hide our greatest lessons. That may sound paradoxical or even cliché, but it's a truth many of us come to realize.

When we're in the midst of suffering, the idea that there might be a valuable lesson hidden within it can seem absurd, if not offensive.

Yet as time goes on and the wounds begin to heal, we may find ourselves drawn back to those moments not out of masochism or a desire to wallow in the pain but out of a sense that there's something important there, something worth understanding.

You see, pain has a way of cutting through the noise and distractions of life and focusing our attention with laser-like precision on what truly matters.

It can reveal our deepest values, our most profound desires, our most authentic selves. It can show us where we're strong and where we're weak, where we're whole and where we're broken.

But to extract those lessons, we must be willing to face the pain head-on, to sit with it and explore it not as a victim but as a student. We must approach our scars with curiosity, compassion, and courage, asking ourselves what they have to teach us, how they have shaped us, and how they can empower us moving forward.

It's not an easy process. It takes time, patience, and often the support of others who understand what we're going through. But the rewards can be immense.

Our scars become not just reminders of where we've been, but signposts pointing the way forward. They become sources of strength, resilience, wisdom, and empathy. They become part of our story, part of who we are, part of how we show up in the world.

So if you find yourself drawn to revisit a painful experience, know that you're not alone. Know that it's a personal expedition worth taking. On the other side of the pain lies something valuable, beautiful, and uniquely yours.

Take your time. Be gentle with yourself. And when you're ready, let your scars speak to you. Listen to what they have to say. Let them guide you towards a future where you're not just surviving but thriving, not just healing but growing, not just overcoming but becoming.

Day 85

We Gather Strength As We Go

Amidst life's ebb and flow, there lies the profound truth of the Latin saying *Vires acquirit eundo*: "We gather strength as we go."

It's a mantra that can guide us through life's twisting paths, a reminder that our strength does not lie dormant, waiting to be uncovered, but rather builds and grows with each passing moment.

Imagine a river that starts as a trickle high in the mountains. As it winds its way down the slopes, it gathers more water and power, becoming a force to be reckoned with. It learns from its trek, from the rocks and the trees and the landscape that shape its path. It doesn't resist its challenges but embraces them, using them to grow stronger and more resilient.

We're like that river. Life doesn't always hand us a map, and our path may not be smooth or straightforward. But with each experience, each twist and turn, we gather strength.

It's not always easy to see, especially in the moments that challenge us most. When we're in the thick of it, facing a steep climb or a seemingly insurmountable obstacle, it's natural to feel weak, tired, or overwhelmed. But that's when this truth shines brightest.

We gather strength as we go.

The challenges aren't hindrances; they're opportunities. They teach us about what we're capable of and what truly matters to us. They shape us, mold us, and forge us into something more potent and powerful than we were before.

Think back to a time when you faced something tough, something that pushed you to your limits. Maybe you stumbled, maybe you fell, but you didn't break. You learned, you grew, and you kept moving forward. That experience, as painful as it may have been, contributed to who you are today.

Embrace your path with all its ups and downs. Recognize that the very things that seem to be holding you back are the things that propel you forward. Trust the process and know that you're gathering strength, wisdom, and resilience with each step.

Don't shy away from the difficult parts. Face them head-on with the knowledge that they're not roadblocks but fuel for your growth.

It's in the crucible of life's experiences that we forge our resilience and fortitude. Embrace the process of continuous improvement and know that with every stride, you are becoming stronger, wiser, and more capable.

Day 86

Letting Go

"*When I let go of what I am, I become what I might be.*"- Lao Tzu

Lao Tzu's words remind us of the power of letting go: the art of shedding old skin to embrace new possibilities. When we release the limitations of who we think we are, we open the door to becoming who we can be.

It is the act of surrendering to change that allows us to bloom into our full potential. Our past does not define us; it is merely a stepping stone to the future.

Embrace the liberation that comes with releasing your self-imposed labels and constraints. In doing so, you unleash the potential to become the magnificent version of yourself that awaits beyond the horizon. Let go of the old narratives, and step into the infinite realm of what you might be with an open heart.

It doesn't mean forgetting or discarding the past. It's about acknowledging it, learning from it, and then releasing it with gratitude to allow space for the new.

By letting go, we're not losing or diminishing ourselves. We're evolving and expanding; we're becoming more aligned with who we truly are and what we're meant to be.

Day 87

Triumph and Disaster

"*If you can meet with triumph and disaster and treat those two impostors just the same...*" –Rudyard Kipling

Triumph and disaster: two powerful words that resonate with all of us. We've all experienced the highs of success and the lows of failure. But what if we consider them both impostors? What if we looked beyond their immediate effects and recognized them as merely fleeting moments in time?

Triumph can be intoxicating. It fills us with joy, pride, and an overwhelming sense of achievement. But if we attach ourselves to it, if we let it define us, then we can easily become complacent or arrogant. We might begin to believe that we're invincible and forget the continuous effort, growth, and humility that true success requires.

Disaster, on the other hand, can feel crushing. It can break our spirit, fill us with doubt, and cause us to question our worth. But if we can step back and view it as an impostor — as a temporary setback rather than a defining failure — we can learn from it, grow, and come back even stronger.

Kipling urges us to treat these two impostors just the same. Why? Because life is full of ups and downs, successes and failures. If we become too attached to either, we risk losing sight of our core values, our true selves, and the bigger picture of what we're aiming to achieve.

By treating triumph and disaster as equals — as transient events rather than defining moments — we maintain our equilibrium. We stay grounded, focused, and true to our path. We recognize that both success and failure are parts of the journey. Neither is more important than the other, and both provide lessons to be learned.

Kipling's words are not just poetic wisdom; they're a guide to a resilient and fulfilled life. They remind us that what truly matters is not the fleeting victories or defeats but how we handle them, learn from them, and continue to strive for what we believe in.

In embracing this philosophy, we take ownership of our lives, our reactions, and our path forward. We become masters of ourselves, unaffected by the external circumstances that might otherwise derail us.

Remember, triumph and disaster are merely guests in the grand scheme of our lives. Treat them as the impostors they are, and yours is the earth and everything that's in it.

It's a path worth walking.

Day 88

Knowing Isn't the Hard Part

Knowing what to do isn't the hard part. You know what you need to do to lose weight, write that book, build that business, or cultivate that relationship. The knowledge is there, often staring us right in the face, sometimes even nagging us in the quiet moments before sleep.

The real challenge isn't ignorance; it's taking action. It's the willingness to pay the price and the understanding that sacrifices must be made. Every choice to pursue a dream carries a cost, be it time, comfort, money, or even relationships. There's always a trade-off.

So why do we hold back?

It's easier to dream than to do.

Dreams are comfortable and risk-free, existing only in the safe confines of our minds. Pursuing them exposes us to the possibility of failure, the pain of rejection, and the discomfort of venturing beyond our comfort zone.

Here's a revelation: Those instances where we stand firm, even when every fiber wants to retreat, are the exact moments that sculpt our growth trajectory.

The path to success is littered with difficult decisions, and every step forward may require leaving something behind. But remember, the price of inaction is often higher than the cost of action. Stagnation, regret, the haunting question of "what if?" — these are burdens far heavier to bear.

Recognize that achieving something of significance isn't just about the end goal; it's about who you become along the way. Embrace the struggles, sacrifices, and triumphs. Each step, each choice, and each price paid is a brick in the foundation of a life well-lived.

And in the end, you'll find that the real treasure isn't just the destination. The real riches are the wisdom, strength, and fulfillment gained from the odyssey itself. The price that once seemed so daunting transforms into an investment in a richer, more meaningful life. That's the trade worth making.

Day 89

All In

See, most of us tiptoe through our days testing the waters, afraid of diving deep. We have this irrational fear of commitment because commitment means risk. What if we're wrong? What if we fail? What if it's not "the thing" for us?

But here's a perspective shift: What if by not committing, by not going "all in," you're missing out on the full spectrum of experiences, emotions, and growth that life offers? What if staying on the sidelines is the bigger risk?

When you go all in on life, you're not just saying yes to an opportunity, you're embracing all that life has — the ups, the downs, the joys, the heartbreaks. You're acknowledging that the journey is as valuable as the destination, if not more.

There's a certain intensity to living this way. It's like turning the volume up on life. Colors become brighter, moments more memorable, experiences more profound. Why? Because you're fully present, fully committed, and fully engaged.

Commitment has a momentum of its own. When you're all in, doors open. People notice. The universe itself seems to conspire in your favor. It's as if life rewards those brave enough to fully commit to it.

But "all in" doesn't mean recklessly throwing everything into chaos. It means a calculated embrace of life with all its uncertainties. It's a mindset; a declaration that you're playing full out regardless of the outcomes.

The Latin root of the word *decide* means *to cut off*. So when you decide to go all in, you're cutting off other possibilities and distractions. You're narrowing your focus to the present, to the magic of the now.

So here's the challenge: Decide to be all in on life. Not half-hearted. Not lukewarm. All in. Because life, with all its unpredictability, is waiting for you to embrace it, to dive deep, to experience it in its fullness.

In the end, remember: Life doesn't ask for perfection, but it does ask for participation. Dive in. Participate fully. Go all in.

Day 90

You're Stronger Than You Think

Sometimes life gets heavy. You know the feeling. Responsibilities pile up and it seems like everything is demanding your attention at once. It's like you're juggling flaming torches and they just keep adding more.

At times like these, it's natural to feel overwhelmed. Doubt creeps in. The little voice in the back of your mind starts to ask, "Can I really handle all this?" "Am I strong enough?" "Will I drop everything and crash?"

Here's the secret: You are strong enough. We all are. You have within you an extraordinary reserve of strength and resilience that you might not even be aware of. It's waiting just beneath the surface, ready to be called upon when needed.

I know it doesn't always feel that way. When you're in the thick of things, juggling everything life throws your way, it's easy to lose sight of your own strength. But it's there, trust me. It's like a deep well within you filled with determination, persistence, and unwavering resolve. Even when you feel like you're running on empty, even when you think you've hit the bottom of that well, there's still more there. You just have to dig a little deeper. Don't be afraid to lean into that hidden reservoir of strength.

Take a moment to breathe, reassess, and remind yourself of everything you've already accomplished. Look back at the times when you felt defeated but pushed through anyway. That's evidence of your strength. You've handled tough situations before, and you can do it again.

And when you come out the other side, you'll be all the more resilient, wise, and strong for having faced it.

Day 91

Habits

Habits. They're these fascinating little creatures that live in the crevices of our daily lives. At first glance they might seem inconsequential, but oh, how they shape us.

Think of a habit as a river cutting through a canyon. One day of water flowing won't make a difference, but give it time, and it will carve a path so deep and so profound that it will dramatically shape the landscape.

Now translate that to your life. Each small action, each repeated behavior, and each daily ritual is like that gently flowing water. And just like the river, given enough time it will carve a path in your life. It's subtle, yes, but over time it's monumental.

Your habits, whether you consciously acknowledge them or not, are declarations of who you want to become. They're like little promises to your future self. Each time you choose to perform a positive action, you're laying a brick on the path to becoming the person you aspire to be.

Here's the beauty and the challenge of habits: They work both ways. Positive habits build you up, creating strength, resilience, wisdom, and grace. Negative habits tear you down, accumulating weakness, stagnation, frustration, and despair.

That's why it's essential to choose your habits wisely. They're not just routines; they're commitments. They are the slow, steady building blocks of transformation.

And the most beautiful part? You have control over them. You can decide what habits you want to cultivate, and you can take the steps to embed them in your life.

It won't be instant, and that's okay. Habits aren't about immediate gratification. They're about lasting change.

So if you want to make a change in your life, look at your habits. They might seem trivial, but their power is immense. They often go unnoticed, operating under the surface, but they're quietly, patiently, persistently working to sculpt you day by day.

And when you realize that, when you really grasp the magnitude of their influence, you unlock a tool that can propel you toward the life you desire.

Remember, your daily actions are not just habits; they're a reflection of who you are and a blueprint for who you'll become. Embrace them with intention, cultivate them with care, and watch how they shape you into the person you've always wanted to be... or not.

Day 92

Earned Success, a Path to Fulfillment

Earned success. It's a phrase that sounds both inspiring and intimidating. But what does it really mean, and why is it so essential to our happiness?

Think of it this way: When you set out in pursuit of a goal — something far from your grasp, something that requires effort, determination, and grit — you're signing up for a transformation.

It's not just about reaching the peak of a mountain. It's about the climb. It's about the sweat, the perseverance, the moments when you feel like giving up but choose to keep going. It's about the person you become as you overcome obstacles, learn from failures, and grow stronger with each step.

In this process, you're not just working towards a goal; you're crafting yourself. You're taking raw materials and, turning them into something new and beautiful through hard work and perseverance.

This is earned success. It's not handed to you on a silver platter. You can't buy it, inherit it, or stumble upon it by luck. You have to work for it. You have to earn it.

The beauty of earned success is that it's yours. No one else can do it for you. Friends and family might support you, but you alone have to fight the battles, make the sacrifices, and navigate the path.

And here's the secret: The joy of reaching the destination is sweet, yet the richness is in the progression towards it. It's in the growth, the discovery, and the understanding that you are capable of more than you thought possible.

Earned success gives you more than a sense of accomplishment. It provides a sense of purpose, autonomy, and mastery. It reminds you that you are the author of your destiny.

It's not about the accolades, recognition, or even tangible rewards. It's about knowing that you stretched yourself, pushed yourself, and emerged a better, stronger, more resilient person.

That's why earned success is a key to happiness. It enriches your soul, builds your character, and leaves you with a sense of fulfillment that goes beyond the surface.

So don't shy away from those goals that seem just out of reach. Embrace them. Chase them with all you've got. Allow yourself to be stretched, challenged, and transformed.

In the end, it's not just about the destination; it's about the person you become along the way. That's a reward no one can take away from you, a treasure that you'll carry with you always, and success that is truly earned.

Day 93

The Beach Ball Effect

Imagine a beach ball in a swimming pool. Now imagine trying to hold it underwater. It seems simple at first. But the deeper you push it, the more resistance you feel. No matter how hard you try, no matter how strong you are, that beach ball wants to float to the surface. If you push it too far and then let go, it doesn't just rise; it erupts out of the water with a force that can be surprising.

Our emotions are a lot like that beach ball.

We all have feelings we'd rather not deal with. They might be painful or uncomfortable, so we push them down. We keep ourselves busy, we distract ourselves, and we tell ourselves we're fine. But just like that beach ball, those feelings don't go away. They're still there under the surface, and the harder we push them down, the more intense they become.

Avoidance doesn't work. Just like that beach ball wants to float, our emotions want to be seen and acknowledged. You can keep avoiding your feelings and pushing them beneath the surface, but at some point, they're going to erupt back up. The energy you use to suppress them doesn't make them disappear; it often makes them stronger.

Resistance amplifies intensity. The more you resist an emotion, the more intense it can become. It's not just that it's still there; it's that it's growing. It's building power like that beach ball being pushed deeper under the water.

Maybe it's time to pause, reassess your current approach, and dare to try something new. Instead of suppressing your emotions, embrace them. Feel them fully.

Ask yourself what they're trying to tell you. Emotions are messengers. They have something to say. Listen.

Remember, it's natural to have emotions, even painful or uncomfortable ones. It's not about getting rid of them but understanding them. Embrace your feelings as they come and learn what they have to teach you.

You can keep pushing them down, but like that beach ball, they will come back up. It's not a sign of weakness but a law of nature.

Day 94

Slow Down to Speed Up

In the world of "go, go, go," the idea of slowing down seems almost rebellious. We're conditioned to believe that faster is always better. Speed, we're told, is the ultimate metric of success. But what if I told you that's not the whole story?

Imagine for a second that you're on a bicycle, pedaling as hard as you can, head down, sweat dripping. But then you look up and realize you've been on the wrong path this entire time. All that effort was not in service of the direction you truly wanted to go. Sounds familiar?

Here's a simple truth: Busyness doesn't always equate to productivity, and constant motion isn't synonymous with progress. In life, it's the pause, the intentional slow-down, that allows us to reset and recalibrate.

Have you ever noticed how the best ideas often come during a leisurely walk or a long shower? When we slow down, we're not just idling. We're creating space to think. Space to breathe. Space to see the bigger picture. By stepping back even momentarily, we gain perspective on where we are and where we want to go.

But here's the real kicker: Once you've slowed down, seen that larger map, and adjusted your course, your forward momentum is not just faster. It's also more aligned and more purposeful. Slowing down allows you to speed up in the right direction.

So next time you feel the weight of the world pushing you to hurry, give yourself permission to resist. Hit the pause button even if just for a moment. It might seem counterintuitive, but sometimes slowing down is the quickest way to get where you truly want to go.

Day 95

The Gift You Give Yourself

Think of forgiveness as a door. Behind that door lies a room filled with all the pain, anger, resentment, and memories you've been holding onto. The door is heavy, and it takes effort to keep it closed. You feel its weight every day, dragging you down and clouding your life with shadows.

Now consider what forgiveness really means. It's not about saying that what happened was okay. It's not about letting someone off the hook for their wrongdoings. It's about putting down the weight of that door and walking away from it.

Forgiving doesn't mean forgetting. It means choosing to focus on the present and future rather than being trapped in the past. It means acknowledging the pain but deciding that it won't define you anymore.

Forgiveness is a gift you give yourself. It's a conscious decision to let go of the bitterness and anger that weighs you down. It's about saying, "I will not carry this burden any longer. I choose to be free."

This act of courage liberates you. It unchains you from the past and lets you step into the now with a clear mind and open heart.

Of course, it's not easy. Forgiveness can be a complex process that takes time and reflection. But the first step is to recognize the power and control that forgiveness puts back into your hands. It's a conscious decision to no longer let the past control your present or future.

Forgive not because the other person deserves forgiveness, but because you deserve peace.

Day 96

Take Off the Mask

Today, something's different. Today, you feel a little lighter, a little freer, a little more yourself. Why? Because today, you've decided to take off the mask.

You know the one. It's that face you put on for others, that version of you that you think the world wants to see. The one that smiles when it doesn't feel like smiling, nods when it doesn't agree, and hides when it wants to shine.

Well, guess what? That mask doesn't fit anymore. It never really did. It's time to take it off. Embrace your authenticity. Let your true self shine, and don't apologize for it. You are one of a kind, and that's something to celebrate.

So why hide? Why pretend? Why not be gloriously, unabashedly, courageously you?

Your imperfections? They're not flaws; they're character. They're the nicks and scratches that tell the story of a life lived, not a life hidden. Embrace them. They make you who you are.

Your uniqueness? That's your gift to the world. It's the color you bring to the tapestry of life. Don't dull it. Don't hide it. Let it shine.

Today is a new beginning — a chance to break free from the constraints of others' expectations and embrace the real you. So go ahead. Take off that mask. Look in the mirror. What do you see?

It's you, in all your wonderful imperfection, all your beautiful uniqueness. It's you as you are meant to be.

Embrace that. Go out there and be you. There's no one else who can.

Day 97

Walking Your Talk

I magine you're part of an orchestra. You can talk all day about the music you're going to play. You can describe it, analyze it, or wax poetic about its beauty. But until you pick up your instrument and play, there's no music. There's only the idea of music. Life is a lot like that.

We can talk about our values, beliefs, and dreams. We can speak eloquently and passionately about what we want to achieve, what we stand for, and what we're against. But without action, those are just ideas. They're not real. They're not alive.

What if instead of talking, we started doing? What if instead of describing the music, we started playing it? What if our actions were so in line with our words that we didn't need to speak at all?

That's where transformation happens. That's where leadership is born. That's where authenticity shines through.

Do you want to inspire others? Don't just tell them what you believe; show them. Live your values. Embody your principles. Walk your talk. It's easy to say you believe in honesty, integrity, kindness, and compassion. But do you live those values? Do your actions reflect them?

In the end, your actions are your legacy. They're what you leave behind. They're your music. Make sure it's a tune that lingers and one that inspires others to move to their own rhythm, to play their own beautiful song.

That's leadership. That's authenticity. That's life fully lived.

Will My Goals Bring Me Happiness?

Goals. We all have them. They drive us, motivate us, and keep us moving forward. But have you ever stopped to think about the goals you're going after? Have you considered whether accomplishing these goals will actually give you what you desire: happiness, peace, and purpose?

It's a critical question, and one we often neglect to ask ourselves. In the rush to achieve, to conquer, or to prove our worth, we can become entangled in the allure of external validation and societal standards. We might find ourselves chasing after worldly achievements without ever discerning if they align with the essence of our true selves.

The problem with this approach is that it can lead to a hollow victory. We might achieve our goals only to find that they don't provide the satisfaction, fulfillment, or joy we were seeking.

This is why it's essential to pause, reflect, and delve into the depths of our being. We need to ask ourselves hard questions like:

- **What do I truly want?**

- **Why do I want this?**

- **Does this goal resonate with my values and authentic vision?**

It's not about abandoning our dreams or dampening our ambition. It's about aligning our aspirations with our core values and purpose.

When we set goals that resonate with our innermost selves, we're not just chasing an arbitrary target. We're moving towards something that has real meaning and significance for us. We're pursuing something that will not only bring success but fulfillment.

So let's take a moment to look beyond the superficial layers of what society deems valuable or successful. Let's go deeper, seeking to understand what truly motivates and inspires us.

Let's strive for goals that reflect who we are, what we stand for, and what we genuinely want in life.

Only by harmonizing our ambitions with our authentic vision and values can we truly savor the taste of fulfillment.

Day 99

Momentum Breeds Momentum

M omentum. It's a powerful force. It can start with something as simple as a small win or a single step forward, and then it grows, building upon itself, gaining speed and strength.

Momentum breeds momentum.

It's one of those truths that's easy to forget but incredibly profound once you grasp it. You don't have to make a massive leap to create significant change. You just have to start — to take that first step and then let the momentum carry you.

Once you take action, something incredible begins to unfold. That first step leads to a second, then a third, then a fourth. Before you know it, you're not just moving; you're rolling. You've got momentum.

What's beautiful about momentum is that it doesn't require constant Herculean effort. Yes, you need to keep moving and pushing, but it gets easier. The more momentum you have, the more natural it becomes to keep going. The effort you put in starts to pay off exponentially.

But it all starts with that first step. It's the key. Without it, nothing happens. With it, anything is possible.

So whatever you want to do, wherever you want to go, don't wait. Don't get hung up on the size of the task or the distance of the journey. Just start. Take that first step. And then let the momentum carry you.

Day 100

How Can I Serve?

"How can I serve?" This question is so simple, yet it holds the power to transform our lives and the world around us. Imagine if it wasn't just a fleeting thought or a one-time query but the central focus of our lives. Imagine waking up every morning with that mantra echoing in our hearts and minds, guiding our actions and decisions.

Service is often associated with volunteering at a soup kitchen, building homes for those in need, or other charitable actions. While those are noble endeavors, the concept of service is rooted in something deeper.

Service is about the way we approach everything in life — our relationships, our work, our community. It's a perspective, a philosophy that sees ourselves not as isolated individuals but as interconnected beings who are part of a greater whole.

When we embrace this philosophy, we begin to see opportunities to serve everywhere. In our relationships, it means being present, listening, understanding, and supporting others in the way they need. In our work, it means focusing not just on personal gain but on the broader impact we can make. In our community, it means recognizing the ways we can contribute to the well-being of those around us.

Service is not about self-sacrifice or neglecting our own health and happiness. Quite the opposite, in fact. When we serve others, we enrich our own lives. We find purpose, connection, and fulfillment. We discover parts of ourselves we didn't know existed.

And we inspire others to do the same.

Imagine if this philosophy spread. Imagine if everyone asked, "How can I serve?" and lived that question. The ripple effect would be profound. Society would shift from competition to collaboration, from isolation to connection, from scarcity to abundance.

The beauty of this approach is that it's accessible to all of us right now. We don't have to wait for some future time or condition. We can start today, at this moment, with a simple choice to see the world through the lens of service.

Ask yourself, "How can I serve?" Let that question guide you. Let it open your eyes to the possibilities around you. Let it reshape your life.

Day 101

The Canvas of Transformation

Within each of us, hidden in the depths of our spirit, lies a most extraordinary gift—the remarkable ability to transform ourselves. This is not just a poetic sentiment but a profound truth, a living reality that we carry within our very essence.

Think about it for a moment. We are not static beings trapped in a single form or defined by past choices. We are fluid, ever-evolving, capable of growth and reinvention.

With each passing day, we hold the power to shed old skin, leave behind limiting beliefs, and break free from patterns that no longer serve us. We can paint the canvas of our lives with vibrant hues, crafting a masterpiece that reflects our deepest desires and highest aspirations.

Why? Because change is in our DNA. It's the essence of being human.

Transformation is not always easy. It requires courage, effort, and determination. It calls for self-awareness, self-reflection, and self-love. It asks us to confront our fears, face our shadows, and challenge our comfort zones.

But the rewards are immeasurable. Transformation leads to new possibilities, greater fulfillment, and a deeper connection with ourselves and others.

So how do we tap into this gift? How do we unleash our potential for change?

It starts with a choice—a choice to recognize our ability to transform and to commit to growth.

It continues with action—small, consistent steps towards our goals, fueled by a sense of purpose and guided by a vision of who we can become.

And it flourishes with patience, perseverance, and faith in the process.

Through the alchemy of intentional evolution, we shape our destinies and sculpt the person we aspire to be. Let us not shy away from change, for it is in the embrace of change that we unlock the truest expressions of our humanity and elevate ourselves to new heights of greatness.

Embrace it. Celebrate it. And most importantly, use transformation. Because in the story of your life, you're both the author and the protagonist. And the best chapters? They're yet to come.

All You Have is One Raspberry, and You Give It to a Friend

I was struck to my core when I came across the story in Benjamin Zander's book *The Art of Possibility*. The tale was set in a place of unimaginable horror, but what unfolded was a profound lesson in humanity, love, and generosity.

Imagine the scene at the Holocaust Memorial at Quincy Market in Boston. Five of the six pillars inscribed with stories speak of cruelty and suffering. But then there's the sixth pillar. A different tale. A beacon of hope amidst despair.

It tells the story of a little girl named Ilse, around six years old, living in the hellish world of Auschwitz. Among all the deprivation, she found something beautiful, something precious—a single raspberry. In a place where mere survival was a daily battle, where kindness was a rarity, this small fruit was a treasure beyond measure.

But what Ilse did with that raspberry is what ripped open my heart and let love flow from it.

She carried it all day, protecting it, cherishing it. And in the evening, with eyes shining with joy and love, she gave it to her friend Guerda on a leaf. Her only possession, the symbol of life and hope in a barren world, she gifted to another.

"Imagine a world," writes Guerda, "in which your entire possession is one raspberry, and you give it to your friend."

Stop for a moment and let that sink in.

This story isn't about a raspberry. It's about the essence of human goodness. It's about the ability to find beauty in the bleakest of places. It's about the strength of spirit that enables a little girl to transcend her circumstances and perform an act of pure selflessness.

What can we learn from Ilse's raspberry?

We live in a world abundant with material possessions, yet how often do we truly share? How often do we give without expecting anything in return? How often do we find joy in the joy of others?

The gifting of a raspberry teaches us that generosity is not about the size of the gift but the size of the heart. It's about seeing beyond ourselves and recognizing the humanity in others. It's about the love, the connection, the empathy that binds us all.

In a world often driven by self-interest and competition, let's remember Ilse's raspberry. Let's strive to cultivate a heart that gives, a soul that loves, and a spirit that uplifts.

No act of kindness is too small. No gesture of love is insignificant.

Let's be the love we wish to see in the world.

Day 103

Gardening the Mind

I sn't it fascinating how our thoughts shape our reality? I've often found myself in awe of the intricate web of human behavior. With a little observation and a dash of introspection, it becomes clear that the origin of every destructive action and regrettable decision can be traced back to the seeds of negative thought.

Negativity is insidious. It doesn't always announce itself with a loud bang but rather creeps into our consciousness, slowly taking root.

These poisonous tendrils infiltrate our minds and poison our perceptions. It might start with a single pessimistic thought, a momentary doubt, or a fleeting fear. But left unchecked, these thoughts multiply, darken, and become a part of us.

I've been there. It's a place none of us want to be.

But here's the good news: Our minds are gardens and we are the gardeners. It's in the crucible of our thoughts that we forge our character and thus the quality of our actions.

So how do we go about gardening the mind?

First, recognize that the mind is fertile soil. It will grow what you plant in it. Plant seeds of doubt, fear, envy, and anger, and you'll harvest a crop of despair, anxiety, jealousy, and rage. But plant seeds of hope, optimism, resilience, and love, and you'll cultivate a life filled with joy, positivity, strength, and compassion.

Identify the weeds. Know what negative thoughts look like. Recognize them when they sprout. Acknowledge them without judgment and actively work to remove them.

Nourish the good seeds. Focus on what you want to grow. Feed your mind with positive affirmations, inspiring books, uplifting friendships, and nourishing experiences.

Protect your garden. Be mindful of what you allow into your mind. Surround yourself with positive influences. Avoid environments that breed negativity. Create barriers that keep the toxic weeds out.

Tend your garden daily. Cultivating a positive mind is not a one-time task but a daily practice. Constantly monitor, nurture, and care for your thoughts.

Celebrate the blooms. Acknowledge and celebrate the growth of positive thoughts and the changes they bring about in your life.

Remember, the garden of the mind is never static. It's either growing or decaying. Make the conscious choice to cultivate a beautiful garden daily.

Day 104

Unshackling From the External

Anchoring your happiness on factors beyond your control is like building your house on shifting sands. It's a perilous game, one that can perpetuate an endless cycle of pain and disappointment.

When our joy depends on external circumstances, other people's opinions, or unpredictable events, we essentially hand over the reins of our contentment to forces that are fickle and fluctuating. We become passengers on a roller coaster of emotions, riding the highs and lows dictated by elements beyond our command.

The alternative, then, is to anchor our happiness in what we can control: our thoughts, attitudes, and reactions.

By rooting our contentment in the fertile ground of our own values, actions, and personal growth, we create a stable foundation that sustains us. We become masters of our emotional terrain, not subject to the whims of external forces.

This doesn't mean ignoring the world around us, but rather engaging with it from a place of inner strength and stability, knowing that our core happiness is firmly planted in our own hands.

Day 105

Spectators of Life

The allure of the future and the pull of the past can be seductive distractions pulling us away from the only moment that truly matters: the here and now.

When our desires leap into the future and our minds wander into the past, we relinquish our presence, becoming mere spectators to our own lives. The now is all we have, yet we often forget that.

We're tempted to dwell on our memories or forecast our future. But where does that leave us? Always a step behind or ahead but never where we are. When we lose ourselves in thoughts of what was or what might be, we miss out on what is. We're not in our lives; we're watching it like a movie on a screen.

It's natural, of course. The past and future can feel safe. The past is known and the future is full of potential. But neither is alive. Neither is real. The now, though? It's uncharted territory. It's full of surprises, joys, sorrows, and infinite possibilities. It's where life happens.

So how do we stay present? How do we resist the thoughts of yesterday and tomorrow? We must engage. Fully. Passionately. Deliberately.

Being in the now happens in the awareness of simple things: the taste of food, the sound of laughter, the feel of the wind on your face. It's in the complex things too: the solving of problems, the forging of relationships, the pursuit of dreams. But it's always now.

For in the end, it's the only place you ever truly are. It's where life is. Don't be a spectator to your own existence. Be alive in it.

Day 106

Your Direction

You've got a direction. Maybe it's a blur; maybe it's crystal clear. But it's yours. In a world obsessed with likes, shares, and nods of approval, we're led to believe that our goals need to be billboard-worthy. Flashy enough for everyone to see.

They don't. Your dreams? They might be whispers now — silent anthems only you can hear. It's enough. Silence has its perks. It's when your wisdom speaks loudest. The world's noise is a fickle symphony. Your inner hum? That's the beat that'll drive you.

The pioneers weren't popular. They were weird, obsessive, out-of-sync. They saw maps where others saw wilderness. It's not about being stubborn; it's about knowing yourself so well that external chatter fades into the background.

Walking alone can feel heavy. Doubt is a sneaky companion. But remember, history is written by the ones who heard a different tune and moved to their own moves anyway.

In every step and stumble, you're proving to yourself that your direction matters.

The endgame? It's not some grand arrival. It's the gritty grind, the transformation, and the sheer audacity to say, "This is my way."

So if you've got that fire, that map nobody else sees, guard it. Walk it. Because knowing where you're going, even when no one else does — that's not just enough. That's gold.

Things Are Impossible Right Up Until They're Not

I t's funny how the mind works. We look at something and say, "That's impossible." But what are we really saying? We're saying, "I can't see how that's possible, so it must not be." But how many things in this world were once deemed impossible?

For centuries, humans looked at the birds and said, "Wouldn't it be amazing if we could do that?" And yet the concept of human flight was seen as an unattainable fantasy, a dream that defied the laws of physics.

Then came the Wright brothers: two bicycle mechanics who refused to be shackled by the impossible. Through sheer determination, curiosity, and creativity, they transformed an impossible dream into a soaring reality.

Why does this matter?

Because the realization of an impossible dream doesn't just change what we can do. It changes who we are. It reshapes our perception of ourselves and our place in the world. The boundaries we once thought were rigid and immutable become fluid, flexible, and negotiable.

And it's not just about grand achievements like flight or landing on the moon. It's about the personal impossibilities we overcome every day. The career we never thought we could have. The relationship we never thought we could mend. The fear we never thought we could overcome.

Once you've tasted the exhilaration of making the impossible possible, something profound shifts within you. The world opens up. You begin to see opportunities where once there were only barriers. You begin to believe in yourself in ways you never thought possible.

And that belief is a powerful thing. It's a spark that can ignite a fire: a fire that burns away doubt and hesitation, leaving only clarity, confidence, and courage.

So what's your impossible dream? What's the thing you've told yourself you could never achieve?

Embrace it. Explore it. Dive into it with all your heart and soul. Allow yourself to be consumed by the possibility of it. Because the truth is, the only limits that really exist are the ones we place on ourselves.

And when you shatter those limits — when you achieve an impossible dream — you don't just change what you can do. You change who you are. You awaken to a new reality, a reality where anything is possible.

Day 108

By Endurance We Conquer

Fortitudine Vincimus: "By endurance we conquer." These words have a way of lingering in my mind and resurfacing when I need them most. This motto is not just a comforting phrase but a way of approaching life itself.

In a world obsessed with speed, instant success, and rapid solutions, this motto stands as a beacon of wisdom, calling us back to an understanding of life that honors persistence, patience, and endurance.

Achieving anything meaningful often requires a long and winding trek. It's not the swift sprint but the consistent pace that takes us to the finish line. If we give up too soon, we never give ourselves a chance to reach our potential.

Mastery takes time.

Whether it's learning a musical instrument, building a business, or nurturing a relationship, patience allows us to grow organically without rushing the process. Life will inevitably bring challenges, failures, and setbacks. *Fortitudine Vincimus* teaches us to endure these trials not by resisting them but by facing them with grace and resilience. It's not about how hard you can hit but how hard you can get hit and keep moving forward.

This motto also encourages us to recognize that strength doesn't mean invulnerability. Strength is about accepting our imperfections, our fears, and our doubts and still choosing to stick to the path.

Most importantly, *Fortitudine Vincimus* is a reminder that we are often far more capable than we believe. By enduring, we discover strengths we didn't know we had.

The spirit of endurance is like a quiet river that keeps flowing regardless of the obstacles in its path. It doesn't rage against the rocks or lament the twists and turns. It simply keeps moving, always forward, cutting through the landscape with gentle determination.

It's a spirit we can all cultivate. When faced with a challenge, we can choose to see it as a roadblock or as an opportunity to grow, learn, and strengthen our character.

So the next time you find yourself on the brink of giving up, pause and whisper to yourself, *Fortitudine Vincimus*. Let it be your rallying cry, a reminder that you have the inner fortitude to conquer whatever stands before you.

It's not just about enduring; it's about thriving in the face of life's complexities and emerging stronger and wiser on the other side.

Day 109

Standing Up... for Yourself

Have you noticed how sometimes the smallest actions carry the most significant weight? Like saying "no" when it would be easier to say "yes," or speaking up when it would be more comfortable to stay silent?

These tiny acts of standing up for yourself might seem insignificant at the moment, but they're like building blocks, creating a foundation for something more profound.

Think about this for a second: You're in a meeting, and someone makes a suggestion that doesn't quite sit right with you. It would be easy to nod along, to blend into the consensus, but something inside you nudges you to speak up. You clear your throat, voice your opinion, and stand up for what you believe, even though it's a small matter. It's just a brief moment, but it's also a declaration of self-respect.

These small acts of standing up for yourself aren't just about that moment. They set a precedent for how you want to be treated and how you choose to live your life.

Standing up for yourself in small ways is practice for when you'll need to do it in more significant, more consequential situations.

But here's the fascinating part: The little things ARE the big things. By standing up for yourself in everyday interactions, you're not only building confidence and integrity, but you're also shaping your identity. You're telling yourself and others who you are and what you stand for.

It doesn't mean you have to be confrontational or aggressive. Standing up for yourself can be done with grace, kindness, and firmness. It's about being true to yourself, honoring your values, and not allowing others to define you.

So here's a gentle challenge for you: Notice those small opportunities to stand up for yourself. Embrace them. Recognize that they're not trivial but essential pieces of the puzzle that makes you you.

Remember, life doesn't just happen in grand gestures and pivotal moments. It's woven together out of the everyday, the mundane, the seemingly insignificant. And in those spaces, you have countless opportunities to define yourself, to grow, and to become the person you wish to be.

Stand up for yourself, even in the smallest of ways, and see where that path takes you. It might just lead you to a more authentic, more empowered version of yourself.

The Hero's Journey

In life, there are patterns and cycles that reflect universal truths. Joseph Campbell's *The Hero's Journey* explores one of those patterns — a template that helps us understand the human experience in a profound way.

The Hero's Journey resonates with storytellers and seekers alike because it describes a universal pattern in the human experience. Broken down into twelve distinct stages, it paints a picture of growth, discovery, struggle, and triumph that we can all recognize in our lives.

The 12 Steps of The Hero's Journey

1. **Ordinary world.** This is where we find ourselves before the adventure begins. It's our comfort zone, our everyday life. But within this ordinary existence, there's often a feeling that something is missing — a whisper that there's more to life.

2. **Call to adventure.** Suddenly, something shakes us out of our routine. It might be a feeling, a person, an opportunity, or a challenge that presents itself. It beckons us to step out of our comfort zone and embark on something new.

3. **Refusal of the call**. Fear and doubt often make us hesitate. We may refuse the call because we're scared of what lies ahead. This refusal, however, is part of the process. It's a natural reaction to the unknown.

4. **Meeting the mentor**. Whether it's a person, a book, or an inner realization, the mentor provides guidance, encouragement, and wisdom to help

us overcome our fears and accept the call to adventure.

5. **Crossing the threshold.** This is the point of no return. We commit to the adventure and leave the ordinary world behind. It's both exciting and terrifying, and it's where the journey truly begins.

6. **Tests, allies, and enemies.** Along the path, we face challenges, meet new friends, and encounter foes. These trials help us learn and grow, and they prepare us for the greater challenges ahead.

7. **Approach to the inmost cave**. We come to the edge of a deep abyss or challenge where we must face our greatest fears and doubts. This is a time of reflection and preparation.

8. **Ordeal: The darkest hour.** We must face our greatest challenge — our most fearsome opponent — which is often a part of ourselves we have been unwilling to face.

9. **Reward: seizing the sword.** Having faced and conquered our fears, we seize the reward, whether it's a physical object, personal growth, understanding, or reconciliation.

10. **The road back**. The journey isn't over yet. There may be new challenges as we find our way back to the ordinary world carrying our hard-earned wisdom with us.

11. **Resurrection**. This is a final test or last initiation, where we must prove that we have truly changed, that we have become something new.

12. **Return with the elixir.** The journey is complete. We return to the ordinary world, but we're transformed. We have something to share — wisdom, healing, or an understanding that can benefit others.

It's more than just a storytelling template; it's a metaphor for our lives. It reminds us that growth requires courage, that the path will not always be smooth, and that the rewards of self-discovery are worth the struggles. Your adventure awaits.

The Unwritten Novel of Life

Imagine your life as an unwritten novel — blank pages crisp and unblemished, ready to record the great adventures of your existence. The weight of the pen feels significant, doesn't it? It's because you're holding in your hand the power to craft a story that's uniquely yours.

Sure, not all of us can pen great novels like the literary legends, but let's pause and consider something even more profound. We can live lives that are just as extraordinary, memorable, and impactful. Each step you take and every decision you make is a stroke of the pen that shapes the narrative of your life. It's not only about the grand gestures and sweeping arcs but also the little details, the subtle nuances that add texture and depth to your story.

Life is full of plot twists, unexpected turns, and surprises. Some chapters are filled with triumph while others are marred by tragedy. But remember, it's not the events that define you; it's how you respond to them. It's about how you choose to write those moments into your life's manuscript.

You're not just a passive observer. You are the author. Your decisions, your actions, and your attitude all contribute to the unfolding plot. You have the creative freedom to choose the themes, the tone, and the direction of your story.

Don't rush through the pages, skimming the surface, missing the profound beauty hidden in each paragraph. Slow down. Engage with your story. Feel the emotions. Learn from the conflicts. Celebrate the resolutions.

Remember, no one else can write this story for you. Only you can determine how the pages will be filled, the chapters unfold, and the story end. Write it well.

Day 112

The Choice

Life can feel like a maze of choices, each one tugging at our hearts and minds. Yet amid the complexity, there exists a simple, profound decision that holds the key to our happiness. Strip away the noise and ask yourself, "*Do I want to be happy?*"

This isn't some glossy magazine advice to plaster on a smile and bypass the gritty realities. No, it's far deeper than that. It's understanding that happiness isn't a passive state that befalls the lucky ones. It's an active choice.

It's not about turning a blind eye to adversities or glossing over our genuine feelings. It's realizing that every situation, whether radiant or challenging, comes with a small, powerful space: the space to choose our reaction.

Choosing happiness is not about ignoring life's challenges or pretending that everything is perfect. It's about recognizing that in each moment, you have the ability to choose how you respond to life's unfolding drama.

By choosing happiness, you start to see the world through a new lens. You recognize that happiness is not something that happens to you but something you create, cultivate, and choose.

Begin here.

- **Start with awareness.** Recognize that happiness is a choice.

- **Pay attention** to your thoughts and feelings without judgment. Notice when you drift into negativity and gently steer yourself back toward a positive focus.

- **Take action** that aligns with your desire for happiness. Choose activities, relationships, and environments that nurture your well-being.

- **Reflect regularly** on your path. Are you following your guiding star? Are you choosing happiness? Be willing to make adjustments as needed. Life changes, and so must your approach to maintaining your happiness.

Choosing happiness is not a one-time decision but a continuous process, a way of life that requires practice, commitment, and love. It's a path that leads to a richer, fuller existence.

Day 113

Reality-Checking Your Dreams

In a world brimming with ambition, we're often told to set our sights high. To dream big. Yet amidst the clouds of lofty goals, many of us get lost. We pour energy and years into aspirations only to be met with the sting of unmet expectations.

But what if there was a question, a sort of litmus test to guide our direction more wisely?

Before diving headlong into your next big endeavor, pause. Reflect. Ask: "What must be true for this plan to work?"

It's not about doubting or curtailing your dreams. It's about grounding them in reality. This question unpacks assumptions, identifies gaps, and clarifies prerequisites. It challenges you to think through the fundamental conditions necessary for your plan's success.

By grappling with this question, you're not just daydreaming — you're strategizing. It's a step toward turning grand visions into tangible results and ensuring that your journey, while ambitious, remains rooted in the realm of the achievable.

Day 114

Perspective

"*I cursed the fact I had no shoes until I met the man who had no feet.*" – Persian proverb

Often we become entangled in the web of discontent, focusing on what we lack rather than what we possess. But the poignant words of the Persian proverb remind us of the power of perspective.

We yearn for more, oblivious to the abundance surrounding us. Yet life has a way of revealing its profound lessons through encounters with those who carry burdens greater than our own.

In the presence of someone enduring unimaginable challenges, we gain clarity and realize the triviality of our complaints. As we shift our gaze from what is absent to what is present, a sense of humility and gratitude takes root within, forever altering the way we perceive the world.

Our perspective shapes our reality. If we focus only on what's missing, we'll never see what's there.

It's up to us to decide whether to curse the lack of shoes or to walk joyfully on the feet we have. By celebrating the abundance in our lives, we can find joy in the simple, profound blessings all around us.

Think today about someone who is going through hardships that are tough to imagine. What would your life be like if you were experiencing the same thing?

Day 115

Unlocking Creativity Through Constraints

U sing limitations to spark creativity is a fascinating paradox that can not only transform our creative work but also guide our everyday lives.

Many people think that creativity thrives on boundless freedom and an endless horizon of possibilities. But often, it's the very constraints that we impose upon ourselves (or find imposed upon us) that fuel our most innovative and creative thoughts.

Constraints, whether in the form of time limits, budgets, or specific rules, force us to think more critically and creatively about how we approach problems. We must find new paths, explore unconventional solutions, and maybe even redefine the problem itself.

When faced with constraints, our mind shifts from autopilot to active engagement. We no longer rely on the tried and true; instead, we must innovate, improvising solutions that fit the unique boundaries of our situation.

In personal development, self-imposed constraints can lead to growth and self-discovery. You might commit to a month without social media, forcing yourself to find new ways to connect with others and enjoy your free time. Or perhaps you decide to limit your spending, leading you to discover simple joys that don't require money. These constraints challenge you, pushing you to develop new skills, habits, and insights.

But what if the constraints are not chosen but thrust upon us? Challenges like a tight budget, a demanding schedule, or a difficult work environment can also be a catalyst for creativity. Embracing rather than resisting these constraints allows us to adapt, innovate, and grow. We learn to see them not as obstacles but as unique parameters that define our problem-solving space, guiding us to creative solutions.

Embrace constraints in both art and life. Recognize them as opportunities to unlock creativity, not barriers that stifle it. By learning to work within limitations, you open the door to new possibilities, discovering fresh perspectives and growing in ways you never imagined.

Constraints aren't roadblocks on the path to creativity; they're launch pads. And the more you practice navigating them, the more adept you'll become at turning limitations into launching pads for innovation and transformation.

Day 116

The Wisdom Within

When we're on a relentless quest for growth and improvement, it's easy to look outward. We scour books, devour podcasts, and seek mentors. External wisdom is everywhere, and we're hungry for it. But hold on a second. What if I told you that one of the richest sources of insight and wisdom is right there within you? It's true.

You have lived, you have learned, you have stumbled, and you have triumphed. There's a unique untold wisdom in your journey — lessons that are yours and yours alone. It's a treasure trove just waiting to be discovered.

So why not pause today?

Why not sit in quiet reflection and dive deep into your own experience? Forget the external noise for a moment. Listen to your own voice, intuition, and wisdom. It's not about rejecting external knowledge but complementing it with the rich insights that only you can provide.

There's a beautiful balance between learning from others and learning from oneself. It's about honoring and valuing your own journey and realizing that you, too, are a sage, a philosopher, and a teacher. Embrace this inner wisdom and let it guide you in making decisions, crafting your path, and growing in ways that resonate with who you truly are.

There's magic in that introspection, a unique form of empowerment that only comes from knowing and trusting oneself. Your life is a library of wisdom. It's time to read that book.

Day 117

86,400 Seconds

Each day, we're handed 86,400 seconds on a silver platter. That's 86,400 fleeting moments to capture, savor, and harness. These aren't just mere seconds ticking away; they're a treasure trove of opportunities, chances, and endless potential.

Now, here's the thing about time: it's unyielding. It marches forward, never hesitating and never looking back. But wrapped up in this seemingly harsh reality is a beautiful challenge. The very fact that time is limited pushes us, nudges us, and often propels us out of our comfort zones. It's within these boundaries that our creativity flourishes, sparking a hunger to achieve more, learn more, and be more.

Each spark, each second, gives us the power to transform, grow, and become more. In this endless parade of seconds, we find the power to redefine who we are and what we can become. With each tick, we have the chance to reclaim our equilibrium, stand tall in the face of challenges, and realign ourselves with our highest aspirations.

These 86,400 seconds — this daily allotment of life's currency — can be spent in endless ways, but they can never be saved, hoarded, or reclaimed. They are the fleeting canvases upon which we paint our existence moment by moment.

How we choose to spend these seconds defines our reality. It's an opportunity and responsibility that's equally exhilarating and daunting, but within this challenge lies the beauty of human existence.

The next 86,400 seconds are yours. A blank page, a fresh start. Will you let them slip away unnoticed? Or will you shape them into a masterpiece of purpose, joy, and fulfillment? The symphony of possibility plays on, and the conductor's baton is in your hands.

Passion, Playfulness, Purpose, Persistence

Envision your life as a vast expedition punctuated by challenges, victories, and countless moments of growth. Within this expedition, you're guided by four essential elements. These are not physical objects but guiding principles, like the four cardinal directions on a map. They are passion, playfulness, purpose, and persistence.

- **Passion** is your driving force, the fire that fuels your engine. It's what makes your heart race and your eyes sparkle. When you engage with what you love, time seems to stand still, and the world around you fades away.

- **Playfulness** is your inner child, ready to explore and laugh. It's a reminder that life doesn't always have to be so serious and that joy can be found in the simplest of things.

- **Purpose** is your North Star, guiding you through the darkest nights. Knowing your purpose gives direction to your actions and meaning to your existence. It's the answer to the age-old question, "Why am I here?"

- **Persistence** is your unwavering commitment, your refusal to give up. It's the grit that keeps you going even when the road is rocky and the destination seems far away.

These Four Ps are not independent of one another but are interconnected, each one enhancing the others. Like the points on a compass, they guide you through life's complex terrain, helping you navigate with confidence and grace.

You Might Be One Step Away

There's a threshold just before success where the darkness is deepest. It's a space where doubt creeps in and the road ahead seems almost impossibly hard. This is the point where many stop, not realizing how close they are to breaking through.

I've often thought about why this happens, and I've concluded that it's partly because of how we perceive effort and progress. We expect a linear path, but in reality, the path to achieving our goals is more like an exponential curve. The closer we get, the steeper it becomes.

The last miles of a marathon are the hardest not just because we're tired but because every additional step requires more from us than the one before. Our resources, be they physical or emotional, are depleted, and it takes real grit to keep pushing.

But this is precisely the time when we must dig deep, tap into our reserves, and find the inner strength to keep going.

Why?

Because these are the moments that define us. These are the moments when we discover what we're really made of.

You see, accomplishing our goals isn't just about the triumph of crossing the finish line. It's about who we become in those final, grueling steps. It's about the character we build, the resilience we forge, and the self-knowledge we gain.

So if you find yourself in that dark place, teetering on the edge of giving up, remember this: You're closer than you think. Sometimes the finish line is just around the corner, hidden from view. Don't let the illusion of distance defeat you.

Your goals and dreams are worth that extra push. They're worth the struggle and the sweat. And you? You're worth the triumph of not just reaching your destination but becoming the person who got there.

So keep going. Don't stop on the brink of greatness. Push a little harder, go a little further, and discover the extraordinary power within you. The finish line is calling, and it's closer than you think.

Broken Hearts and Clearer Vision

We've all been there: a failure so profound it not only breaks our hearts but shakes our belief in ourselves. But what if we looked at this not as a setback but as a moment of revelation?

Something that seems to crush us can also enlighten us, revealing a new way forward and a clearer path to our real desires.

Think of a career dream that didn't work out. At the moment of realization, it feels like the end of the world. But give it time, reflection, and honesty, and suddenly the disappointment may unveil a more authentic desire.

What we thought was a dream was only a shadow. The true aspiration is now clear, no longer obscured by ego or others' expectations.

Consider a relationship that broke your heart. The pain feels unbearable, yet with time may lead to a realization of what you truly need and want in a relationship. It can guide you to a more fulfilling connection with yourself and others.

These broken-hearted moments are tough teachers, but they are teachers nonetheless. They have lessons to teach us about our true selves, our genuine goals, and the unvarnished truths of our lives. But we have to be willing to listen.

Here's how we might embrace these moments.

- **Accept the pain.** Don't run from it. Feel it, know it. It's part of the process.

- **Reflect with honesty.** Ask yourself what this defeat is really about. What is it teaching you?

- **Realign with your values and vision.** Sometimes defeat shows us where we were off course. It's a chance to get back on track.

- **Embrace transformation.** Let the pain reshape you. It's working on you, sculpting you into something new.

- **Move forward with clarity.** Use this newfound understanding to guide your next steps. You know the way.

Heartbreaks and failures aren't just stumbling blocks. They're opportunities. They help us see ourselves more clearly, understand our desires more fully, and navigate our lives more successfully. It's not easy, but if we let them, they can guide us to a life more in tune with who we really are and what we genuinely want. That's not a defeat; it's a triumph.

The Exquisite Space

I magine a spectrum. On one end, there's comfort — the familiar, the known. It's cozy and safe, but it's not particularly stimulating. On the other end, there's the impossible — grand, exciting dreams that seem so far out of reach that we hardly dare to think about them.

But right in the middle? That's where the magic happens.

This space is where our limitations start to stretch. It's where we push ourselves just enough to feel the thrill but not so far that we're paralyzed with fear. It's a sweet spot that's neither too comfortable nor too daunting.

It's where we should aim to be.

In that exquisite space between comfortable and impossible lies the playground of endless possibilities where the magic of growth and transformation unfolds.

It's not complete relaxation, but it's not overwhelming either. It's like a playground teeming with opportunities, each swing and slide offering a lesson, a discovery, an adventure.

Why does this space matter? Because this is where growth feels like a game, where challenge intertwines with fun. In this delicate balance, we are pushed just enough to stretch but not enough to break.

So let the adventure begin, and revel in the beauty of that enchanting space between comfort and impossibility where dreams take flight and you soar to new heights.

Day 122

I Don't Know

It's a simple phrase, but it carries immense weight: "I don't know." Three little words that can be incredibly hard to say. Why? Perhaps it's because we live in a world where knowledge is power, where expertise is revered, and where admitting ignorance can feel like a failure.

But let's take a step back and examine that belief. The pressure to know everything is a myth. It's an unattainable standard that we've somehow convinced ourselves is necessary. But in reality, it's a trap. Pretending to know everything closes doors, stifles curiosity, and blocks growth.

When we fake knowledge, we miss the opportunity to learn. We shut down the conversation and limit our understanding. In trying to appear competent, we may become less so.

Now imagine the freedom that comes with saying "I don't know." It opens doors. It invites collaboration. It sparks curiosity and encourages exploration. Saying "I don't know" is an admission of humility. It's a sign that we're aware of our limitations and open to growth. It's a starting point, not an endpoint.

Embracing "I don't know" is the beginning of a journey. It's the first step on the path to understanding. It's a catalyst for growth, collaboration, and discovery. Every great adventure or mind-bending discovery began with someone standing at the precipice of the unknown.

It's time to recognize that not knowing is not a failure but an opportunity. It's a chance to grow, connect, and explore.

Day 123

The Power Beyond Goals

S etting goals is exhilarating. It gives you a clear target, a tangible sense of direction, a single point to aim for. Goals can provide motivation, pulling you forward and inspiring you to give your all to reach that specific outcome. But what happens once you achieve that goal? Often the thrill fades, the drive diminishes, and a sense of aimlessness can settle in. Goals can sometimes feel like chasing a high; a fleeting satisfaction that leaves you wondering, "What's next?"

Others approach life's game differently. Instead of fixating on individual goals, they develop systems. They're not just aiming to win once. They want to win over and over again.

Systems are not about chasing one-time achievements. They're about creating habits, structures, and routines that lead to ongoing success. A system isn't a finish line; it's a pathway.

A writer's goal might be to complete a novel, but a writer's system is writing every day. An entrepreneur's goal might be to build a successful business, but an entrepreneur's system is continually evaluating and improving business processes. An athlete's goal might be to win a championship, but an athlete's system is consistent training, recovery, and learning.

In systems, the magic isn't in the end result but in the process. The focus shifts from "What do I want to achieve?" to "What can I do every day to get there?" It's about ongoing growth, not fleeting success. It's about building something that endures.

Is it possible to have both goals and systems? Of course! Goals give you direction while systems guide your daily actions. But the real power lies in understanding the role of each and leveraging them effectively. Set inspiring goals, but don't let them dictate your self-worth or satisfaction. Build robust systems that align with your values, and let them drive you forward.

Remember, winning once might feel great, but winning repeatedly brings something deeper. It's about mastery, growth, resilience, and fulfillment. It's not about a one-time victory but a life built on continuous success.

In the grand game of life, systems are the secret to playing and winning the long game. Let them be your guide.

Day 124

The Self-Imposed Cage of Limitation

Limitation, like a self-imposed cage, can become the mental dwelling where many individuals unwittingly reside. It starts as a fleeting thought or mere whisper of doubt, but left unattended, it takes root and grows into a crippling belief. With every passing day, this belief gains strength, shaping the contours of reality until it becomes the very fabric of existence.

This cage of limitation isn't constructed by others. We build it ourselves with the bricks of doubt, fear, and complacency. It's comfortable inside, but it's a confinement nonetheless. We peer through the bars, longing for what might be yet afraid to step outside.

What was once a mere thought can be unlearned, unshackled, and replaced with a liberating mindset. Sometimes the keys to this cage are hidden in plain sight. A question, a curiosity, a willingness to ask "What if?" can be enough to turn the lock. It may be a change in routine, a new hobby, or a connection with someone who sees the world differently.

Once we dare to question the boundaries of our potential, we open the door to unbounded growth and transformation. The walls that once seemed so solid begin to crumble under the force of determination, persistence, and a newfound belief in possibility.

Remember, the cage was never locked. The door was always open. It's time to step out, breathe the fresh air of freedom, and explore the landscape of limitless possibility. The world is waiting, and so is the best version of you.

Day 125

A Decision Framework

Decision-making is a daily activity we often do without giving it much thought. But some decisions carry weight, and their implications stretch far beyond the immediate moment. How do we navigate these crossroads and make choices that align with our long-term goals and values? Here's a simple framework to try that involves a perspective of time.

Consider the decision in front of you and ask yourself: Will this matter in 10 years? Will it still be significant in 10 months? What about 10 minutes from now?

- **The ten-year perspective.** Think about the long-term. Will this decision impact your life a decade from now? If the answer is yes, then it's a choice that deserves careful consideration. It's likely connected to your core values, life goals, or long-term aspirations. Reflecting on this perspective ensures that your decisions align with where you want to be years down the road.

- **The ten-month view.** Now narrow your focus a bit and consider the mid-term effects. Will this decision matter in 10 months? If it will, then it's probably tied to ongoing projects, relationships, or commitments. This perspective helps you align your choices with the progress and direction you want to maintain in the foreseeable future.

- **The immediate impact: ten minutes.** Finally, think about the immediate future. Will this decision matter in 10 minutes? If the answer is no, it might be a smaller, less critical choice. But if it's yes, then it may be something that affects your immediate well-being or comfort. This perspective ensures that you're not overlooking the present moment and your immediate needs.

By examining a decision through these three lenses, you gain a holistic view of its potential impact. You're considering the future, the present, and everything in between. You're not just reacting to the moment but aligning your choices within a broader context.

This framework isn't about overthinking every little choice. It's about having a tool in your toolbox for when you're facing decisions that feel weighty or significant. It's a way to ensure that your choices reflect not just the urgencies of the present moment but also the path you want to walk in the future.

Remember, time offers a unique perspective. It allows us to see beyond the immediate and consider the enduring. By applying this time-based framework, we can make decisions that resonate with who we are, where we are, and where we want to go. It's a simple method with profound potential for guiding us to choices that stand the test of time.

Day 126

Embracing the And

L ife has a funny way of presenting us with binary choices. We often feel pressured to choose between this or that, here or there, one path or another. But what if life isn't an endless series of either/or decisions? What if we could embrace the richness of 'and' instead of the limitation of 'or'?

It's not about career *or* family, but career *and* family. It's not about being an artist *or* an entrepreneur but being an artist *and* an entrepreneur. It's about integrating seemingly contradictory parts of life into a harmonious whole.

The idea of living a life of 'and' instead of 'or' is not about having it all in the sense of accumulating more. It's about embracing the full spectrum of who we are and what we love. It's about recognizing that life's various aspects don't have to compete with each other but can complement and enrich each other.

Here are a few ways to start doing that.

- **Recognize the possibility of *and*.** The first step is to recognize that *and* is an option. Society, culture, or even our upbringing might have ingrained in us the idea that we must choose one thing over the other. Challenge that notion. See the possibility of embracing more.

- **Explore your multifaceted self.** We all have different roles, interests, and passions. Acknowledging and honoring them doesn't create conflict; it creates completeness. You can be a parent and a writer, a teacher and a student, a businessperson and a poet.

- **Find the connecting threads.** Look for connections between seemingly disparate parts of your life. Maybe your love for nature feeds into your entrepreneurial venture. Perhaps your artistic creativity enhances your scientific pursuits. The connections are there if you look for them.

- **Create your unique blend.** There's no one-size-fits-all approach here. Your unique blend of *and* will be different from anyone else's. It's about crafting a life that honors all parts of you.

- **Let go of judgment and comparison.** Others might not understand your path, and that's okay. The *and* approach is deeply personal and might not fit neatly into conventional categories.

- **Regularly reflect and adjust.** Your blend of *and* will evolve over time. Regular reflection and adjustment can keep you aligned with your values and aspirations.

Living a life of *and* instead of *or* is a liberating and enriching choice. It's about refusing to be boxed into artificial categories and choosing instead to flow with the complexity, diversity, and richness of life.

It's an approach that invites depth and breadth, integration, and expansion. It's an approach that respects all facets of who you are and your vast potential... one that recognizes that life's richness is not in its either/or choices but in the boundless opportunities of *and*.

Day 127

What Will You Pass On?

As you reflect on your life, ask yourself this deeply personal and significant question: What are the three most important pearls of wisdom I want to pass on to the next generation?

1. The pearl of your greatest lesson. What has been your greatest lesson? What did you learn from it? How has it shaped your perspective, your choices, your path? This is the wisdom born from experience, often hard-won, that can serve as a guiding star for those just setting out on their journey.

2. The pearl of universal truth. What life lessons or hard truths have shaped you most? What universal truth has guided you, comforted you, or provided clarity in moments of confusion? This pearl offers the chance to connect with others on a profound level, transcending the boundaries of individual experience.

3. The pearl of hope and inspiration. What inspires you? What fills you with hope and motivates you to strive, to grow, to overcome obstacles? This pearl represents the spark that ignites passion, the gentle encouragement that can lift someone up and set them on a path filled with purpose and joy.

These three pearls are more than mere words or abstract concepts; they are the essence of what you believe, what you've learned, and what you wish to share. They are a legacy, a gift to the future, a way to reach across time and touch the hearts and minds of those who will come after you.

So what wisdom will you pass on? What are your three pearls?

Day 128

Don't Compare Your Behind-the-Scenes to Someone Else's Highlight Reel

In the age of curated social media feeds and meticulously crafted online personas, it's easy to fall into the trap of comparison. We scroll through endless images of perfection, achievements, and joyous moments, often feeling that our own lives pale in contrast. However, it's vital to remember that what we see online is but a fraction of someone's reality, a carefully selected highlight reel of their best moments. Meanwhile, we're intimately aware of our own struggles, insecurities, and behind-the-scenes challenges.

In my work, I've had the privilege of seeing behind the curtain of some of the world's best athletes and CEOs. And the revelation has been eye-opening.

When it comes to refining their craft and pushing their own boundaries, these top performers aren't juxtaposing their daily grind with someone else's picture-perfect moments. They're too engrossed in their own craft and too involved in their own processes to be derailed by the highlight reels of others.

Dr. Michael Gervais said it best: "The fear of people's opinions is one of the greatest constrictors of human potential."

Comparing our everyday struggles and unfiltered moments to someone else's curated best moments is unfair to us and can distort our perception of reality.

Social media might show us a constant stream of achievements and successes, but remember, behind every highlight is an untold story of grit, perseverance, and relentless pursuit. It's in the late-night practice sessions, the failures, and the come-backs where the essence of greatness lies.

To truly achieve, we must shun the instinct to constantly measure our journey against someone else's destination. Embrace the missteps, cherish the learning, and revel in the small victories that pave the path to greatness.

So the next time you're scrolling through someone's achievements, remember: Every highlight had its backstage. Embrace your own process, celebrate your small victories, and don't shy away from showcasing the raw, imperfect, yet beautiful journey that is uniquely yours.

Shedding the Cloak of Self-doubt

For years, self-doubt has followed you like a shadow you couldn't shake, wrapping you in its stifling embrace. Woven with threads of insecurity and uncertainty, this cloak has convinced you it's an essential part of your attire. Every time you face a mirror, it's been there, subtly altering the reflection, masking the brilliance beneath.

However, this cloak isn't your skin. It's a layer you've donned, perhaps unconsciously, perhaps out of self-preservation. But over time, it's grown heavy and burdensome, suffocating the vibrancy of your true self.

Hidden underneath is a version of you that's been patient, biding its time. This authentic self is resilient, brimming with potential, and radiates a unique light. It's the part of you that dreams, hopes, and loves fiercely — the you that is resilient in the face of challenges and shines even in moments of despair.

Today, right now, is that pivotal moment where you gently unclasp and shrug off that heavy cloak of self-doubt that's been draped over your shoulders for far too long.

As you do, you'll see — perhaps for the first time — the outline of possibilities, the shape of dreams yet to be pursued, and the silhouette of the person you've always been destined to become. Remember, potential isn't something we acquire; it's something we uncover.

Begin today. Shed the doubt and unveil your extraordinary.

Day 130

That Magical Space Between Stimulus & Response

You know, there's an underlying assumption in our culture — a sort of unspoken rule — that goes something like this: Life is supposed to be a constant stream of cloudless skies and sunny days. In the narrative we tell ourselves, our aim is to navigate through life untouched, unscathed, and unscarred.

But one evening as I was tracing the steps of my life journey, a realization dawned upon me: To end this voyage with an untouched heart is not just impossible—it's undesirable.

Our hearts, like a vast canvas, accumulate strokes of various colors as we live. Some strokes are vibrant and happy while others are dark and melancholic. But they all come together to form the masterpiece that is our life.

Consider this for a moment. Every person you've ever admired, every inspiring biography you've read, and every story that made you sit up and think all came from scarred hearts. It's not the untouched hearts that inspire; it's the scarred ones, the ones that have seen, felt, and been through the most only to emerge resilient.

Now think about your favorite music, the kind that reaches right into the depths of your soul. More often than not, it comes from places of profound pain, love, hope, or despair. That song that gives you goosebumps? It's probably a product of a scarred heart.

But why is it that we understand the value of these scars in art, music, and stories yet try so hard to avoid them in our own lives?

Being untouched is safe. Yes, it is. But it also means being untested, untried, and unproven. Scars, on the other hand, are a testament. They say, "I've been through the battles of life, I've been touched deeply, and I've emerged... not unharmed, but definitely stronger."

To love passionately, to engage deeply, to risk boldly — these all come with the promise of scars. But they also come with the promise of life lived fully. As I often remind myself, the depth of your scars is directly proportional to the depth of your experiences.

If I were to put my entire life on a timeline, the segments that stand out — the ones where I learned, grew, and evolved the most — were those where my heart got its scars. Be it a failed venture, a broken relationship, or moments of intense vulnerability, each scar is a chapter in my book.

So here's a thought I'd love for you to sit with: Embrace the inevitable scars on your heart. They're not just signs of pain but badges of honor, signaling a heart that dared to touch, feel, and engage.

And as we go through life, let's remember this essential truth: An untouched heart might never hurt, but it also never truly knows the boundless landscapes of love, loss, and life. It's in our scarred hearts that we find our stories, our songs, and our soul's symphony.

Day 131

Reclaiming Fun

Yesterday, while absorbed in the carefree antics of my kids, I had a thought. Their entire world orbits around a singular, potent word: fun. Whether it's a simple game or just a walk outside, they infuse it with gleeful abandon and infectious enthusiasm. It's as if they wear fun-filtered glasses, turning even the mundane into magical.

Then there's us, the adults. Along the path from sandbox to boardroom, our lenses seem to have shifted. They became tinted with the weight of responsibilities, obligations, and the 'serious' business of adulthood. It's as if we traded those fun glasses for a more practical, albeit grayer, pair.

But here's something to ponder: Must adulthood be devoid of the fun that defined our younger selves? Sure, we have duties that can't be ignored. But could we perhaps revisit our days with a sprinkle of that childlike spirit?

Maybe it's dancing in the kitchen while cooking, singing loudly in the shower, or just allowing yourself a full-bellied laugh over a silly joke. Tiny acts, when viewed through the fun lens, can reinvigorate our days.

So here's a nudge: Slip on those fun glasses once again. You might just see the world in colors brighter than you remember. After all, if life is the grand adventure we're all navigating, wouldn't it be better with a little more fun on the map?

Day 132

The Mountain Ahead

All of us are standing at the base of a giant mountain in life, looking up at the dizzying height and quivering ever so slightly on the inside, wondering how we can ever conquer such a monumental task. It's an overwhelming sensation, that feeling of insignificance in the face of something so vast and imposing. It's natural to feel intimidated, to question our abilities, and to doubt our strength.

But let's take a breath, pause, and change the perspective.

Instead of focusing on the entire mountain, shift your attention to the path right before you. Look at the stones, the rocks, the tiny elements that make up this grand challenge. Each one is a step, a moment, a small but crucial part of the climb.

The wisdom here lies in the simplicity of progress one small step at a time. It's not about attempting to climb up the entire mountain at once, for that would be an overwhelming feat. It's about breaking down the colossal into the manageable. Embrace individual steps and recognize that each one, though seemingly insignificant on its own, accumulates into a force of change.

Each tiny step forward, even if it doesn't seem like much at the moment, contributes to the transformational journey ahead. It reshapes the landscape of your life brick by brick, stone by stone.

This approach applies to any significant goal or challenge in your life. Whether it's a personal dream, a professional ambition, or a relationship that needs nurturing, the principle remains the same. Break it down. Focus on the now. Embrace the small actions that lead to big changes.

Acknowledge the power of consistency and focus. Commit to the small actions every day knowing that they will add up. Trust in the process knowing that every effort, no matter how small, is part of your transformation.

So next time you find yourself at the base of a mountain, either literal or metaphorical, remember this principle. Look to the stones, not the summit. Focus on the step, not the entire path.

And one day, you'll find yourself at the summit, looking down at the path you've traveled, realizing that you conquered the mountain one small stone at a time. It was always within your power. You just needed to take that first step.

Day 133

Daring to Dream Big

In the grand theater of life, where many prefer the familiar comfort of well-rehearsed acts, the spectacle of someone who dares to dream big and fearlessly challenge the imposing hurdles in their path is a mesmerizing performance. It's a portrayal that kindles a spark within the deepest recesses of our being, a spark that illuminates the cavernous potential lying dormant within our souls.

Witnessing the triumphant dreamer who surmounts what appears as formidable odds is like witnessing a radiant beacon of light slicing through the murky shroud of self-doubt and self-imposed limitations.

It's a spectacle of such rarity that it leaves us captivated, enraptured by the raw display of human potential and resilience.

This stirring scene awakens within us a profound realization: that we, too, are not just spectators but actors on this grand stage. We, too, are imbued with the potential for greatness if we dare to stoke the embers of courage and fan the flames of our dreams with unwavering determination.

As you embark on today, let your life be the stirring performance that leaves others in awe and instills inspiration. Be the luminary who showcases what unfathomable wonders can unfold when one fearlessly answers the call of their heart, embarks on the daring adventure to scale their personal peaks, and unlocks the resplendent potential that is their birthright.

Today, shine not just for yourself but for others, too, reminding them of the extraordinary spectacle that is a life lived with courage and passion.

Day 134

Anchors in the Storm

Every odyssey, regardless of its nature, presents its set of storms — those unforeseen obstacles that threaten to divert our course or capsize our vessel entirely. It's during these tumultuous times that we find ourselves yearning for some semblance of stability, something to cling to.

That's where the twin anchors of faith and courage come into play.

Faith isn't just a religious concept; it's a deeply personal belief in the unknown. It's the assurance that there is a dawn beyond the darkest night and a silver lining to every cloud. Faith serves as our internal compass, constantly pointing us toward our true north. Even when the map is unclear and the terrains treacherous, faith reminds us that there's a purpose to our excursion — that every challenge is but a chapter in our grand narrative.

Faith tells us that even if the path is uncharted, our footsteps are not aimless. Faith knows the beauty of destinations that are found not with sight but with insight. It whispers to us the tales of those who tread before, assuring us that the mists of uncertainty eventually lift to reveal the landscape of our dreams.

Courage, on the other hand, is the fire that fuels our forward motion. It's the raw, untamed force that looks adversity in the eye and declares, "I will not be stopped." While faith whispers hope into our hearts, courage roars in defiance against our fears. It's the spirit that drives sailors to brave uncharted waters, explorers to tread unknown lands, and dreamers to chase stars.

But courage isn't just about grand acts of valor; it's also found in the subtle, everyday decisions: the choice to stand up after a fall, to voice an unpopular opinion, and to persist when the odds are stacked against you. In the moments when we summon the strength to move forward, courage shines brightest.

Together, faith and courage form the bedrock upon which our lives are built. While faith assures us that our journey is meaningful, courage ensures that we continue to forge ahead regardless of the challenges. In this dance of assurance and action, we not only navigate our path but also transform it, turning obstacles into stepping stones and trials into testimonies.

As you tread through life, clutch these anchors tight. With faith lighting your path and courage powering your steps, there's no storm too fierce, no mountain too high. In the union of these twin forces lies the magic to turn every voyage into a legend.

Day 135

Finding the Next Track

Life is often likened to a trail, path, or road that stretches out before us. But this road isn't straight or clearly marked. It's more like a labyrinth of interconnected tracks, winding and weaving, full of twists and turns.

You don't have to figure out your entire life right now. That's an overwhelming task filled with pressure and anxiety. Instead, follow the next step that feels aligned with who you are and who you want to become.

Imagine standing at the edge of the jungle with many tracks leading in different directions. You don't have to see the end of each track to make a choice. You don't have to know where every track leads. You just have to select one that feels right at this moment.

The beauty of this approach is in its flexibility and forgiveness. Certain tracks you follow will lead you nowhere, and that's okay. That's not a failure or a dead end. It's a learning opportunity. It's a chance to understand what doesn't resonate with you or what doesn't align with your values or goals.

When you find yourself on a track that's not working, you can stop. You can reset. You can take a breath, look around, and start finding the next track.

Each track you follow and each step you take is a discovery. It's a chance to learn more about yourself and to understand what makes you feel fulfilled, what ignites your passion, and what brings you joy. It's an opportunity to grow, evolve, and become more authentic to who you truly are.

The tracks of life are not rigid or permanent. They're fluid and changeable.

You're not locked into one path. You have the freedom to choose, to explore, to experiment. And with each choice, you're not just moving forward; you're shaping your course and defining your road.

So don't be daunted by the unknown. Don't be paralyzed by the fear of choosing the wrong track. Embrace the uncertainty as a beautiful aspect of being alive. Relish the opportunity to explore, to learn, to grow.

Follow the track that calls to you now. Trust in your intuition to guide you.

And remember, you have the power to change tracks whenever you need to. You have the control to navigate your life in the way that feels most aligned with you.

Day 136

Taking Charge

Fourth grade. Most kids worried about math homework or which toy was the coolest. But for me, the weight of my own body was a far greater concern. Literally. I was the kid in class others poked fun at. The so-called fat kid.

But let me tell you a secret: Inside that bigger frame was a heart just as large, teeming with a spirit that refused to be defined by a number on a scale. At the ripe age of 10, when most children are playing and carefree, I made one of the most significant decisions of my life. I chose to step up and rewrite my story.

No, it wasn't easy. Shedding the weight was a challenge, yes. But what was harder was the discipline, the daily grind, the tiny decisions to choose health over momentary comfort. That said, every bead of sweat was a tiny victory, a small reassurance that I had the power to reshape not just my body but my destiny.

As I sit here reminiscing about that younger me, my message for you emerges clearly: If a 10-year-old can turn their life around amidst jeers and judgment, what's stopping you? Your challenges may be different, but the spirit to overcome them is universal.

Don't wait for the world to define you. Seize your narrative. Because trust me, if I could do it with my young heart bursting with hope and determination, you can too. You've got this.

Day 137

The Great Equalizer

I n the vast gallery of human attributes, one singular power stands tall, dwarfing others in its grandeur: willpower.

Willpower? It's that quiet, steadfast voice inside you, nudging you forward when everything else suggests you retreat.

Willpower is a choice — a deliberate commitment to stick to your path, even when (especially when) it's the path less traveled. It's an invisible yet potent force dwelling within each individual that walks the Earth. It cradles the master key that unlocks our potential.

Willpower does not discriminate; it courses unfettered through the veins of humanity, infusing us all with its transformative potency.

Unlike talent or privilege, which oscillates from person to person, willpower emerges as the ultimate equalizer, instilling the might to rise above our circumstances and forge our own path.

Willpower is nestled deep within us. It patiently awaits the moment we decide to fully embrace its staggering power and let it out. So let it out. Stop holding back and looking for excuses. You possess this great power that can transcend the chains of limitations.

Today is the day to unleash your willpower and let it transcend your limitations. Discover what's been inside of you all along.

Day 138

Counter Clockwise

Ellen Langer, a renowned psychologist, ventured into the uncharted territory of understanding aging through the lens of mindset. Her experiment, famously known as Counter Clockwise, unraveled an aspect of aging that we often overlook: how our minds shape our aging experience.

Langer took a group of elderly men and placed them in an environment that was created to resemble the world twenty years earlier. The surroundings, conversations, even the mirrors were manipulated to transport them back in time. They were instructed to live as if it were that time, essentially immersing themselves in their younger selves.

What unfolded was nothing short of extraordinary. Within a week, these men started to exhibit physical and mental changes that were aligned with a more youthful state. Their strength improved and flexibility increased; even their vision got better. They began to walk upright and show a spark in their conversation, laughing and engaging like their younger selves.

The results of the experiment were not just about reversing the clock but about shedding light on a profound truth: that our beliefs and mindsets about aging play a significant role in how we age. Ellen Langer's experiment tells us that this isn't just wishful thinking; it's a possibility grounded in science and human potential.

The Counter Clockwise experiment is more than a scientific curiosity. It's a call to action, a challenge to each of us to examine our beliefs and consciously choose a mindset that empowers us. It reminds us that it's never too late to change our minds, and in doing so, we might just change our lives.

Day 139

Awakening from Life's Slumber

L ife has a funny way of lulling us into a hypnotic trance. We find ourselves stuck in the routine, repeating the same tasks, engaging in the same conversations, and watching the same shows. It's like a record stuck on repeat, playing the same tune over and over. It's comfortable, familiar, and safe.

Often this repetitive cycle isn't a conscious choice but a default setting. We find ourselves sleepwalking through life, our eyes half-closed, missing the vibrant colors and thrilling melodies that surround us.

Breaking free from this trance is more than an escape from monotony; it's a radical wakeup-call to the richness of life. It starts with a question: How can I shake up my day and my routine?

You see, a great life isn't a cookie-cutter template that fits all. It's a unique blend of experiences, relationships, and pursuits that resonate with who you are and what you value.

The path to awakening isn't about drastic changes or sudden transformations. It's about small shifts in awareness, intentional choices, and a willingness to explore the unknown.

Imagine taking a new route to work, joining a club, learning a skill, or connecting with a stranger. These simple steps can stir the waters of routine, creating ripples that reach far and wide.

As you begin to explore, you may find that the fog of repetition lifts, revealing a landscape filled with opportunities and adventures. You'll discover passions you never knew you had and connections that enrich your life in unexpected ways.

The beauty of awakening from life's slumber is that it's never too late to start. But it requires courage — courage to question the familiar, step into the unknown, and embrace the uncertainty that comes with growth.

And it requires commitment — commitment to invest in yourself, nurture your curiosity, and pursue what lights you up.

In the end, a great life isn't about grand achievements or flashy success. It's about the richness of experiences, the depth of connections, and the alignment with your true self.

So take a moment to pause and reflect. Are you sleepwalking through life, or are you living it fully, eyes wide open, heart beating with excitement?

Day 140

Failures of Kindness

"When I look back at my life, what I regret most is failures of kindness." These simple yet profound words from award-winning author George Saunders reflect not just personal sentiment but a universal truth that many of us can relate to.

How often have we passed up the chance to extend a hand, offer a smile, or simply listen? How many times have we been so caught up in our own world that we overlooked an opportunity to make someone's day better?

Saunders' insight into the human condition reminds us that kindness is more than an act; it's a way of living. It's not just about doing nice things for others but about cultivating a mindset that seeks to understand, connect, and empathize.

But Saunders' reflection is not a condemnation; it's a gentle reminder. It nudges us to think about our interactions, decisions, and approaches to life. It encourages us to look beyond ourselves and recognize the impact we can have on others.

Kindness is not a finite resource but an infinite possibility. It's a choice we make every day in every interaction. It's a philosophy that guides our actions, shapes our relationships, and influences our understanding of the world.

Saunders didn't just share his regret; he shared his wisdom. He illuminated a path that we can all follow, a way of living that transcends the ordinary and touches the extraordinary.

Day 141

Silent Battles

Life often unfolds in a hurried mixture of noise, motion, and emotion. In the midst of it all, we interact with others, sometimes taking mere seconds to make judgments, form opinions, and move on.

But what if we paused? What if we took a moment to consider that each individual we encounter, every person we pass on the street, every coworker, friend, or stranger, is shouldering a burden unseen to the naked eye?

It's easy to forget that behind the casual "I'm fine," and smile is private struggle, hidden pain, and silent battles. These are the things we don't see, the challenges we don't know about, and the weights people carry with them, often shrouded in silence and obscured by the bustling clamor of daily life.

This understanding of the complexity and depth of the human experience is more than a fleeting thought. It's a call to action. It's an invitation to nurture a culture of empathy, compassion, and benevolence. It's a prompt to approach others with a mind willing to see beyond the surface.

We can never fully comprehend the magnitude of the silent battles others wage within themselves. We can never truly know the pain they feel, the doubts they harbor, or the fears they face. But we don't have to know everything to be kind, empathetic, and understanding.

Empathy is not about full comprehension; it's about connection. It's not about having all the answers; it's about being present, listening, and caring. It's about recognizing that we are all, in some way or another, fighting battles, facing challenges, and striving to make sense of our lives.

Day 142

The Mundanity of Excellence

Sociologist Daniel Chambliss conducted an extensive study on what separates truly excellent swimmers from the rest. The findings were not grand secrets or hidden techniques. No, Chambliss found something more ordinary at the heart of their success. He termed it "the mundanity of excellence."

When we watch exceptional performers, we often look for that "magic ingredient" that sets them apart. We seek the extraordinary, the spectacular, the secret sauce that makes them who they are. But Chambliss found that excellence often resides in the mundane: the simple daily practices that are easily overlooked.

The excellent swimmers didn't possess a magic touch or have access to hidden knowledge. They practiced with diligence, focused on technique, and paid attention to details. Their excellence was built on a foundation of mundane tasks performed consistently with dedication and purpose.

They showed up every day. They worked on their strokes, their turns, their starts. They listened to their coaches, analyzed their performances, and made incremental improvements. It was about the everyday grind and the relentless pursuit of mastery in the small things that eventually led to their extraordinary performance.

It's a lesson that transcends swimming. It's a reminder that greatness doesn't necessarily spring from a single moment of brilliance, flash of genius, or secret formula known only to a select few.

Greatness is often about doing simple things extraordinarily well. It's about commitment, focus, and a love for the process. It's about embracing the mundane, the repetitive, and the ordinary and transforming them into something extraordinary through sheer persistence and dedication.

It's a call to focus on the fundamentals, appreciate the beauty in the basics, and recognize the value in the everyday. It challenges us to see excellence not as a distant mountain peak accessible only to the chosen few but as a path that's available to all of us.

So whether you're an athlete, an artist, a writer, an entrepreneur, or just someone striving to be better in some area of life, remember the lesson from Chambliss's swimmers. Embrace the mundane. Focus on the process. Commit to the daily grind.

Day 143

The Illusion of One Best Way

In our endless search for success, happiness, or meaning, many of us become ensnared in the belief that there must be one best way to achieve it all. This belief is seductive, promising a clear and direct path to everything we desire. But it's also a perilous trap that can lead us astray.

The notion of a "one best way" is tantalizing but deceptive. It implies that there's a perfect formula — a singular method that, if only we could find it, would unlock all the doors, solve all the puzzles, and guarantee success.

But life is not a linear equation. It's a complex and ever-shifting collection of experiences, opportunities, and challenges. There's no one-size-fits-all solution, no universal blueprint for success or fulfillment.

Chasing after this mythical 'one best way' can lead us down a path of confusion and despair. We compare ourselves to others, desperate to emulate their successes, and feel inadequate when we fall short. We cling to rigid strategies, convinced that deviation from the prescribed path will lead to failure. We become paralyzed by indecision, terrified of making the "wrong" choice.

But what if we were to embrace the notion that there is no single "right" way? What if we were to recognize that our journey is uniquely ours and that what works for someone else might not work for us?

The truth is, the "one best way" is a mirage. It's an illusion that keeps us chasing shadows, never quite feeling fulfilled or content. The real path to success and happiness lies in embracing our individuality, recognizing our unique strengths and passions, and forging our path.

This doesn't mean disregarding the wisdom of others or ignoring proven strategies. It means adapting them to our unique circumstances, listening to our intuition, and being willing to experiment and learn.

Life is too complex and multifaceted to be reduced to a single formula. We must be willing to explore, take risks, fail, and learn from those failures. We must be open to the idea that our path may look very different from someone else's — and that that's not only okay but beautiful.

Let's liberate ourselves from the burden of believing in an elusive "one best way" and instead embrace life as it unfolds with all its twists and turns, ups and downs.

In the end, our path is ours to walk. Focus on finding *your* way. That's where the magic happens.

Day 144

Embracing the Winding Path

It's a strange contradiction, isn't it? We often find ourselves trying to create a straight, smooth path through life. We aim to avoid hardships, steer clear of failure, and make our lives as easy and uncomplicated as possible.

But we look up to those who have faced the very obstacles we try to avoid. We admire those who have stumbled, fallen, and risen again. We respect those who have suffered and failed but learned from those failures to climb out of their depths and reach the pinnacle of success.

Why is that?

Perhaps it's because we recognize deep down that the winding path — the road filled with bumps and turns — often leads to growth, wisdom, and resilience.

It's easy to desire a life without failure, but it's in failure that some of life's most potent lessons are hidden. Every stumble teaches us something about ourselves and our limits, desires, strengths, and weaknesses.

Failure is not a dead end; it's a crossroads, a junction where we get to choose our next step. It's a teacher, a guide, and a mentor that helps us refine our approach, mindset, and strategy.

And those who have failed and risen again? They embody the essence of human potential. They remind us that it's not about the fall but the rise. It's not about the pain but the recovery. It's not about the defeat but the triumph.

They turn their hardships into stories of inspiration. They transform their failures into fuel. They don't shy away from the twists and turns of life; they embrace them. They don't see the winding path as a curse; they see it as an adventure filled with lessons, growth, and transformation.

They know that the straight, easy path might be comforting, but it's the winding, challenging path that's truly enriching.

So next time you find yourself longing for a smooth, obstacle-free road, remember the people you admire and respect. Remember the paths they've walked, the battles they've fought, and the victories they've won.

The winding path is not your enemy; it's your teacher. It's not a hindrance; it's an opportunity.

And it's waiting to guide you toward the pinnacle of your potential. All you have to do is embrace it, trust it, and let it lead you to the places you never thought you could reach.

The Pursuit of Substance Beyond Success

Scaling the peaks of success is often portrayed as the ultimate achievement, the grand culmination of years of hard work, perseverance, and sacrifice. But what happens when we finally reach that pinnacle and find ourselves feeling strangely hollow?

"Is this all there is?" This question can become a haunting refrain for those who have realized their dreams only to discover a disconcerting emptiness at the summit.

You see, it's a common misbelief that success itself is the ultimate reward. We spend our lives chasing goals, accumulating accolades, and building our resumes, all in pursuit of that glorious moment of triumph. But what if that moment, though exhilarating, leaves us unfulfilled?

This is where we need to explore the concept of substance beyond success. It's about recognizing that the fulfillment we seek may not lie solely in achievements, titles, or material wealth. These may be gratifying, but they are transient and external.

Real fulfillment, the kind that resonates deep within our soul, comes from connecting with something greater than ourselves. It's about finding purpose, engaging in meaningful relationships, contributing to a cause, or pursuing a passion that brings joy and enriches our lives.

Many have stood on that lofty peak, basking in the glory of accomplishment, only to feel a nagging emptiness tugging at their hearts. It's not an indictment of success, but rather an invitation to look beyond it, to delve into what makes us truly alive.

This may mean reevaluating our priorities, redefining what success means to us, or embracing a new path that aligns with our values and passions. It might involve giving back, mentoring others, or investing in personal growth and self-discovery.

Success is not the problem. It's how we view it, how we chase it, and what we expect from it that can leave us feeling hollow. If we pursue success as the end-all-be-all of our existence, we may find ourselves standing atop that peak, staring into the echoing void, wondering what's next.

We can embrace it without being consumed by it. We can enjoy the journey without becoming lost in the destination. The echoing void at the zenith of success is not a failure but a call to explore deeper dimensions of ourselves.

So as you scale the heights and strive for success, remember to infuse your life with substance, connect with what truly matters to you, and embrace a life that resonates with more than just accomplishments.

The Limits of Cynicism

Cynicism can be alluring. It's often seen as insightful or intelligent. But when we delve deeper, we realize cynicism isn't impressive. It's a hindrance to our growth. It limits our perspective and narrows our worldview.

A true measure of wisdom is found in the ability to recognize and celebrate the value in others, not in pointing out their faults.

Imagine cynicism as looking at the world through a narrow slit in a wall. What we see is limited, confined, and often darkened. Faults are magnified and virtues minimized. It's a perspective that cuts us off from the true depth and beauty of human experience.

But there's another way. By recognizing the value in others, we open to a more expansive, beautiful view of the world. This isn't about ignoring faults; it's about understanding the whole person in both their strengths and weaknesses and acknowledging our shared human experience.

Cynicism isn't wisdom; it's a refusal to see the full, rich complexity of the world. By choosing to recognize the value in others, we not only enrich our lives but help build a world filled with compassion and connection.

So choose to approach today not from the lens of a cynic but from the lens of wisdom.

Day 147

The Game of Life

Life is an intriguing game, isn't it? You sit down at the table, and you're handed a set of cards. These cards represent the circumstances you were born into, the talents you possess, the opportunities you encounter, and the challenges you face.

Some people look at their hand and feel defeated right away. They see the cards they were dealt and think, "That's it. I can't win with these." They focus on what they don't have, the resources they lack, or the obstacles in their path.

Others look at those very same cards and see potential. They recognize that the game of life isn't about having the perfect hand; it's about playing the hand you have to the best of your ability. It's about strategy, creativity, resilience, and determination.

It's about perspective. How often have you heard stories of people who turned seemingly impossible circumstances into incredible success? It happens more often than we think, and it's usually because they refuse to see their circumstances as limitations.

Your cards represent a snapshot in time. Depending on how you choose to view them, they can be either obstacles or stepping stones. The same card that looks like a hindrance to one person might look like an opportunity to another.

Strategy over luck. Though we often associate card games with luck, the best card players in the world know that strategy, psychology, and skill are what win the game in the long run. In life, relying solely on luck is a losing proposition.

Creating a plan, understanding your environment, knowing when to take risks and when to play it safe, recognizing when to stand firm and when to adapt — these are the marks of a skilled player in cards and in life.

Embrace the unknown. No matter how well you play your hand, there's always an element of the unknown. Unexpected things happen. That's life.

It's not about avoiding surprises but about learning how to handle them. Can you take an unexpected turn of events and turn it to your advantage? Can you remain calm and focused when the unexpected occurs?

Relationships matter. In many card games, understanding your opponents is as important as understanding your own hand. The same holds true in life.

Building relationships, understanding others' perspectives, learning to cooperate, and knowing when to compete are all vital skills. The way you interact with others can be a game-changer, turning an ordinary hand into a winning one.

Reflection and growth. Every game is a learning experience. Win or lose, there's always something to be learned. What worked? What didn't? What could you do differently next time?

Life is no different. Reflecting on our experiences allows us to grow and evolve. It's not about dwelling on past mistakes but learning from them and using those lessons to improve and innovate.

Remember, we don't all start with the same hand, and that's okay. The beauty of life is not in the cards themselves but in how we play them. The seemingly weakest hand can turn into a winning one with the right attitude, strategies, and actions.

So take a good look at your cards. Appreciate them for what they are, not for what they aren't. And then play them with everything you've got. You might just surprise yourself with what you can achieve.

Finding the Questions You're Truly Asking Yourself

Sometimes life seems to be a continuous series of questions, each leading to another, forming a complex web of inquiry. Yet, amidst all these questions, we often overlook the ones that are most vital and essential to our growth and understanding. These are not the questions posed by others or demanded by circumstances; these are the questions that reside deep within us.

Our inner landscape is rich with wisdom, insights, and queries that await discovery. When we take the time to look inside, we may find that the questions we are genuinely asking are not the ones we articulate to the outside world.

It's a subtle art, this process of tuning into our inner dialogue. It requires patience, stillness, and the willingness to listen without judgment. Hearing the quiet voice within means pushing aside the external noise, the expectations of others, and the pressures of daily life.

Perhaps you find yourself feeling discontented or restless, and you're not sure why. Maybe you're at a crossroads, uncertain about which path to take. Or perhaps you're grappling with a relationship or personal challenge and feeling stuck and frustrated.

The answer often lies not in seeking more advice, more data, or more opinions, but in turning inward and exploring the questions that your heart and soul are asking.

What is truly important to you? What are your deepest values and desires? What is your gut telling you? These questions might not have straightforward answers, but they can guide you towards clarity, alignment, and purpose.

The beauty of this inner inquiry is that it is deeply personal and unique to each individual. Your questions are yours alone, shaped by your experiences, dreams, fears, and passions.

By looking inside yourself and searching for the questions that truly resonate with who you are and who you wish to become, you create the space to live more in tune with your essence.

So take the time to pause, reflect, and explore. Listen to the whispers of your inner voice. Seek the questions that resonate with your core. In doing so, you may find that the path to understanding, fulfillment, and joy becomes clearer one thoughtful question at a time.

Day 149

Lean In

In its uncanny wisdom, life has a knack for serving up difficult moments: ones that push us, pull us, and force us to confront what we'd rather not.

But here's the crux: These are the moments when we grow the most. This is where real transformation happens.

It's when we feel discomfort, resistance, and friction that we know we are on the precipice of something significant. Because that resistance, that discomfort, is not just pain. It's a signal, a beacon illuminating the path to our better selves.

When you find yourself in the throes of a challenging moment, lean in. Look that challenge in the eye and understand it for what it is: not a blockade but a catalyst.

Let's make "lean in" more than just a phrase. Let's make it our way of life.

Lean into the fear. Lean into the uncertainty. Lean into the discomfort. Embrace it, wrestle with it, learn from it.

Because on the other side of that discomfort is a version of ourselves we've yet to meet.

And isn't that something worth leaning into?

Day 150

Life Is the Ultimate Teacher

We live in an age of information. The answers to most questions are just a click away, and there's a book or a blog post or a video tutorial for almost everything. It's tempting to think that we can learn everything we need to know from someone else's wisdom.

But let me tell you something: Life is the best teacher.

Books can give you information. People can give you advice. But life? Life gives you lessons. Real, deep, meaningful lessons that you can't get from merely reading about something.

Life teaches you how to be resilient when you face adversity, how to be compassionate when you see someone in need, how to be patient when things don't go your way. These aren't lessons you can simply read about and understand. You have to live them.

Want to learn about love? Fall in love. Want to understand loss? Lose something precious. Want to know what success feels like? Work hard and achieve something meaningful. Want to comprehend failure? Try something and fail.

Living these experiences — feeling them in your bones, understanding them in your soul — is where real learning happens. That's where you not only know something in your head but feel it in your heart.

So yes, read books. Listen to advice. Take in all the information you can. But don't forget to live. Don't forget to step out of your comfort zone and try new things. Make mistakes. Fall down. Get up. Try again.

Day 151

This Is Who We Want to Be Around

In the intricate web of human interactions, an intriguing commonality emerges among those who profoundly impact the lives of others: energy transference. Picture the individuals you are drawn to, the ones who leave an indelible mark on your heart and mind. They possess a certain aura, an energy that captivates and uplifts. It's not mere coincidence; it's an art they've mastered: the ability to transfer their energy in a way that resonates deeply.

This phenomenon goes beyond the surface. It's not just about the charismatic extrovert or the larger-than-life personality. While such individuals may possess a captivating energy, it's the subtle currents beneath the surface that truly make the difference. The energy that draws people in isn't just big and bold; it can also be grounded, wise, and steeped in authenticity. It's the kind of energy that makes you want to linger in their presence, absorbing their essence like a sponge soaking up water.

As we navigate our own journeys, it's worth contemplating this energy transference. How can we cultivate an energy that uplifts those around us? How can we become people others seek to be around?

It's not about pretending to be someone we're not; it's about channeling our inner wisdom, embracing our uniqueness, and letting that energy flow naturally.

Day 152

Disentangling from the Digital

In our hyper-connected, always-online world, there's a soft, distant whisper that often goes unnoticed. It's the call of the wild, the tug of our natural roots nudging us to step outside the digital maze and reconnect with the earth beneath our feet.

Consider the devices we're so attached to. They are masterpieces of human ingenuity. They connect us, inform us, and entertain us. They also buffer us. They keep us a step removed from the raw, tactile experience of life.

When was the last time you felt the earth, not as a fleeting moment between Uber rides or as a scenic backdrop for a photo, but genuinely felt connected to it? There's something inherently grounding about nature. It reminds us of rhythms older and more profound than any algorithm: the change of seasons, the ebb and flow of tides, the cycle of day and night.

This isn't about renouncing technology. That's neither practical nor desirable. Instead, it's about balance. It's about recognizing that for all the benefits our digital world offers, there's something irreplaceably nourishing about nature... something that touches a part of our soul no app can reach.

So make it a habit. Once a week, once a month — whatever feels right — step away from the screen. Walk in a park. Hike up a hill. Dip your toes in a stream. Feel the world not as pixels and bytes, but as wind, water, and earth. In doing so, you might find you're not just reconnecting with nature but also with a deeper, more authentic version of yourself.

Day 153

Breaking Free

In our minds, we often build elaborate monuments to our past. We revisit old memories, analyze past mistakes, and dwell on roads not taken. While reflecting on our history can provide valuable insights, there's a crucial distinction to be made between learning from the past and becoming a prisoner of it.

The past, with all its triumphs and failures, is over. It's a collection of experiences that have shaped us, not an unbreakable chain that binds us. We are not fated to relive yesterday's mistakes or restricted to yesterday's horizons.

Let's dive into the understanding that today, right here and right now, we stand at the crossroads of countless possibilities.

Let's anchor ourselves in these truths.

- **The past is a teacher, not a master.** Embrace the wisdom your past has offered, but understand that it doesn't dictate your future. It's a part of your story, but it doesn't have to be the entire tale.

- **You are the author of your life.** Each decision, action, and thought you entertain is a stroke of the pen in the manuscript of your life. You have a remarkable capacity to shape your destiny.

- **Embrace the power of now.** Recognize the potential that this very moment holds. What you choose to do today can alter the trajectory of your life, leading you toward an extraordinary future.

- **Shed the weight of old burdens.** Old disappointments and failures can weigh heavily on our shoulders. It's time to lay them down. Acknowledge them, learn from them, and let them go.

- **Transcend limiting beliefs.** The barriers we face are often not external but within our minds. Break free from self-imposed limitations. Challenge yourself to see beyond the constraints you've accepted in the past.

- **Craft a vision.** Create a vivid and compelling vision for your future. Allow it to guide you, inspire you, and propel you forward.

- **Commit to continuous growth**. Embrace a mindset of growth and transformation. Seek to expand your horizons and constantly evolve.

The beauty of life lies in its dynamism — its potential for change, growth, and reinvention. You are not bound to a fixed path; you are an adventurer on a journey that's uniquely yours.

Your past is a rich tapestry filled with lessons and insights, but it doesn't have to determine your future. Break free from its grip and chart a course toward the extraordinary.

Embrace the power that lies within you: the capacity to create, change, aspire and achieve. The future awaits, and it's a blank canvas waiting for you to make your mark.

Day 154

The Illusion of Stagnation

Progress is a beautiful and mysterious thing. It's like an ever-expanding horizon, always calling us to move forward to reach higher and become more than we are. It knows no limits, even amidst the infinite, and its beauty lies in its very boundlessness.

But here's the thing about progress: It's not always visible. It doesn't always announce itself with fanfare and triumph. Sometimes it's quiet, subtle, and hidden beneath the surface like seeds germinating in soil, unseen but full of potential.

These are the moments that test us. They challenge our faith and our resolve. It's easy to feel discouraged, to lose heart, or to question whether we're really getting anywhere at all. But these seemingly stagnant moments are often where the most profound transformations take place.

Think about it: A seed doesn't burst into vibrant life overnight. It takes time, patience, and nurturing. It grows in darkness, silence, and stillness. When the conditions are right, it emerges strong and beautiful and full of life.

Your journey is no different. Those moments when you feel stuck or wonder if you're making any progress at all may be the moments you grow the most. They are the moments you're building strength, resilience, and wisdom to lay the foundation for the next leap forward.

So don't be deterred by the illusion of stagnation. Don't let doubt creep in and steal your fire. Keep going undeterred, for progress does not always wear a visible cloak.

Speed up Success

If you want to be better at something, the path is already paved by those who are exceptional at it. Success doesn't happen by chance; it leaves clues all over the place. You just need to be curious enough to find them.

Think about athletes, writers, entrepreneurs, or any field of excellence. They didn't reach their pinnacle overnight. They studied, practiced, and most importantly, learned from others who were already at the top.

If you want to excel at something, find those who are masters at it. Study them deeply. Don't just admire their results. Look at their process. See what they do differently, how they think, how they practice, and what they read.

You don't have to reinvent the wheel. Learn from others' mistakes and successes, and then put your unique spin on what you learn. That's where creativity meets mastery.

So pick something you want to improve at. Find three people who are exceptional at it, and study them. Read their books, watch their videos, understand their habits, discipline, and mindset. Learn the patterns. Emulate them, but make it your own.

The clues are there. Success is whispering its secrets all the time. Are you willing to listen and act? The path is there, waiting for you. Don't just walk it; own it.

Day 156

Overcoming Setbacks

When confronted with failure or setbacks, we must adopt a three-tiered approach to overcome them.

- **First, eliminate all debilitating negativity.** Address the situation without distorting its severity, thereby preserving a lucid and concentrated state of mind. This will help prevent a minor setback from ballooning into an insurmountable problem in your mind.

- **Next, seize the moment as an opportunity for learning**. Extract invaluable lessons and insights from the situation, turning perceived failures into catalysts for personal growth. Look at the scenario with a lens of curiosity the same way a scientist would look at an experiment.

- **Finally, divert your energies towards constructive solutions that drive progress.** Instead of brooding over the setback, dedicate your efforts toward positive action that leads to tangible progress, rekindling your resolve to surmount any barrier.

Failure is not a wall but a gate, and the key to unlock it lies within your response. See the situation with clarity, not distortion. Approach setbacks with curiosity, not despair. Focus on positive action, not passive brooding.

Setbacks don't have to define us. They can refine us.

The Rule of Progress

One of the foundational stones of sustained personal growth is a simple yet immensely powerful axiom: never miss two days in a row.

The human journey is overflowing with unpredictability and turmoil, causing us to falter and occasionally miss a day in our pursuit of progress. However, a key to growth lies in preventing these hiccups from morphing into a recurring pattern. Consistency is the golden thread that weaves success.

This philosophy is about more than the task at hand; it's about cultivating discipline, resilience, and a commitment to growth. It's about recognizing that we all have off days, but we mustn't allow them to become off weeks, months, or even years.

"Never miss two days in a row" is a safeguard against the spiral of procrastination and neglect. Miss one day, and it might not make much difference. Miss two, and it's the beginning of a trend; it's the birth of a habit, and not a good one.

By adhering to the two-day rule, you're recognizing that it's okay to stumble, to be imperfect. But you're also making a pact with yourself that stumbling won't become a collapse — that imperfection won't lead to abandonment.

Day 158

The Mysterious Boundaries of Human Capability

Our lives are filled with invisible boundaries. They shape our actions, thoughts, and essence, yet we often don't realize they exist. They are the borders of our comfort zone, the edges of what we think we can achieve.

But here's the thing about boundaries: they're not usually real. They're constructs, figments of our imagination. We create them, and we can erase them.

The landscape of human capability is one of enigmatic beauty and profound depth. It's filled with peaks and valleys, smooth plains and rugged terrains. And it's shrouded in mystery.

Why? Because we don't know what we can truly achieve until we test ourselves by pushing beyond the familiar. That's the beauty of the human spirit. We can reach further than we ever thought possible if we're willing to stretch ourselves.

To discover your boundaries, you must venture into the unknown. You have to take risks, push yourself, and be willing to fail (and perhaps fail again). You have to let go of the comfortable.

In that discomfort, in that space where you're unsure, where you're stretching and growing, you find your real limits. And often you find that those limits are far beyond what you thought was possible.

How do you embark on this journey into the uncharted terrain of your capabilities? Start by questioning the boundaries you've set for yourself. Why are they there?

What evidence do you have that they're real? Challenge them. Test them. Push against them.

And then go beyond. Set new goals. Aim higher and reach further. Create a new boundary and then push past that one, too.

Your limits are waiting to be found, defined, and shattered. All you have to do is take that first step into the unknown.

Don't be afraid of the uncharted terrain. It's where your greatness lies hidden beneath the surface like treasure waiting to be unearthed. All you need is the courage to dig and the will to explore.

So venture beyond the familiar. Embrace the mystery and unlock the unlimited potential that lies within you. In the enigmatic limits of human capability, you'll find not only your boundaries but your boundless potential.

Day 159

Allies in Disguise

Life is filled with teachers if you know where to look. One of the most transformational principles that significantly reshaped my worldview is the practice of seeing every person as an ally.

It's so easy to dismiss people — especially those who challenge us or don't immediately seem to have something to offer. But what if we shifted our perspective? Imagine walking into a room, and instead of seeing strangers or adversaries, you see allies. Every person you lock eyes with holds a key, a lesson, something that could help you grow.

What does this mean in practice?

It means that the person who challenges you the most might be offering you the most valuable lessons about yourself or the world. Embrace the challenge. Learn from it. Grow from it.

It means that inspiration can come from the most unexpected places. That person you overlook might hold insights that can open new doors for you. Listen to them.

It means that everyone you meet, no matter how fleeting the encounter, is a potential mentor. Even if their life seems utterly disconnected from yours, there's something you can learn. Find it.

This practice changes everything. It's a mindset that invites continuous growth, curiosity, and connection.

You'll start to see opportunities for learning in every conversation, encounter, and moment of your day.

You'll see the rich reservoir of knowledge that exists all around you. You'll realize that opportunities for growth don't just lie within books, classes, or formal mentorship. They're in every human interaction.

By embracing this mindset, I've learned to appreciate the complexity and beauty of human connection. I've learned that every person is a world of experiences, thoughts, and wisdom, and that I can tap into that richness if I'm willing to see them as an ally.

But it's more than a strategy for personal growth. It's a way to enrich your life and deepen your relationships. It's a way to build bridges and foster understanding. It's a way to see the humanity in others even when it might be hidden behind differences and disagreements.

So try it. See every person as an ally. Look for the lessons they have to offer. Embrace the challenge. Seek inspiration. Find mentors in your everyday life.

You'll be amazed at how this simple shift in perspective can transform your life. It's more than a principle; it's a way of living. It's a path to a richer, more connected, more insightful life.

Day 160

25 Things To Do Before You Die

L et's do something right now that could change your life forever. Grab a pen and paper. No, really, do it. You're going to make a list of 25 things you want to do before you die.

Why 25? It's big enough to make you think, but not so big that it's overwhelming. These are the dreams and experiences you don't want to miss out on.

Now look at that list. Feels exciting, right? Maybe a little intimidating? That's okay. Let's turn it from a list into action.

Pick the first one. That's your starting point. Don't worry about the other 24 right now. Just focus on that top one.

What's your plan? How are you going to make it happen? Break it down into steps. What's the first step? What's the second? Keep going until you have a roadmap.

Now here's the crucial part: Start. Take that first step. Today. Not tomorrow, not next week. Today. Because those dreams on your list are not going to happen by themselves.

Your life is happening right now. Those 25 things? They're part of your life. But they won't be unless you make them so.

So take that list, and make it real. Start with the top one. Make a plan, and then make it happen. And once you've done that first one, move on to the next. Because you've got 25 amazing things to do. You've got a life to live.

Day 161

The Dinner Guest

Imagine getting the chance to invite anyone in the world to dinner at your table: a renowned artist, a genius inventor, a compassionate leader, or perhaps a friend who has inspired you.

In choosing a dinner guest, we're not just selecting someone we find interesting or admirable. We're unveiling a mirror that reflects the traits, values, or passions that resonate deeply within our own selves. It's a glimpse into who we are and who we aspire to become.

The qualities that draw us to others are often those we admire or wish to cultivate within ourselves. Your choice may also reveal a path you wish to explore or a journey you're already on. Sometimes our choice reveals the core values that guide us.

This simple exercise of imagining a dinner guest can be a powerful tool for self-discovery. It's an invitation to reflect on what really matters to you, what you admire, what you yearn for, and perhaps what's missing from your life.

- What qualities in this person resonate with you?

- What dreams or ambitions does their story inspire in you?

- What can you learn from them that could be applied to your own life?

- How does this choice challenge or affirm your current path?

Take time to delve into these questions, allowing yourself to uncover the underlying meanings in your choice. It's not just about a fascinating conversation over dinner; it's a glimpse into the depths of who you are and who you hope to be.

Day 162

The Myth of Having It All

There's a common notion that success, as portrayed in the media and popular culture, means having it all figured out. We see images of celebrities, entrepreneurs, authors, and other figures who seem to have unlocked the secrets of life living in a state of constant fulfillment and unshakable confidence. But here's the unvarnished truth: It's a myth.

I've had the privilege of conversing with hundreds of people from various walks of life, many of whom are considered extraordinarily successful in their fields. You might expect that these individuals would exude an aura of absolute certainty, possessing all the answers to life's complexities.

But the reality is quite different. What I find in these conversations is a shared humanity and an understanding that no matter how accomplished we might appear, we're all grappling with something. Whether it's self-doubt, personal relationships, health, or existential questions, everyone wrestles with uncertainties and feels inadequate at times.

This realization is not a cause for despair but an invitation to authenticity and compassion. The myth of having it all figured out can be a heavy burden to bear. It can lead to comparison, discontent, and a never-ending chase for an unattainable ideal. But when we release ourselves from this illusion, we discover a richer and more rewarding way of living.

It's a liberating experience to recognize that it's okay not to have all the answers. It's okay to be human, with all the complexities and contradictions that come with it. It's okay to be you in all your beautiful imperfection.

The Heart of Culture

When we speak of culture, our minds often gravitate towards grand concepts like organizational values in business, team dynamics in sports, or national traditions and customs. We explore ways to foster a healthy work environment, build team cohesion, or celebrate our shared heritage. While these aspects of culture are significant and valuable, there's a fundamental cultural space we tend to overlook: our homes and relationships with our loved ones.

Home is more than a dwelling place; it's a living ecosystem that influences and shapes who we are. It's the space where we laugh, cry, grow, and discover the essence of our being. It's a sanctuary, school, workshop, and playground all woven into one complex tapestry.

The culture we create at home — the unspoken rules, the shared values, the rituals, and the emotional climate — affects us profoundly. It's not just about the physical arrangement or aesthetics of our living spaces, but the interactions, communications, and connections that take place within them.

Think about family dinners where conversations blossom, bedtime stories that nurture dreams, acts of kindness that affirm love, and honest dialogues that foster trust. These aren't mere activities but the building blocks of a thriving home culture.

Consider these vital aspects of crafting a positive culture at home.

- **Intentionality.** Culture doesn't just happen; it's cultivated. What are the values you want your family to embody? What behaviors do you wish to encourage? It begins with mindful choices and intentional actions.

- **Communication.** Open, honest, and clear communication lays the foundation for understanding and empathy. It's not merely about talking but in truly listening, seeing, and feeling each other.

- **Rituals and traditions.** From simple morning hugs to yearly family vacations, rituals and traditions create a sense of continuity, belonging, and identity. They're the threads that connect the present to the past and future.

- **Flexibility.** Families grow and change, and so should the culture. Adaptation, openness to new ideas, and willingness to evolve are crucial in keeping a home environment vibrant and alive.

- **Support and encouragement.** A home should be a place where every member feels supported and encouraged to be themselves. It's where we celebrate successes, learn from failures, and lift each other up.

- **Love and respect.** Above all, love and respect are the cornerstones of a healthy home culture. They transcend disagreements, heal wounds, and create a space where everyone can thrive.

Building a great culture at home isn't about rigid rules or forced conformity. It's about creating a living, breathing space where everyone can be themselves, feel valued, and grow together. It's about little things done with great love, small gestures that make big impacts, and daily choices that shape a lifetime.

In a world where we invest so much time and energy in cultivating external cultures, let's not neglect the most sacred space of all: our homes. For it's here that we find our roots and wings, our challenges and triumphs, our tears and joys. It's here that we shape and are shaped by the most important culture of our lives.

The Trap of Tradition

I've seen it happen time and again. We get comfortable with a way of doing things. Maybe it's a workflow, a method, or even a philosophy. We've always done it this way, so it must be the best way, right? Wrong.

This assumption is a dangerous trap, one that I call the Trap of Tradition. It's the belief that just because something has always been done a certain way, that way must be the best. It's a comfortable fallacy, but it's a stifling one. When we assume that the way we've done something in the past is the best way, we close ourselves off to the possibility of improvement. We become resistant to change. We become defenders of the status quo.

And in a world that's constantly changing, that's a dangerous position to be in. It can lead to stagnation, complacency, and eventually, irrelevance.

So how do we break free from this trap? How do we open ourselves to the possibility that there might be a better way?

The first step is awareness. Recognize that just because you've always done something a certain way doesn't mean it's the best way; it's just the way you've done it.

Next, cultivate curiosity. Ask questions. Why are we doing it this way? What other ways could we do it? Could a different approach be more efficient, effective, or joyful?

Finally, be willing to experiment. Try new ways. Take risks. Learn from failures. Embrace the possibility of *better* even if it means stepping out of your comfort zone.

Day 165

Be the Only

Striving to be the best is an endless race. There's always someone better, faster, smarter, or more skilled. It's an external competition that never ends, always pushing you to one-up someone else. But the path to true success and fulfillment doesn't lie in this race. It's not about being the best. It's about being the only.

Being the only is about carving a unique path, embracing what makes you distinct, and cultivating your authentic self. It's not about comparing yourself to others or conforming to external standards. It's about understanding what you have to offer the world that no one else does.

Imagine you're an artist. There are millions of skilled artists in the world, and trying to be the "best" among them can be a futile pursuit. But what if you focus on creating something that only you can create? What if you embrace your unique perspective, your individual style, and your personal experiences to craft something truly original? Suddenly, you're not competing with anyone else. You're the only one doing what you're doing.

Being the only one doesn't mean you don't strive for excellence or continuous improvement. It means that your metric for success isn't about being better than others but about being more fully yourself. It's about finding the intersection of your passion, your skills, and the needs of the world, and focusing on that unique space where only you can operate.

Don't get lost in the endless race to be the best. Focus on being the only one who can do what you do in the way you do it. That's where you'll make a mark that is uniquely yours.

Day 166

Arête

T he saying that has had the most profound impact on my life is the ancient Greek philosophy of *Arête*, which represents the pursuit of excellence and virtue in all aspects of life. It emphasizes the cultivation of one's character, wisdom, and moral integrity.

Rather than chasing fleeting accolades or transient gains, *Arête* encourages us to weave our core values into the fabric of our daily actions, relentlessly striving to become the best versions of ourselves.

The true beauty of *Arête* is that it doesn't consider excellence as a destination or single pinnacle to reach. Instead, it views excellence as a continuous journey, a constant evolution of our intellectual and moral prowess.

This philosophy reframes life as an invaluable playground filled with endless opportunities for self-improvement, each one beckoning us to rise to our highest potential. Every conversation, every task, and every moment gives us the opportunity to embrace our best. That's what *Arête* is all about — delivering your absolute highest and best self in each and every moment.

By embracing *Arête*, we're propelled towards a life not just of doing, but of being — embodying the principles of virtue, wisdom, and integrity in our every thought, action, and interaction. This relentless pursuit of excellence becomes the cornerstone of our personal evolution, lighting our path towards a fulfilling and virtuous life.

Day 167

The True Measure of Success

In a world that often equates success with comparison, remember that the true measure of success resides not in outdoing others, but in constantly surpassing your own potential.

It's not about being better than others; it's about being better than the person you were yesterday. It's not about standing above others on a podium; it's about standing tall on the pedestal of your personal growth.

Bear in mind that the most defining competition isn't one that unfolds in the external world; instead, it takes place within the confines of yourself. This is where the fiercest battles are fought — not against others but against your own limitations, doubts, and fears.

The real contest is against your past self and the constraints you've set for yourself. As others engage in the external race, remember to focus on the competition within. Strive to break your own records each day, push your boundaries further, and shatter your own glass ceilings.

The greatest reward you can ever attain is not a glittering trophy or applause from a crowd, but the deep, unparalleled satisfaction of knowing that you've evolved into the person you aspire to be.

The greatest reward is seeing the reflection of your best self in the mirror, knowing that you've nurtured your potential, overcome your limitations, and grown into a better version of yourself.

That, in its purest form, is the true measure of success.

Day 168

Your Track Record of Overcoming Adversity

C lose your eyes for just a moment and reflect on something we often overlook when we're in the thick of a battle: your track record of overcoming adversity.

Remember that time when you thought you couldn't go on but you did? Remember that situation you believed you would never get through but you managed? Remember the challenges that seemed insurmountable but you overcame them?

These are not mere accidents or lucky breaks. These are testaments to your resilience, determination, and grit. With each challenge met, you've gained wisdom, perspective, and strength. You've learned about yourself and your abilities.

These experiences are your personal treasure chest of lessons learned. They're assets to draw upon.

So here you are again, facing another challenge, feeling the weight of uncertainty. But now you know something powerful: You've been here before. You've overcome before. And you will do it again.

It's not about denying the difficulty of the situation. It's about recognizing your ability to handle it as you have in the past.

I know it's easier said than done. But consider embracing the journey even when it's tough. Your current challenge is another opportunity for growth, another chapter in your ever-evolving story.

Day 169

Coloring Our Perception

Feelings have a way of enveloping us, guiding our actions, shaping our relationships, and coloring our perception of the world. But one of the most profound realizations I've come across in my own exploration of self-awareness is this: Feelings are not objective facts.

Emotions are deeply personal, springing from our unique blend of experience, belief, and personality. They provide valuable insight into our inner world, but they don't necessarily depict an accurate portrayal of external reality.

Think of a time when you felt overwhelmingly afraid or anxious about something that in hindsight wasn't a threat at all. Or a moment when love or infatuation blinded you to the more nuanced truth of a situation. These emotions, while undeniably real and potent, were colored by your subjective experience.

Recognizing this distinction between feelings and facts is not about discounting our emotions. On the contrary, it's about embracing them as personal indicators rather than universal truths. By examining them, we can uncover the underlying beliefs or past experiences that shape them.

However, there's a delicate balance to be struck. We must learn to respect our feelings without being led astray by them. This involves developing an inner awareness that allows us to feel deeply while also recognizing that our emotions are not the definitive word on reality.

Ask yourself: What is this feeling trying to tell me? Where might it be coming from? Is there another perspective I could consider?

Day 170

Getting to the Root

We've all done it at one point or another. We identify a problem, react to the symptoms, and work hard to fix what's on the surface. It's a natural response, but unfortunately, it may be just a temporary fix. The issue may seem to disappear for a while, but it tends to resurface, sometimes even stronger than before.

What's going on here? The answer lies in the difference between treating symptoms and understanding the root cause.

Think of a weed in a garden. If you simply snip off the leaves and stem, it might look like you've solved the problem. But the root remains, ready to grow again. The same is true for many problems in our lives. Whether it's in our relationships, work, or personal development, focusing only on the symptoms is a bit like cutting off the top of that weed. It's an approach that might bring temporary relief but fails to deal with the underlying cause.

Finding the root cause is not always easy. It often requires us to look deeper, question our assumptions, and face uncomfortable truths about ourselves or our situation. It might require us to admit that we've been avoiding something or that we need to change something fundamental about our approach.

Here are some steps to digging deeper.

- **Ask "Why?" repeatedly.** Sometimes you have to ask "Why?" multiple times to get to the real underlying issue. Keep digging. Each answer can lead you closer to the root.

- **Look beyond the obvious.** It can be tempting to stop at the most apparent reason, but that may just be another symptom. Look beyond what's right in front of you.

- **Seek outside perspectives.** Sometimes we're too close to a problem to see it clearly. Friends, mentors, or professionals can provide valuable insights.

- **Be honest with yourself.** Facing the root cause may require you to admit something about yourself that's difficult to face. Honesty is crucial here.

- **Make a plan to address the root cause.** Once you've identified it, create a clear and actionable plan to address the root cause. It may require more effort in the short term but will likely lead to a more lasting solution.

Getting to the root cause of an issue is more complex and time-consuming than treating a symptom. It requires patience, introspection, and sometimes courage. But it's a process that leads to real, lasting change. It's an approach that enables you to solve problems at their core rather than continually battling the same issues over and over again.

So the next time you find yourself faced with a persistent problem, take the time to dig deeper. Go beyond the immediate symptoms and look for the underlying cause.

Day 171

A Lesson from Nietzsche

Nietzsche wisely proclaimed that the presence of a compelling *why* in our lives can empower us to endure and overcome any *how* that comes our way. A profound sense of purpose provides us with the fortitude and resilience to navigate the most challenging circumstances and adversities.

A clear and meaningful reason to live serves as a guiding light, illuminating our path and offering solace during the darkest of times. Our *why* becomes the anchor that steadies us amidst the storms of life, enabling us to hold on and find strength in the face of uncertainty. Embrace your *why*, for it will be the driving force that propels you forward, empowers you to overcome obstacles, and imbues your life with profound meaning and fulfillment.

Take some time today to uncover the *why* behind your actions, and let it propel you forward.

- Why do I do what I do every day?

- Why is that important to me?

- Why do I value that?

- Who matters most to me, and why do they matter to me so much?

Day 172

Dead Time and Alive Time

We live in an era of instant gratification and perpetual connection. Our devices buzz and ping, drawing us into a vortex of emails, tweets, likes, and follows. We've become so accustomed to filling every waking moment with digital distraction that we've forgotten something crucial: the power of stillness and the art of being present.

I call this phenomenon the dance between dead time and alive time. And understanding it might just change the way you live your life.

Dead time is found in those gaps between activities, the pockets of space we've unconsciously trained ourselves to fill with distraction. You know the moments I'm talking about: waiting in line, sitting at a traffic light, pausing between tasks. These are the moments we reach for our phones, scroll through social media, or get lost in an endless stream of information.

There's a price we pay for this constant engagement.

Our bandwidth — our mental and emotional capacity — is a finite resource. Every tweet we read, every infuriating post we react to, and every email we respond to eats away at this bandwidth. In those actions, we're compromising our alive time: those precious periods when we're fully present, engaged, creative, and at our best.

Alive time is where life happens. It's the space in which we create, connect, reflect, and grow. But to tap into this rich reservoir of potential, we need to recognize the toll that dead time is taking on us.

So what can we do about it?

- First, we must **become aware of the dance**. Notice how often you reach for distractions and begin to question why. Is it a habit? Is it anxiety? Is it boredom? Understanding the *why* behind the behavior is the first step toward change.

- Next, **reclaim those pockets of dead time.** Instead of reaching for your phone, take a deep breath. Look around. Be present with yourself and your surroundings. You might be surprised at what you discover in those brief moments of stillness.

- Finally, **cultivate a practice of mindfulness**. This doesn't have to be a formal meditation practice (though it can be). It's about making a conscious effort to be present and engage with life as it unfolds rather than losing ourselves in distraction.

Remember, our bandwidth is precious. How we choose to spend it determines the quality of our lives. In recognizing the dance between dead time and alive time, we can reclaim our focus, creativity, and well-being.

So the next time you find yourself reaching for that phone, pause. Breathe. And ask yourself: Is this a moment of dead time or alive time? The answer might just transform your life.

Day 173

Pause to Progress

Priest and psychotherapist Anthony de Mello once shared a wisdom gem: "The day you stop rushing, you will arrive." Let that sink in for a moment.

We live in a world where speed is often synonymous with success. The fastest wins the race. But life isn't a sprint; it's a marathon, a journey. In our obsession to reach somewhere, we often forget to appreciate where we are. The rush becomes routine. The moments blur. And ironically, the very destination we're hurrying toward keeps seeming further away.

Stopping the rush isn't about inaction. It's about intentional action. It's about understanding that the journey is as crucial as the destination. When you pause, you notice. You appreciate. You recalibrate. You connect. It's in these non-rushed moments that epiphanies strike, relationships deepen, and true growth happens.

De Mello's words are a reminder that you don't have to always be on the move to move forward. Sometimes taking a step back, pausing, and soaking in the moment finds you the right direction. And when that happens, you don't just arrive at a destination. You arrive at a realization, a deeper understanding of your journey and yourself.

So next time you find yourself rushing, ask: Where am I really trying to go? And could I get there faster by simply slowing down?

Day 174

Why Goals Slip Away

I've been there. We set ambitious goals fueled by midnight epiphanies only to watch them dissolve as quickly as they appeared. Reflecting on this, I've pinned it down to a tricky trio — three culprits that often thwart our aspirations.

- **Not motivating.** Imagine setting a goal because someone said you should or because it's the societal norm. Such goals lack a personal connection and hence, the intrinsic motivation to chase them. When a goal doesn't resonate with your innermost desires and values, it's like trying to light wet wood — it just doesn't catch fire.

- **Not specific.** "I want to be fit" sounds noble. But what does "fit" look like? Can you measure it? Goals without clarity are like ships without navigation. They drift. A more specific goal, such as "I want to run a 5K in under 25 minutes by December," gives you clarity and a tangible target.

- **Not accountable.** Here's a secret: When goals are kept private, it's easy to adjust them downward in the shadows of our minds. But when shared with, say, a trusted friend or a mentor, there's external accountability: someone to nudge you, ask about your progress, and celebrate the small victories with you.

Recognizing these three pitfalls is half the battle. The next time a goal flashes in your mind, ask: Is this truly what I desire? Is it crystal clear? And who can I share this journey with? Then watch as your aspirations transform from fleeting thoughts to tangible realities.

Day 175

Idea Catching

When an idea flares up with the potential to set your world ablaze, there's a tendency to want to ponder it, analyze it, and maybe overthink it. But I've learned something valuable over the years: Those moments of inspiration demand our swift embrace before they fade into the abyss of forgotten dreams.

So what do you do? You write it down. You sketch it out. You act. You tell someone. You make that phone call. You do something to capture the essence of that spark.

In the realm of creativity, timing is everything. Those brief flashes of brilliance are delicate and ephemeral. They won't wait for you. They don't care about your convenience. And the moment you say, "I'll remember this later" is often the moment you lose it forever.

The habit of nurturing these sparks into flames is a practice, an attitude of staying alert, receptive, and ready to move when the idea strikes. It's about honoring the creativity within you and recognizing that these ideas are fleeting gifts.

Urgency is not about stress or panic. It's about recognizing the value in the moment and understanding that the opportunity is *now*. It's a constructive energy that propels you to act not out of fear but out of respect for the potential.

Those sparks, flares, and shooting stars of ideas carry the power to fuel your journey towards remarkable heights. They are the seeds of possibilities, the whispers of what could be. Treat them with the care and urgency they deserve. Let them set your world ablaze. Cultivate the habit of catching them, nurturing them, and watching them grow.

Day 176

Unveiling the Unseen

Sometimes the most important discoveries are hidden in plain sight. It's the way we look at things and the perspective we bring that reveals their hidden value. Your way of seeing is a powerful tool.

You and I can look at the same piece of art or hear the same piece of music and perceive it differently. What might seem ordinary to others could strike you as extraordinary. What others overlook might catch your eye. This distinction in perception isn't something to be brushed aside. It's a signpost pointing towards your distinct strengths and talents.

I think of it as having a distinct lens through which you see the world. Your lens is shaped by everything you've been through, everything you know, and everything you value. It's a culmination of your experience, and it's unlike anyone else's. To truly unlock your potential, you need to become attuned to these unnoticed gems in your thinking. You need to embrace the practice of keen observation and curiosity.

Start by noticing what catches your attention. What intrigues you? What do you see that others seem to miss? These are clues — the starting points of your unique path. Your unique perception is your gift. It's your tool for creativity and growth. It's how you'll find those unseen gems in your life, in your work, and in others.

It's not about being better or smarter; it's about being you. In your distinction lies your strength. In your perception lies your path. Follow it. Trust it. It's showing you something wonderful.

One Foot at a Time

I recently had a conversation with a Navy SEAL friend that I think you'll find fascinating, especially if you've ever found yourself overwhelmed by the future.

He shared with me some insights from BUDS, the grueling training program that every Navy SEAL goes through. Specifically, he talked about the people who quit. BUDS is known for pushing people to their physical and mental limits. It's not just about fitness. It's about resilience, grit, and the ability to handle intense pressure.

My friend said, "You know what's common among those who quit? They were always thinking about the future. Everything that was to come. They weren't focused on what was happening right now. They weren't thinking about just putting one foot in front of the other."

Think about it. When you're overwhelmed by the entire journey ahead of you, it's easy to succumb to fear and anxiety. The future is unpredictable and vast. It's full of uncertainties and unknown challenges that can seem insurmountable.

But what if you bring your focus back to the present? What if you concentrate solely on the step you're taking right now? This idea of "one foot at a time" is more than a strategy for survival in a rigorous training program. It's a philosophy for life.

Whether you're facing a challenging project at work, a tough period in a relationship, or any big goal you want to achieve, the concept remains the same. Break it down. Focus on the present. Put one foot in front of the other.

The Power of Visualization

As each dawn breaks, we're gifted with the chance to prepare for our day through the art of visualization. By closing our eyes and envisioning our desired outcomes, we tap into a vital tool available to us in every moment. By conjuring vivid, immersive images of our desired outcomes, we effectively map a blueprint for our minds to follow.

- **Identify your goals.** Begin by clearly defining what you want to achieve. The more specific you can be about your goal, the better.

- **Visualize in detail.** Close your eyes and imagine your goal as vividly as possible. Engage all your senses. If your goal is to run a marathon, imagine the sound of your footsteps, the feeling of the pavement beneath your shoes, and the sight of the finish line.

- **Embody the emotion.** One of the key aspects of visualization is to feel the emotions you would experience if you achieved your goal. Feeling the joy, satisfaction, or pride as you visualize strengthens the impact of the exercise.

- **Create micro-moments of practice.** Visualization can have profound effects when done for just a minute at a time multiple times throughout the day. Have a few minutes between meetings? Opt to tap into visualization instead of picking up your phone.

Visualization is a skill that gets better with practice. The more you use this tool, the more naturally it will come to you, and the more powerful its effects can be.

Day 179

What's More Important?

The pursuit of knowledge and personal growth often begins with a simple yet profound question: Are you more attached to being right or to learning?

Being right feels good. It validates our sense of self-worth and reinforces our beliefs. It gives us a temporary sense of victory and superiority. But attachment to being right can become a shackling force that confines us to a limited perspective.

On the other hand, an attachment to learning is liberating. It acknowledges that we don't have all the answers and that that's okay. It's an open door, an invitation to explore, question, and grow. It places us in a state of humble curiosity, allowing us to approach life with an open and receptive mind.

When you are attached to being right, every disagreement becomes a battle and every differing opinion a threat. This mindset fosters defensiveness and close-mindedness. It inhibits growth, stifles creativity, and often leads to strained relationships. But when you are attached to learning, differing opinions become opportunities to expand your understanding. Disagreements transform into dialogues, and the unknown becomes a thrilling exploration. It's a mindset that promotes collaboration, innovation, and personal growth.

This philosophy can be applied to all aspects of life from personal relationships to professional pursuits. It's a perspective that recognizes the fluidity of truth and the infinite potential for growth.

So ask yourself this question regularly: Are you more attached to being right or to learning? Your honest answer to this question reveals much about your character, your approach to life, and ultimately how far you will go.

Day 180

Escaping the Pull of Mediocrity

In modern society, there's a relentless push towards conformity — an invisible hand nudging us towards a standardized definition of success and normality. Media, advertisements, and even well-meaning friends and family can all send the message that there's a specific path we should follow. That path often leads to what's considered average.

Is average really something to aspire to be? This isn't a condemnation of what's considered ordinary or typical. Many find happiness and fulfillment in pursuing traditional goals and living conventional lives. There's nothing inherently wrong with that. The danger arises when we pursue *average* not out of a genuine desire for those things but out of fear, conformity, or lack of self-awareness.

In many ways, *average* is a societal construct, a comfort zone. It's a place where you're unlikely to be criticized, ridiculed, or misunderstood — but it may also be a place where you're unlikely to fully explore your unique potential, passions, and purpose. Aspiring to be something other than average doesn't necessarily mean seeking fame, fortune, or extreme paths. It means striving to be the most authentic version of yourself. It means aligning your life with your values, passions, and strengths, even if those don't align with societal expectations.

The pursuit of average can lead to a life that's satisfactory. But the pursuit of authenticity can lead to an extraordinary life.

So take a moment to step back and ask yourself: Is average what you genuinely aspire to be? Or is there something deeper, more personal, and uniquely you that's waiting to be explored?

Day 181

Harness Your Strengths

It's worth taking the time to contemplate on this: What strengths do you have that lay forgotten and unused?

These untapped reservoirs of potential and prowess are the very essence of what makes you unique and effective, whether it's your ability to connect with others, your knack for problem-solving, your creative spirit, or your tenacity in the face of adversity.

It's these attributes that constitute your greatest assets. But it's not enough to merely acknowledge them. The real magic lies in leveraging them, in weaving them into the fabric of your daily life.

Today, task yourself with a mission. Consciously utilize these latent strengths. Apply them to your tasks, your interactions, and your goals. Let this not be an exercise in vanity but a demonstration of your inherent power. By utilizing your strengths, you create an environment that not only enhances your productivity but also feeds your soul.

And remember, there's strength in vulnerability as well. The courage to lean in, embrace it, and use it as a platform for growth is perhaps one of the greatest strengths you possess. Harness it, hone it, and let it lead the way.

From Problem-Focused to Solution-Oriented

In the thick of challenges, it's natural to get consumed by the problem itself — dissecting it, wrestling with its weight. But what if we change our perspective? Imagine shifting the focus from the obstacle to the path stretching ahead.

Here's the game-changer: *Ask solution-oriented questions*. By doing so, we flip the script, steering our thoughts away from what's blocking us and toward what could catapult us forward. It's like transforming roadblocks into springboards.

Instead of pondering "Why are sales plummeting?" ask, "What steps can we take to enhance our sales and customer engagement?" It's not just wordplay; it's a mindset makeover that ushers in a whole new way of tackling issues.

Likewise, let's ditch the "Why am I always sad?" question for "What brings me joy?" It's about paving a path towards positivity one query at a time. By switching our mental lens, we unearth solutions, see opportunities in the midst of challenges, and tap into our innate resourcefulness.

So the next time life throws you a curveball, don't fixate on the problem's intricacies. Turn your attention to the possibilities that emerge from within you. Embrace the transformational magic of solution-oriented thinking and watch as challenges evolve into catalysts for growth, propelling you toward the radiant future you deserve.

Day 183

The Price of Waiting

There's a line by spiritual teacher Eckhart Tolle that's stayed with me: "How much more pain do you need before you can make the choice?" It's a bold question. Raw. It prods and pokes right where it hurts, but for a good reason.

We often imagine change on a distant horizon that will come at the "right time." But waiting can be a comfortable illusion, one we afford at the cost of enduring repeated pain. It's like touching a hot stove and waiting to get burned a few more times before deciding to pull away.

Take the case of someone wanting to get in shape. They believe they'll start their fitness journey when they find the perfect gym, when work is less hectic, or at the beginning of a new year. But years roll by, and they're still at square one. If they had begun with simple home workouts, even 10 minutes a day, they'd be in a far better place physically and mentally today.

Why do we do this to ourselves? Is it fear? Comfort in the familiar, no matter how painful? A sense of undeservingness? Maybe a mix of them all. But here's the thing: Every moment is a crossroads and every second is a fresh chance to choose.

Tolle's words remind us that we don't need to hit rock bottom to start climbing up. We don't need more heartaches, regrets, or 'should-haves' to make a change. We just need the present moment and the choice to say, "Enough."

So if you're waiting for a sign, this might be it. Ask yourself: How much more pain do you need? Or is now the perfect time to choose a different path?

Transcending the Weight of the Past

There is a saying that life is a journey, and each of us carries a backpack filled with memories, experiences, and emotions. Sometimes this backpack becomes heavy with the burdens of past failures, fears, guilt, and regret. We hunch under the weight, forgetting that these burdens are not permanent fixtures. They are not the entirety of our existence, nor do they define us.

Instead, these burdens are navigational markers on the roadmap of life. They signal areas of growth, strength, and resilience that have been, and continue to be, shaped by these challenges. But remember, it's our choice to decide how long we want to carry these weights.

It's within our power to put them down — to unpack the backpack and make room for forgiveness, acceptance, and new experiences.

Your heart is not a vessel for sorrow, but a beacon of light that guides you forward, illuminating your path with hope and love. Every step you take forward without these burdens is a victory, a testament to your strength, and a promise of a brighter, lighter tomorrow.

Day 185

Ever Upward

Latin phrases seem to have timeless allure in my life, and among them, *excelsior* shines brightly as a beacon of aspiration and determination. Directly translating to "ever upward," *Excelsior* is more than just a word—it's an exhortation to continual growth, progress, and a relentless pursuit of greater heights.

Embracing *excelsior* means adopting an unwavering commitment to self-improvement and personal evolution, constantly setting our sights higher, and challenging ourselves to transcend our comfort zones.

It embodies the belief that our potential is not fixed but rather a landscape of boundless opportunity waiting to be explored. It's a potent reminder that life's journey is not a flat terrain but an upward climb where every summit we conquer becomes a new vantage point, offering an expansive view of uncharted territories.

Excelsior serves as a cue that life's journey is a constant upward trajectory, and every milestone reached becomes a launchpad for even greater achievements.

So today, embrace *excelsior* and bring its ever-upward pursuit into everything you do.

The Art of Mental Decluttering

Decluttering isn't an exercise reserved for our physical spaces; it is equally critical for the expanse of our minds. Our thoughts are akin to a bustling marketplace, filled with a ceaseless hum of ideas, worries, memories, and plans. It can be tempting to hold onto everything and believe that every piece of mental debris carries significance. But the true treasures of our inner selves can only shine brightly when we clear away the clutter.

We must learn to let go — to untangle the knots of unnecessary thoughts and complications that only serve to cloud our vision and disrupt our inner harmony. By actively discarding what no longer serves us, we make way for what truly matters: the clarity of purpose, the serenity of peace, and the joy of unburdened thoughts.

This act of mental decluttering is deeply liberating. It is akin to stripping away the extraneous layers to reveal the radiant authenticity beneath. Embracing simplicity isn't about eliminating complexity; it's about making room for what truly enhances our lives. Within this spaciousness, the symphony of our soul can resonate unhindered, painting our existence with rich, harmonious hues.

Day 187

Eudaimonia

M any believe that the pursuit of happiness revolves around immediate gratification and fleeting moments of pleasure. The ancient Greek philosophers
introduced us to a more profound concept: *eudaimonia*. This form of happiness
isn't just about ephemeral joys; it's about truly and deeply flourishing.

Imagine a doctor working in a remote village. The work is challenging and lacks
the monetary rewards of a city-based practice. Yet the doctor feels an overwhelming
sense of fulfillment because they believe in the importance of offering healthcare to
those who need it most. Every life they touch and improve gives them a profound
sense of purpose and meaning. A nice car won't touch them to the core like this
will.

Philosophers like Aristotle and Socrates emphasized the value of eudaimonic happiness. They spoke of life not as a series of events to be experienced but as an opportunity for personal growth, purpose-driven endeavors, and authentic connections.
Their teachings remind us that genuine happiness is derived from living in alignment with our true nature, passionately chasing our potential, and contributing
meaningfully to the world around us.

In our pursuit of such fulfillment, the idea is to delve beneath the obvious. Instead
of skimming the surface of life for quick pleasures, we should be diving into its
depths, seeking meaningful engagements, nurturing intrinsic goals, and fostering
communal bonds. Let's shift our focus from momentary delight to lifelong fulfillment — not just living a life of fleeting happiness but embracing one rich in
purpose, depth, and lasting contentment.

Day 188

The Mind's Marathon

Just as an athlete prepares tirelessly for their race — pushing their physical limits, improving their endurance, and perfecting their technique — so must we condition our minds to perform optimally in life's greatest race. Our mind, like any muscle, needs consistent, deliberate training to enhance its capabilities, resilience, and agility.

Here are some workouts to train your mind for life's race.

- **Build mental endurance.** An athlete needs stamina to sustain the pace of the race; our minds need endurance to overcome life's challenges. This can be built through practices like mindfulness and meditation, which strengthen our capacity to manage stress.

- **Enhance mental agility.** Life is filled with unexpected twists and turns, so our minds need to be flexible and adaptive. We can enhance this by constantly learning, embracing new experiences, and being open to different perspectives.

- **Cultivate a growth mindset.** Athletes view setbacks as opportunities for growth, and we must see life's hurdles as chances to learn and improve. Always ask yourself, "What can I learn from this?"

- **Practice regularly.** Just as an athlete trains regularly to keep in shape, our mental training should be consistent. Whether it's daily meditation, reading, or journaling, find a routine that works for you and stick to it.

Day 189

Eye Level With Everyone

B e at eye level with people. It's a simple yet profound metaphor. Don't look up and don't look down on people. Treat everyone with the same level of respect, dignity, and understanding.

Looking up at someone might mean putting them on a pedestal, idolizing them, or feeling inferior. It creates a distance and a barrier, making a genuine connection difficult.

Looking down on someone, on the other hand, implies a sense of superiority, judgment, or arrogance. It dismisses the value and humanity of the other person, stifling empathy and consideration.

Being at eye level means recognizing the inherent worth and humanity in everyone you encounter. It means approaching people with an open heart and a mind without preconceived notions or judgments. It means understanding that every person you meet has dreams, struggles, and triumphs just like you.

Being at eye level embraces the idea that no one is above you and no one is beneath you. It's a recognition that we are all on this journey together, each with our unique path but all deserving of kindness, respect, and empathy.

And here's the beautiful thing about eye level: It doesn't diminish your worth or accomplishments. It doesn't mean you have to agree with everyone or accept every viewpoint. It simply means approaching others with the recognition that they are fellow human beings with their own insights, perspectives, and value. It's not about looking up or down; it's about looking straight ahead, right into the heart of what makes us human.

Internal Mastery Through Acceptance

L ife throws countless events our way. But often, it's not the events themselves that shake us; it's our resistance to them.

Picture life's ever-flowing stream of events as a river. Now imagine a dam blocking it. That's our resistance turning smooth flow into chaos.

Life's happenings? They're neutral. Rain simply falls. If you curse it for ruining your plans, you're resisting. But adjust and move on, and it's just water. The difference? Your reaction.

While many life events are beyond our control, our responses are firmly in our hands. Acceptance isn't passivity; it's recognizing that resistance amplifies discomfort. With acceptance, you can act with clarity.

When stress looms, ponder: Is it the event or my resistance causing this unrest? Grasping this can help pivot you from tension to tranquility.

In life, don't be the obstructing dam. Let events flow. True peace lies in mastering your responses, not in altering the uncontrollables.

Day 191

Life in a Day

Every day is a mini-lifetime.

It starts fresh, unfolds with a universe of possibilities, and concludes, leaving behind memories, lessons, and impacts. How we move through these daily rhythms and small lifetimes is indicative of the larger melody of our existence.

Today is not just another day. It's a chance to iterate, innovate, and maybe even redefine who you are.

So ask yourself: If today were the blueprint for the rest of your life, what would you do? How would you act? What choices would you make to ensure it's a day you'd cherish, relive, and replay in your mind's theater?

We often dream of monumental days: big events, life-changing moments. But the truth is, greatness is cultivated in the ordinary: in the small acts of kindness, the choices to learn, the pauses to reflect, the courage to love, and the decision to embrace every moment with zest.

Make today that kind of day — one where, when the night comes, you'd say, "I'd live it all over again." Because in shaping your days, you're sculpting your life. Remember, it's not about grand gestures; it's about sincere moments.

So find the magic in the mundane, and make today not just another day, but a day that reflects the best version of you.

Tonight, wouldn't you love to look back and whisper, "I'd relive this"?

Day 192

Efficiency

We live in a world obsessed with efficiency. There's a tool, an app, or a system for everything, all designed to help us do things faster, better, more effectively. But in our pursuit of efficiency, we sometimes lose sight of the big picture.

There is no bigger waste of time than doing something efficiently that shouldn't be done at all. The time and energy spent on it are gone, never to be recovered.

Efficiency is a valuable tool, but it's not an end in itself. It's a means to an end, and it only makes sense in the context of a clear, meaningful goal. So before you dive into the *how*, take a moment to reflect on the *why*. Make sure you're not just doing things right but doing the right things. Don't waste your time on efficiency for efficiency's sake. Focus on what truly matters, and let the rest go. That's not just efficient; that's wise.

So how can we avoid this trap?

Start with your *why*. Before diving into how to do something, ask yourself why you're doing it. Is it aligned with your goals, values, and vision? If not, no amount of efficiency will make it worthwhile.

Question assumptions. Just because something has always been done doesn't mean it should continue to be done. Challenge the status quo. Maybe there's a reason to stop doing it altogether.

Prioritize. Focus on what's truly important and contributes to your larger purpose. Let go of the rest, even if you can do it efficiently.

Day 193

The Continuous Craft of Confidence

There's a secret I need to share with you: Confidence isn't something you're born with. It's an ability honed through conscious, deliberate, and mindful actions.

Confidence isn't born from thin air. It's not an abstract concept that materializes with wishful thinking. No, confidence is forged in the crucible of preparation and honed through countless repetitions. But let's be honest: Even those who've clocked thousands of reps can wrestle with lingering doubt. Just ask the athlete battling the infamous yips.

Repetition alone doesn't guarantee unwavering confidence. It's a necessary step, yes, but it's not the whole journey. A foundation of relentless practice and diligent preparation is essential. Confidence isn't about constructing castles in the sky; it's about solidifying your fortress on unshakable ground.

Yet even after this arduous groundwork, a gap remains. This gap is where your internal dialogue comes into play. Your self-talk becomes the bridge connecting the practical to the psychological. And here's the kicker: your self-talk is a skill you can refine.

Your self-talk isn't a realm of grandiose fantasies or falsehoods. It's a sanctuary of focus, directing your attention toward elements within your control. Saying, "I'll win this game!" has its place, but true potency lies in affirmations grounded in what you can manage: "I'll exert exceptional effort on defense. I'll dominate the boards with relentless hustle." These are the variables you can command.

The secret sauce here? Root your self-talk in evidence: moments when you've embodied these traits before. You've been tenacious on defense; you've infused energy into presentations. You have the proof. That's where confidence emerges — in the overlap of control and demonstrated capability.

But let's talk about the uncomfortable zone, those early days when you're short on reps and heavy on uncertainty. This is where courage enters the picture. Courage isn't a byproduct of confidence; it's its own force, igniting action despite fear. It's the fuel that propels you forward when confidence is still in gestation.

Waiting for confidence to manifest is a futile endeavor. Instead, embrace the interplay between courage and control. The cycle begins with preparation fueled by self-talk rooted in tangible command. It's nurtured through evidence and powered by courage, that audacious leap into the unknown.

Know this: Confidence isn't a finish line. It's a spectrum that stretches from courage to command, and with each step, you carve out a stronger, more resilient version of yourself.

Day 194

Time is Slipping Away

I magine your future self looking back on this very moment. What would you tell your younger self? What advice, reminders, and wisdom would you share?

One profound truth might be this: "I would pay any amount of money to be able to rewind the clock and relive this moment."

Why? Because life is made of moments. Moments of joy, pain, growth, love, loss, and everything in between. Each moment is a chance to be, to feel, to connect, to live.

But we often miss these moments. We let them slip away while our minds are elsewhere, preoccupied with what's next, what's past, or what might never be.

The future version of you will want this time back. So don't let it slip away while it's here.

How can you honor this insight?

Your future self is whispering to you across the years, a gentle reminder of the preciousness of now. Listen.

Live the moment that's right in front of you with all the passion, awareness, and appreciation you can muster. For one day, this moment will be a memory, and you'll wish to have it back.

Make it a memory worth revisiting. Make it a life worth living.

Day 195

Tuning the Mind's Engine

I often think of the mind as a turbo-charged engine. Seriously, it's like this super-powered race car inside our skulls, buzzing with potential and ready to zoom towards any finish line we set. But like all high-performance vehicles, it needs daily maintenance to keep running at its peak.

Think about your favorite physical workout. Maybe it's a brisk run in the morning or that killer cycling class. One session is fantastic. It gets the blood pumping and the muscles working. But no one expects that single workout to sustain their fitness indefinitely. The body needs consistent training to stay in shape. In the same vein, our mental prowess also requires consistent upkeep.

Every day, we need to recalibrate and refocus our minds. We can't just rest on yesterday's laurels and hope they'll carry us through today, tomorrow, and the next month. This isn't about doubt or questioning your capacities; it's about daily re-calibration. Refining our focus, refreshing our intentions, and renewing our clarity.

Kick-starting the day with mindful actions is like warming up the car engine in the winter. Starting each day with intention means giving your mind the workout it craves. Whether it's through meditation, journaling, reading, or even just sitting in silence for a few minutes, find what recalibrates you. Use that practice daily, and witness the improved mental horsepower you'll have to race towards your dreams.

So next time you're feeling a bit off track or your mental engine seems a bit sluggish, remember: daily maintenance, daily recalibration. Because when you consistently refuel and recalibrate that magnificent engine of yours, the path to greatness is smooth and unswerving.

Day 196

Prioritizing Self-Care

Your body is the only home your soul will have in this lifetime. It's a temple not just in metaphor but in the most profound sense. Your body is the only place you experience life, love, joy, pain, growth, and all the wonders of existence. But in the whirlwind of daily life, amid the noise, the hurry, and the endless to-do lists, we often forget this simple truth.

We neglect our bodies. We treat them not as sacred spaces but as machines, expecting them to run tirelessly without proper care, nourishment, or love.

Here's a gentle reminder: Your body and your health — both physical and mental — is the foundation of everything else in your life. The quality of your thoughts, your work, your relationships, and your dreams all hinge on the well-being of this singular temple.

So pause for a moment. Ask yourself: "How am I tending to my health today? How am I honoring this incredible body and mind that serve me?"

It's not about grand gestures or extreme measures. It's about small, consistent actions — choices made with intention and respect for yourself. These choices aren't about immediate gains. They're about laying down bricks one by one to build a wall of health that supports you not just today but for the long haul.

Your body and mind are not separate from you; they are you. They are the vessels through which you experience and contribute to the world.

Cherish them. Nurture them. Love them.

Day 197

A Race of One, Cheering for All

Embracing the mindset of competing against yourself while cheering for every-one else is a powerful and transformative approach to life. When we focus on our own growth and progress rather than comparing ourselves to others, we free ourselves from the burdens of envy and jealousy.

Instead of feeling threatened or insecure by others' achievements, we genuinely root for their success, knowing that their triumphs do not diminish our own potential. This mindset fosters a sense of unity and collaboration, creating a community of support and encouragement.

As we celebrate others' victories, we find inspiration and motivation to pursue our own goals with renewed vigor. It is a mindset that embodies humility and self-compassion, recognizing that we are all on unique journeys and that each of us has the capacity to achieve greatness in our own way.

So let us compete against our former selves while lifting others up and celebrating their triumphs as if they were our own.

In this spirit of camaraderie, we can forge meaningful connections and collectively rise to new heights of success and fulfillment.

Day 198

Working at the Source

I once heard of a village constantly battling with the aftermath of a flooding river. The villagers exerted all their energy, resources, and time in managing the catastrophes brought by the raging torrents. Then one old woman, considered the wisest in the village, suggested planting trees way upstream. The villagers were perplexed. They were dealing with a river, not a forest. But she persisted.

Fast-forward several years, and the floods lessened. The roots of the trees helped manage the flow of water, reducing the regular catastrophes. This wise woman understood something fundamental: Instead of constantly dealing with aftermaths, it's often more effective to go to the source and work there.

Taking care of matters at their outset can seem indirect or even irrelevant. It's upstream work, far from where the apparent issue lies. But it's these early interventions that ripple into significant changes down the line.

Many of our challenges seem overwhelming when viewed downstream. But if we trace them back to their nascent stages, we might discover simpler, more manageable points of intervention. And often it's at these points where the most transformative changes can occur.

So next time you're faced with a challenge, consider tracing it upstream. What's its source? How can you address it there? By shifting our approach from reactive to proactive, we set ourselves on a path of true mastery.

Day 199

How Long Will It Take?

We often find ourselves asking, "How long will this take?" But when it comes to chasing a great life, that question might be missing the point.

Imagine your life not as a series of deadlines but as a continuous journey towards growth and learning. The pursuit of a great life doesn't fit neatly into a schedule. It's not about reaching a destination at a specific time; it's about relentless curiosity, a passion for stretching beyond boundaries, and a commitment to lifelong learning.

Think about your personal growth not in terms of months or years but in terms of depth and breadth. Are you learning? Are you growing? Are you challenging yourself and pushing your boundaries? Are you engaging with life in a way that feels meaningful to you?

When you shift your focus from "how long" to "how deeply," the pursuit of a great life becomes a rich and fulfilling experience.

So the next time you catch yourself wondering how long it will take to achieve something, remember that the real question might be, "How deeply am I willing to engage with this journey?" Because a great life isn't measured in minutes or hours; it's measured in growth, understanding, and the relentless pursuit of something more. It's a lifelong adventure, and the clock has nothing to do with it.

Day 200

Real Magic

Magic. It's a word that brings to mind images of wizards and sorcerers, sparkling wands and impossible feats. But real magic, the kind that leaves people in awe, often isn't about supernatural powers at all. Sometimes it's about commitment, dedication, and the willingness to invest more time and effort into something than anyone might reasonably expect.

Consider a musician who practices a single piece of music for thousands of hours, an artist who spends months refining every detail of a painting, or a craftsman who perfects a piece of furniture with loving care. To an outside observer, the end result might seem magical, but the creator knows the real secret: It's about time.

Time not in a hurried sense, but in a focused, deliberate way. It's about shutting out distractions and being fully present in the craft. It's about going beyond what's required or expected and embracing the process as a labor of love. "This matters to me, so I'm going to give it everything I have."

That kind of magic doesn't require wands or spells. It's accessible to all of us in whatever we do if we're willing to invest ourselves fully. The "trick" is no trick at all, but a choice. It's in the extra mile, the unseen hours, and the choices that say, "This is worth my time."

Remember, magic isn't confined to stages and storybooks. It's alive in our daily lives in the way we approach our work, our passions, our relationships, and our dreams.

So next time you witness something magical, know that you're seeing the visible tip of a hidden iceberg. And next time you set out to do something, ask yourself how you might add a touch of magic to it.

Day 201

Love's Infinite Reach

Sometimes life hands us nuggets of wisdom so profound that they resonate deeply, altering our perspective. Brunello Cucinelli, a name synonymous with not just luxury fashion but also profound thought, penned a line that's worth more than a pause. He said, "After all these years and experiences, I know nothing, nothing at all, that compares to the love for another person when it comes to reaching immensity and infinity."

It's humbling, isn't it? Here we are, chasing grand dreams and grander achievements, often losing ourselves in the quest for more. Yet at the heart of existence, it's the simple, pure, and profound emotion of love that trumps all. It's the compass that directs us toward what truly matters.

So how do we take action on this knowledge?

Begin by taking a moment each day to reflect on the love present in your life. Nurture it, cherish it, and make it a cornerstone of your daily intentions.

Invest in the people and relationships that bring this kind of love into your life. Reach out, express gratitude, and ensure that you're not just acknowledging this love but actively deepening it.

Prioritize those meaningful relationships, cultivate deeper bonds, and remember that it's through love that we touch the infinite.

Day 202

Success Structures

Success isn't an accident. It's a structure. It's a system you design, consciously or unconsciously, that governs how you live, work, and play. Your success structures are the habits, routines, and practices that bring you more vitality, more energy, more life.

So today, let's get intentional about it. Take a moment to map out what those success structures are for you. What are the things that make you feel alive, focused, and fulfilled?

Maybe it's a morning run, meditating, or spending quality time with loved ones. Maybe it's working on a project that really matters to you or taking the time to prepare a nourishing meal.

Whatever it is, write it down. Be specific. Get clear on what these success structures are for you. Now look at that list. That's your roadmap to vitality.

But having a roadmap isn't enough. You have to travel it. So make a plan. How can you implement these success structures more frequently in your life? What changes do you need to make? What do you need to prioritize and let go of?

Then commit to it. This is your life, and these are the things that make it worth living. Commit to them. Commit to yourself.

Don't let this be just an exercise. Let it be a turning point. Let it be the day you decide to live with more intention, purpose, and vitality. Start today, because vitality isn't something you find; it's something you create.

Day 203

Pain + Reflection = Progress

I want to share with you a simple equation that's as profound as it is powerful. It's something I learned from Ray Dalio, one of the most successful investors of our time, and it's an equation that's been instrumental in shaping his life and career.

Pain + Reflection = Progress

Sounds simple, right? But like all profound truths, there's depth here that's worth exploring.

Pain. No one likes pain. Whether it's physical or emotional, our instinct is to avoid it, to run from it, to pretend it's not there. But pain is a signal. It's a message. Something isn't right. Something needs attention. Something needs to change.

Reflection. Reflection is the process of looking deeply and honestly at the pain, understanding its root causes, and deriving lessons from it. It's about asking the tough questions: Why did this happen? What went wrong? What can I learn from this? What will I do differently next time?

Reflection turns pain from useless suffering into a valuable lesson. It transforms a negative experience into an opportunity for learning and growth.

Progress. And that leads us to progress. By facing pain and reflecting on it deeply, you gain insights and lessons that allow you to move forward, to progress.

So next time you find yourself in pain, don't run from it. Embrace it. Reflect on it. Learn from it. Grow from it. And remember, Pain + Reflection = Progress.

Day 204

Letting Go

In a march, every step is planned. Every move is calculated. You know exactly where you're going and exactly how to get there.

But in a dance, it's different. You don't know exactly what's coming next. You have to be flexible and responsive, in tune with the music, your partner, and the moment.

Trying to control life is like trying to turn a dance into a march. It's frustrating, exhausting, and ultimately futile. Life won't follow your plan. It won't march to your beat. It has its own rhythm, its own flow, and the more you try to control it, the more you'll feel out of control.

So let go. Surrender. Stop trying to force life into your preconceived notions of how it should be. Stop trying to predict every twist and turn. Stop trying to manipulate every event and outcome.

Instead, dance with life. Move with it, flow with it, be with it. Embrace the uncertainty, unpredictability, and beautiful chaos of it all. Allow yourself to be surprised, to be moved, to be alive.

This is not about being passive or resigned. It's about being active and engaged in a different way. It's about being in harmony with life, not in conflict with it. It's about working with what is, not against it.

It's a gentle embrace, not a tight grasp. It's a way of being that's soft yet strong, flexible yet grounded, and open yet centered.

If You Want to Learn to Swim, Jump in the Water

You can read all the books in the world about swimming, but until you jump in the water, you won't really know how to swim. Life is like that. There's a difference between knowledge and wisdom. Knowledge is something you can accumulate from books, lectures, and study. Wisdom comes from experience — from living life in all its raw, messy glory.

Books can point the way, sure. I hope this one is helping you in that regard. But they're only maps. They're not the territory itself. You can't just read about life. You have to live it. You have to engage with it, struggle with it, love it, hate it, win, lose, succeed, fail, laugh, cry, and everything in between.

There's a whole universe out there humming with life, vibrating with energy, teeming with opportunities and challenges, joys and sorrows, highs and lows. And it's all waiting for you. Not in the abstract, theoretical sense but in the real, tangible, touchable sense.

You've got to get out there and live it. You've got to step into life and really engage with it, not just as an observer but as a participant. As a player. As a liver of life.

So put down the book (even this one!) and go live your life. Embrace it with all its imperfections and inconsistencies. Flow with it, play with it, wrestle with it, learn from it. Let it shape you, mold you, transform you into the person you aspire to be.

Because life isn't something to be studied from a distance. It's something to be lived up close and personal. And there's no better time to start than right now.

Day 206

The Puzzle of Pride

L ife sometimes feels like an abstract jigsaw puzzle: pieces scattered in disarray, an unclear picture, and a sense of aimless trial and error. In your hands, you might hold a piece that seems odd, its shape awkward, its pattern unrecognizable. You might find yourself trying to force pieces together, sometimes out of frustration, other times out of sheer stubbornness.

But here's the thing about puzzles, about life: It's in the patience, the persistence, the belief that even if the image isn't clear today, it will be one day. It's in the quiet moments of solitude and reflection that you might notice something — a slight edge, a curve, a pattern — that resonates. That's the moment when, quite unexpectedly, the pieces start to click together. And what they reveal is sometimes far more beautiful and intricate than you had ever envisioned.

That overwhelming sense of pride, the deep exhalation, the 'aha' moment where everything finally makes sense? It's on the horizon. Maybe it's not right now, maybe not tomorrow, but it's there, waiting for you in a future chapter of your story.

When that day comes, when you look at what you've built, at who you've become despite the odds and the unclear path, you'll feel an immeasurable pride. Not just because of the end result, but because of the journey you undertook, the uncertainties you faced, and the resilience you showcased.

Until then, cherish each piece, experience, challenge, and victory. It's all contributing to a larger picture that you're still painting. And trust me, when you see it in its entirety, it will be a masterpiece I promise you'll be proud of.

Day 207

Your Environment Shapes You, So Shape Your Environment

Your environment shapes you. It's a silent influence that you might not notice, but it's there, nudging you, guiding you, and affecting you in subtle ways.

Look around at the spaces you spend time in. Are they supporting, invigorating, and inspiring to you? Or are they just there, neutral at best, dragging you down at worst?

We spend so much time in these spaces, yet we often neglect them. We let them be even if they're not serving us. Today, let's change that.

Pick one space. Just one. Maybe it's your bedroom, your office, your kitchen, or even your car. Choose a space you spend time in that matters to you.

Now make it immaculate. Make it exactly how you want it. Clean it, organize it, decorate it. Add some plants, some art, some music — whatever makes you feel alive and inspired. Make it a space you crave to be in, a space that when you walk in, you feel a surge of energy, a spark of creativity, and a sense of peace.

Why? Because you deserve it. You deserve to be in environments that lift you up, make you feel good, and help you be your best self. And because it matters. It's not just about aesthetics. It's about how you live, how you work, how you think, and how you feel. Your environment is part of you, so make it a part that you love.

Your spaces shape you, so shape them in return. Make them a reflection of who you are and who you want to be. Make them spaces you love, and they'll love you back.

Do It Now

Do it now. That's the mantra.

Time does not afford us endless opportunities. The realization that one day we'll wake up without the chance to fulfill our aspirations is a sobering thought — but therein lies the motivation to transcend procrastination and indecision.

Time is ticking, and every moment we wait, we lose a chance to act on our dreams. Think about that the next time you postpone something you really want to do.

Remember, life's clock never stops, and it doesn't care about our hesitation.

Start now. Not tomorrow, not next week. Now. Your future self will thank you.

What's the one thing you've been pushing off that you're going to start today?

From Imagination to Reality

L ook around. Everything you see began as an idea. Someone's wild thought became real. The songs you love, the phone you use, the car you drive, the roads you drive on — someone had to imagine all of them first. That's how creation begins.

It's a cool thought, isn't it? You see the proof everywhere you look.

It's not just the geniuses and artists who possess this transformative potential; it resides in all of us. Imagination is the essence of our creativity, our innovation, and our very humanity.

And it's not a passive attribute; it's a call to action. It's an invitation to dream big, to envision a better world, to strive for something greater.

What's your idea? What's your "crazy" dream?

Start it, build it, write it, create it.

The world is filled with things that were once just a spark in someone's mind. Now it's your turn. Turn your spark into a flame.

Your Final Moments

How would you show up if these were your last few moments in life? Let that question sink in. Feel the weight of it. Embrace the urgency it evokes.

We get caught up in the hustle of daily life, chasing after things, rushing through tasks, and often missing out on what truly matters. But what if we pause and consider: What if this were my last day on earth? How would I spend it? Who would I spend it with? What would I say? What would I do?

These are not mere hypothetical questions to ponder abstractly. They are real, tangible guides that can transform the way we live.

If this were your last day, would you still rush through your meals, conversations, and connections, or would you savor each bite, each word, each touch? Would you still get caught up in petty arguments, trivial concerns, and insignificant distractions? Or would you focus on what's truly important and what really resonates with your soul?

Would you still hide behind masks, facades, and pretenses? Or would you show up fully, authentically, vulnerably?

This question is not about dwelling on mortality or living in fear of the end. It's about embracing life in its fullness, richness, and beauty. Recognize that each moment is a gift, a precious opportunity to be alive, to connect, to create, to love.

Tomorrow is not promised, but this moment, this very breath, is yours to seize and savor. Make it count. Make it meaningful. Make it yours.

Day 211

You Have More Power than You Think

I love this thought: *The most common way people give up their power is by thinking they don't have any.* It's so simple yet so profound.

Power is a funny thing. Most of us associate it with status, influence, and control. We see it as something external — something to be acquired or grasped.

But true power, the kind that really matters, isn't about hierarchy or domination. It's not about having control over others. It's about having control over yourself. It's about the choices you make, the actions you take, and the thoughts you cultivate.

Here's the thing: You already have this power. It's not something you need to earn or purchase or win. It's something you possess right now at this very moment. It's inherent to your being.

But so often, we give it away. We give it away when we believe we're powerless. We give it away when we let others dictate our thoughts, feelings, or actions. We give it away when we fail to recognize our own worth, strength, and ability to shape our lives.

So here's a radical idea: What if we stopped doing that? What if we stopped giving away our power? What if we started claiming it, owning it, using it?

Imagine the transformation. Imagine the possibilities. Imagine the impact. You have power. Don't give it away. Claim it. Use it. Make it count.

Day 212

How Beginning with the End Unlocks Your Path

Whenever I set out to complete a new project or endeavor, I often think about a powerful strategy: Start with the end in mind and then reverse-engineer the steps to get there. It's a simple yet incredibly effective way to approach challenges, and here's how.

- **Visualize the outcome.** Starting with the desired result. What does success look like for you? Is it a published book? A profitable business? Whatever it is, get as detailed as possible in your vision.

- **Map the milestones.** Now that you know your end goal, what major milestones will mark your progress towards it?

- **Break it down.** With the major milestones in place, break each one down into smaller tasks. These are your action steps.

- **Set a timeline.** With tasks and milestones outlined, assign a timeline. This will keep you accountable and give you a clear picture of the journey ahead.

- **Review and adjust.** Even with the best planning, real-world execution can throw curveballs. Periodically review your plan. Are you on track? If not, adjust your strategies but keep your end goal in mind.

Next time you find yourself at the beginning, daringly jump to the end and then chart your path back. It's enlightening.

Day 213

Not the What, But the Why

In life, we often get caught up in the *what* — the tasks, achievements, and things we do. But what really matters is the *why*. Why are we doing these things? What's the deeper motivation or purpose behind our actions?

By connecting with this *why*, we create an anchor for ourselves. It's not about the job title, salary, or accolades. It's about the underlying reasons for our choices and our work. This understanding turns the ordinary into the meaningful. It adds depth to our actions. It's a guiding principle that can see us through transitions and changes, providing a continuity that's rooted not in the external world but in our own internal values and goals.

It's not a one-time discovery, either. Your *why* can change and grow with you, offering fresh insights and guidance as you move through different stages of life. But having that anchor, that connection to your deeper self, provides a stability and direction that can make all the difference. This is the philosophy that guides many successful people, and it can guide you, too.

Your *why* is the core of everything you do. It's the reason behind your actions, the purpose that drives your decisions, and the belief that fuels your passion. But discovering your *why* is not always easy. It requires introspection, self-awareness, and a willingness to explore the depths of your soul. It demands that you question your assumptions, challenge your beliefs, and embrace the journey of self-discovery.

So don't shy away from the questions. Dive deep, explore your inner world, and let your *why* lead the way.

Day 214

Dominoes to Disappointment

Have you ever caught yourself getting frustrated because something didn't go exactly the way you planned? Maybe it was a small detail — something trivial in the grand scheme of things — but it bothered you nonetheless. It's an easy trap to fall into, and I've been there myself.

The more we insist that things or situations need to be right or done in a specific way, the more opportunities we create for frustration and disappointment. It's like setting up a row of dominoes, each one representing a specific expectation. One falls out of place, and the whole line collapses.

Life is unpredictable and constantly in flux. People have different perspectives, things change, and surprises happen. If we cling too tightly to specific ideas of how things should be, we become rigid and brittle, setting ourselves up for constant disappointment. The more we relax our grip and allow for life's natural flow, the happier and more at peace we become.

This doesn't mean we should abandon our standards or stop striving for excellence. But there's a balance to be found — a sweet spot between having a vision and being flexible enough to adapt when life takes an unexpected turn.

Here's a challenge for you: The next time something doesn't go exactly as you planned, instead of feeling frustrated, try pausing for a moment. Ask yourself, "Why does this need to be this way?" and "What can I learn or gain from this unexpected turn?"

Day 215

Eliminating the Nonessentials

We fill our lives with nonessentials. Just as a gardener trims away excess branches to nurture a plant's growth, so must we prune the nonessentials from our lives to cultivate our true potential.

Today, the mission is clear: Focus on removing the dead weight that hinders progress. We all possess those time-consuming pursuits that offer little value yet manage to creep into our schedules. These are the distractions that dilute our focus and sap our energy. It's time to bid them farewell.

Here's one process to do so.

- **Inventory.** Begin by taking an inventory of your commitments, activities, and relationships. Create a list of everything that occupies your time and energy. This could range from work tasks to social obligations and hobbies.

- **Value evaluation.** Assess each item on your list for its value and alignment with your goals. Ask yourself: Does this activity contribute to my overall well-being? Does it help me progress toward my aspirations? If an item doesn't offer significant value, consider it a candidate for pruning.

- **Prioritization**. Prioritize your list based on importance and impact. Identify the activities that truly matter to you and directly contribute to your growth, happiness, and purpose. These are the ones to preserve and nurture.

- **Identify nonessentials.** Now pinpoint the nonessential activities that consume your time without offering substantial returns. These might be habits that have become routine or obligations you've taken on without careful consideration.

- **Let go.** This step requires courage. It's time to bid farewell to the nonessentials. For each activity or commitment that doesn't align with your goals, consider reducing your involvement or completely letting it go. It's liberating to free up your time and energy for what truly matters.

- **Mindful commitment.** Moving forward, be discerning about new commitments. Before saying yes to a task or project, evaluate whether it aligns with your priorities. This will prevent unnecessary clutter from accumulating in your life.

- **Regular review.** Pruning is an ongoing process. Regularly review your commitments and activities to ensure they remain in alignment with your goals. Over time, you'll refine your ability to recognize and eliminate nonessentials.

Remember, practical pruning isn't about deprivation; it's about creating space for what truly enriches your life. By intentionally letting go of the nonessentials, you're actively crafting a path that aligns with your purpose. The journey might start with small steps, but the impact will be profound.

Day 216

Belief, Behave, Become

Believe, then behave to become. Sounds simple, but it's a profound journey. Think of it as a road you're paving for yourself.

First, you need a belief. That's your foundation. You've got to truly believe that change is possible and that you can become something more. That's where it all begins. But belief alone won't get you there.

Next, you need to start to behave in ways that align with that belief. Take consistent action. It's like laying the bricks on your road.

And finally, after enough time and persistence, something incredible happens. You become the very thing you believed you could be.

The road is complete, and you're standing there not just imagining or acting, but being. It's transformation at its core.

It's not about grand gestures or sudden changes. It's about small, deliberate steps taken with intention and direction. Don't underestimate the power of this progression.

Embrace it. Start with a belief, align your actions to it, and witness how you evolve. It's within your control, and it's a beautiful process.

The Impact of a Simple Thank You

We "like" posts on social media and send brief thank-you texts, but how often do we take the time to truly articulate what someone's positive influence has meant to us?

Take a moment today to do something different. Write a letter or make a phone call to someone who's been a positive force in your life. Tell them in your own words what they've done for you. Describe the true and lasting impact they've had. Make it personal, authentic, and heartfelt.

Why? Because that small act of gratitude can be profound for both you and the person you're thanking.

For you, it's a chance to reflect on the positive forces in your life, to acknowledge what's good, and to feel the warmth of appreciation. It can be a reminder of your values, your connections, and what's truly important.

Your words can have a profound impact on the person you thank. You never know how much your gratitude might mean to them. Maybe they're going through a tough time and your words are a bright spot in their day. Maybe they don't realize how much they've helped you, and your acknowledgment is a beautiful surprise.

So take that time today. Write that letter, make that call. Thank someone who's made a difference in your life.

Day 218

Fear of Others' Judgments

Isn't it strange how often we give away our internal happiness to people who don't even know us that well? We become prisoners to their judgments, their offhand comments, and their fleeting opinions. And for what? So we can feel accepted in the short term while sacrificing our long-term happiness, authenticity, and self-worth?

Here's something you should know: Their opinions are theirs, not yours. They come from their experiences, biases, and worldviews. They don't define you.

The fear of other people's opinions is a formidable invisible barrier that holds us back from reaching our full potential and living an enriching life. But you don't have to let it be.

Here are three things that help me when I start to feel the fear of other people's opinions.

- **Dig deeper into your values**. Do you know what truly matters to you? Spend some time reflecting on what you genuinely value. Write it down, ponder it, and adjust as needed.

- **Set boundaries.** Recognize that not everyone's opinions need to matter to you. You can respect others' perspectives without letting them sway your core beliefs.

- **Celebrate your uniqueness.** There's only one you, and that's your superpower. Don't shy away from them; embrace them and let them shine.

Day 219

The Measure of Authentic Growth

In the realm of personal evolution, a bold litmus test for your advancement is your capacity to outshine your mentors. Yes, you read that right, outshine your mentors. This isn't a contest or ego-driven conquest; it's an unwavering commitment to transcend your limits and blaze your trail of progress.

Picture mentors as torchbearers illuminating the path with their insights, skills, and wisdom. They are catalysts propelling you forward, but the destination isn't to mimic their footsteps; it's to sprint beyond, forging your trajectory in the terrain of originality.

Mentors' teachings become your launchpad. They ignite sparks of innovation that transform you from a follower into a pioneer. This transition isn't about dismissing their wisdom; it's about fusing their guidance with your insights to craft an unprecedented narrative.

Surpassing mentors is a symbolic shift from apprentice to architect, from learning to shaping. It marks the perpetuation of your growth journey. It's a testament to your ability to absorb, evolve, and then redefine the landscape. As you ascend, you don't just tread forward; you become the guidepost for others. Your journey emboldens them to seek their path.

So let the torch you inherit from mentors illuminate your uniqueness. Embrace the discomfort of stretching beyond their grasp. It's not about diminishing their significance; it's about honoring their influence by becoming a beacon that shines even brighter, inspiring the next generation of seekers and surpassers.

Day 220

Life's Competitive Advantage

In the world of business, we're obsessed with discovering those golden nuggets of sustainable competitive advantage that set us apart from the rest. But let me tell you, these gems of wisdom aren't confined to the boardroom. They hold the key to life's most rewarding successes, too.

- **Learn faster, soar higher.** In business, staying ahead means learning faster than your competition. In life, it's no different. The more you learn, the more you grow. The world is evolving rapidly; be the one who keeps up and capitalizes on emerging opportunities.

- **Empathy: your secret weapon.** In business, empathy is the bridge that connects you with your customers' hearts. In life, the same principle applies. Understand those around you, listen to their stories, and grasp their perspectives.

- **Master the art of communication.** Business thrives on clear, effective communication. Life thrives on it, too. Being a better communicator than your competition doesn't just mean speaking well but listening deeply. It's about fostering an environment where ideas flow, conflicts dissolve, and understanding flourishes.

- **Delayed gratification: the ultimate patience.** In business, waiting can be a strategic move allowing you to seize opportunities at precisely the right time. In life, patience is just as potent. Don't rush into decisions; let them marinate. Delayed gratification teaches us resilience and helps us make choices aligned with our true desires, not just fleeting impulses.

Day 221

Doors Waiting to be Opened

Isn't it fascinating? Many of the walls we see in front of us aren't made of brick or stone; they're made of thought.

Imagine this: You're walking in a desert, and you see water in the distance. You hurry towards it, thirsty and hopeful. But as you get closer, the water vanishes. It was a mirage, an illusion. Similarly, many of our perceived limitations are just mirages. They look real from a distance, but upon closer inspection, they vanish.

We tell ourselves stories. "I can't," "I'm not good enough," "It's impossible." But are they true, or are they just safe narratives that keep us in our comfort zones?

Time and again in my life, I've confronted these self-made boundaries. Each time I edged closer and pushed a little more, that looming barrier receded, proving itself to be nothing more than a figment of my imagination.

It's a curious paradox. The barriers look impenetrable until you approach them with the intention to move through them. And when you do, you often find there is nothing stopping you but yourself.

Challenge your preconceptions. Test your boundaries. Embrace the uncertainty, the risk, the thrill of discovery. Dive into the mystery of your own capability and see how far you can go.

You might just find that the limits you thought were holding you back are simply stepping stones to something greater.

Day 222

The Rock Tumbler

Steve Jobs once shared an insightful story that has profound implications for our personal lives. In an interview, Jobs recounted an encounter with an old man from his childhood neighborhood. This man introduced Jobs to a rock tumbler, setting the stage for a powerful metaphor that would shape his perspective on teamwork and collaboration.

Jobs and the man gathered dull rocks, placing them into the tumbler with liquid and grit powder. After sealing the container, the man instructed Jobs to return the next week. When they opened the can, the once unremarkable rocks had transformed into exquisitely polished gems, all achieved through the friction within the tumbler.

Just as the rocks experienced transformation through interaction, individuals working collectively undergo a similar evolution. In the cauldron of collaboration, where ideas and perspectives collide, a profound refining process takes place.

The beauty of this metaphor is in its simplicity: It illustrates the inherent potential of teams to elevate one another even amidst disagreements and noise. Through shared challenges and a dedication to a common cause, individuals polish one another, uncovering brilliance that may have remained dormant otherwise.

As we navigate the journeys of our professional endeavors and personal lives, let us embrace the beauty in the chaos of collaboration, understanding that collective friction shapes our ideas and polishes our potential. Just as ordinary rocks transform into gems, our collaborative efforts have the power to unveil the extraordinary within us.

Day 223

All In

In the realm of human potential, stories often emerge that astound us with their audacity and innovation. One such story is that of Daniel Kish, a man who didn't let blindness define his limits but rather ignited a beacon of inspiration through his relentless pursuit of seeing the world in his unique way.

Imagine a life where the visual sense — a lifeline for most — is suddenly extinguished. This was the reality that faced Daniel Kish when he lost his sight. But instead of allowing darkness to shroud his dreams, he embarked on a remarkable journey to illuminate his path through a technique named *echolocation*.

Through echolocation, Daniel taught himself to navigate the world using sound, a feat that would leave anyone in awe. By emitting clicks and listening to their echoes, he could perceive his surroundings with astonishing accuracy. But the true revelation came when he was asked, "If you can teach yourself this technique, could others learn it too?" His response was a testament to the essence of achievement: "The reason I was able to do it is because I was all in."

Daniel's dedication was unwavering. His commitment to mastering echolocation wasn't half-hearted; it was total. He plunged into his endeavor with a wholehearted belief that he could overcome his challenges. His "all in" mentality propelled him to achieve what seemed impossible, demonstrating that remarkable feats require unwavering dedication.

Daniel's journey echoes a universal truth: Greatness is not an endeavor for the half-hearted. Whether it's mastering a skill, overcoming adversity, or striving for personal growth, being "all in" is the catalyst that propels us toward the extraordinary.

Day 224

Creating the Conditions You Don't Want

One of the more challenging questions we should ask if we want to grow is this: How am I complicit in creating the conditions in life I say I don't want?

This question requires us to step back and examine the actions, decisions, and even inactions that have contributed to our present condition — those conditions we say we don't want. It's about recognizing that in some way, we may have allowed or even fostered these conditions to exist.

Perhaps it's through tolerating behavior that goes against our values, avoiding confrontations that are necessary, making decisions out of fear instead of conviction, or repeatedly choosing comfort over growth. These subtle actions or lack of actions accumulate over time, often leading to situations we say we don't want.

The power of asking this challenging question lies in the control and accountability it returns to us. Instead of seeing ourselves as passive victims of circumstances, we become active participants in shaping our lives. We empower ourselves to recognize where we've gone wrong and make conscious decisions to steer in a direction more aligned with our desires and values.

It's not about self-blame but about empowerment and responsibility. It's about making an ongoing commitment to be more aware of our complicity and consciously choose different actions that lead to a more fulfilling life.

This process may be uncomfortable and demanding, but it's a path towards genuine growth, self-understanding, and personal freedom.

Day 225

Six Things to Focus on Today

1. **Focus on what you can control.** So much of life is outside of our control. We can't dictate the weather, the traffic, or other people's behavior. But we can control our reactions, our attitudes, and our efforts. Focus there.

2. **The privilege of a lifetime is being who you are.** Celebrate your quirks, your passions, and your dreams. This is your life, your story. Own it. Be you. Anything less is a disservice to yourself.

3. **Be a good ancestor: Do something a future generation will thank you for.** We're all part of a continuum, inheriting the world from our ancestors and leaving a legacy for those who come after us. How will you make it better?

4. **The things that matter most must never be at the mercy of things that matter least.** Life's too short to lose sight of what truly matters. Keep your priorities clear.

5. **The greatest teacher is called doing.** You can read, plan, and theorize, but nothing replaces the learning that comes from action. Dive in. Make mistakes. Learn. Grow.

6. **Be grateful for everything and entitled to nothing.** Entitlement can lead to dissatisfaction and complacency. Gratitude, on the other hand, fuels joy and humility. Recognize the gifts and opportunities in your life, even the small ones.

Day 226

Amplify What Comes Naturally

We often become preoccupied with our shortcomings and let them overshadow the unique strengths that define us. Isn't it strange how we tend to focus on what we're lacking rather than what we excel at? Our natural talents often go unnoticed or uncelebrated simply because they come so effortlessly to us. These are our unsung strengths.

Take some time to recognize what you naturally do well. Is it your innate creativity that flows without conscious effort? Maybe it's your resilience, bouncing back from setbacks as though they were mere hiccups. Perhaps it's your empathetic nature, the ability to step into someone's shoes and see the world from their perspective.

Once you've identified these strengths, the next step is to ask yourself how you can apply them more deliberately. How can you use your creativity to enhance your work or personal projects? How can you harness your resilience to overcome current challenges? How can your empathy improve your relationships?

Remember, the more you use these natural talents, the more they'll grow. It's like a muscle: The more you exercise it, the stronger it gets. By recognizing and utilizing your unsung strengths, you're not just improving yourself; you're stepping into a space of self-awareness that allows you to thrive in your unique way.

Celebrate what comes naturally to you. Don't let your inherent gifts go to waste. Embrace them, hone them, and watch how they transform your life. There's incredible power in playing to your strengths, and it begins with recognizing what they are and giving them the stage they deserve.

Day 227

A Daily Compass for Growth

These three questions, when practiced daily, become a compass guiding you toward a more directed and fulfilling life. It's a simple practice, yet its effects can be profound. Here are three questions that help bring mindfulness, intentionality, and alignment to your life.

1. **What will I let go of?** This question is about releasing what's holding you back, be it a grudge, a negative thought, an old habit, or something else. By consciously choosing to let go of these burdens, you clear space for new opportunities and growth. It's a daily commitment to lighten your load, forgive, move past disappointments, and become more present in your life.

2. **What am I grateful for?** Gratitude has the remarkable power to shift our focus from what we lack to what we have. This question helps you focus on the positive aspects of your life, big or small. By appreciating what's already there, you nourish contentment and joy. It's a reminder to cherish the present moment and the blessings you have rather than constantly reaching for more.

3. **What will I focus on?** This question guides your attention to your priorities and goals. It's about consciously choosing what you will give energy to each day. Maybe it's a project at work, a relationship, a personal goal, or a simple act of kindness. Whatever it is, defining your focus gives direction to your day. It's a commitment to align your actions with your values and aspirations.

Day 228

Igniting Minds

You may have heard the phrase, "Education is not the filling of a pail but the lighting of a fire." It's an old but profound metaphor that shifts our understanding of education from a passive act to an active one.

If education were the filling of a pail, then the role of the teacher would be to pour knowledge into a student's mind, filling it up like a bucket with water. The student's job would simply be to hold still and receive.

But this metaphor falls short. Education is not about stuffing minds full of facts. It's about inspiring, igniting curiosity, and fostering a love for learning. It's about lighting a fire. And guess what? We're all educators to someone.

When you light a fire in someone's mind, you're not giving them something they can hold, measure, or contain. You're starting a process. A spark leads to a flame, and that flame can grow, spread, and become a roaring blaze.

Great teachers don't just relay information; they inspire students to question, explore, and keep learning long after they've left the classroom. They guide students to see that learning is not about memorizing facts but about understanding the world and oneself.

To light this fire is to help people find what excites them, what they're passionate about, and what they want to dive deeper into. It's to help them see that education is not a task to be completed but a lifelong journey.

Remember, the mind doesn't need to be filled; it needs to be ignited. Once that spark is there, the possibilities are endless.

Day 229

The Four Pillars

When things feel off and you're not operating at your best, it's tempting to look for complex reasons or external circumstances. But often the answer is much closer to home. It lies in one or more of these four fundamental areas: sleep, health, nutrition, or the mind.

Sleep. Feeling foggy or unfocused? Maybe you're not getting enough rest, or perhaps the quality of your sleep is lacking. Your brain needs time to rejuvenate and process. Shortchanging sleep is like shortchanging your brain's capacity to function.

Body. Feeling lethargic or uninspired? It might be a lack of physical activity. Movement not only keeps the body healthy but can stimulate the mind. A well-functioning body supports a well-functioning mind.

Nutrition. Feeling tired or sluggish? Consider what you're putting into your body. Just as a car needs the right fuel to run efficiently, your body needs proper nourishment. Eating poorly can lead to energy crashes and a lack of focus.

Mind. Feeling stressed or overwhelmed? Maybe it's a lack of mental clarity or mindfulness. The way you cultivate and take care of your mental space significantly affects how you perceive and interact with the world.

The beautiful simplicity here is that when you're feeling off, you have a checklist to turn to. Rather than searching for external culprits, you can introspectively assess these four areas. These aren't just parts of a routine; they're essential aspects of your life. They're foundational. And when the foundation is strong, everything else becomes more stable and more capable.

Day 230

Brute Force Won't Win the War

We often admire strength and force. We applaud those who "power through" or "muscle their way" to success. But here's a little secret: Anything achieved through brute force never lasts. It's like trying to hold water in your hands by squeezing it tightly. No matter how hard you squeeze, it slips through your fingers.

Brute force is about exerting effort against resistance — overcoming obstacles through sheer power. But here's the problem: Those obstacles are often symptoms of a deeper structure. And unless you change that underlying structure, the obstacles will keep coming back.

Think of it like a garden filled with weeds. You can go in there with a machete and chop down all those weeds. But if you don't get to the roots, they'll just grow back. You've got to dig down deep and change the soil, the environment, the very structure that's allowing those weeds to grow in the first place.

This is true in almost every area of life. Want to change a behavior? Don't just suppress it; understand the underlying beliefs and values that are driving it. Change those, and the behavior changes naturally, without force.

Want to make a lasting impact on an organization? Don't just impose new rules and policies. Understand the culture, shared assumptions, and norms that shape how people behave. Change those, and you change the whole system.

Brute force might win you a battle, but it won't win you the war. To do that, you have to change the game entirely. That's where real, lasting success is found: not on the surface, but deep down at the very core of things.

Day 231

The Right Attire for Any Storm

There's a saying that applies both to the way we dress for the weather and to how we approach life's challenges: "There's no such thing as bad weather, only inappropriate clothing."

Think about it. When we're faced with a sudden downpour, we don't call the rain "wrong." It's just rain. It's the natural course of things. If we're soaked, it's because we didn't carry an umbrella, not because the weather is inherently against us.

Now apply this idea to life. When we encounter difficulties, setbacks, or unexpected challenges, it's easy to label them as "bad" or "unfair." But like the weather, these events are simply a natural part of our human experience. They are conditions to navigate, not judgments against us.

What if, instead of resisting or complaining about these conditions, we asked ourselves, "What's the appropriate response here? What tools, mindset, or objects do I need to navigate this effectively?"

If we're facing a "storm" in our relationships, maybe we need the "raincoat" of patience, understanding, and open communication. If we're navigating the "icy roads" of a career transition, perhaps we need the "snow tires" of persistence, new skills, or a flexible mindset.

By shifting our focus from labeling the situation as "bad" to finding the appropriate response, we empower ourselves to navigate any weather with grace and effectiveness.

This approach doesn't mean ignoring our emotions or denying that some situations are painful or challenging. It simply encourages us to see them as conditions to navigate rather than as judgments or insurmountable barriers. It's about adopting a mindset that says, "I can handle this, and I can choose how to respond."

So the next time you're faced with a life "storm," remember that it's not about the weather; it's about the clothing. Equip yourself with the right attitude, tools, and resilience, and you'll find that you can weather anything. With the right preparation, you can find your way, grow, and thrive even in the harshest conditions.

Day 232

The Weight of Each Decision

Each decision, no matter how seemingly small, carries the power to shape the person we are becoming. It is in these moments of choice that we cultivate our character, values, and aspirations.

With every decision made, we affirm the direction we wish to steer our lives. So let us approach each decision with conscious intent, aware that the accumulation of these choices culminates in the portrait of the person we ultimately become.

The path to personal growth is paved by the consistent actions that align with our truest selves. As we move through life, let us be deliberate in casting our votes for the kind of person we aspire to be: a person who embraces authenticity, kindness, resilience, and purpose.

Life is an ongoing election, and we are both candidates and voters. Each day we are presented with countless decisions, from the mundane choices of what to wear or eat to the more profound determinations that alter the course of our lives. Each of these decisions, no matter how seemingly insignificant, is a vote — a vote for the person we are and the person we want to become.

Every decision and conscious choice takes us in a certain direction. Step by step these decisions form a path that illustrates our character, values, and aspirations.

The daily decisions we make are not isolated occurrences but part of a continuous process that shapes our existence. It's a beautiful and democratic idea: We have the power to elect ourselves, to become the person we aspire to be.

However, this power requires responsibility and intention. It's not merely about choosing but understanding the why behind each choice. Why do we vote for this action and not that one? What does this vote say about us? How does it align with our truest selves?

This intentionality transforms the mundane into the meaningful. It turns each decision into a reflection of our inner world and a manifestation of our authenticity, kindness, resilience, and purpose.

So let us approach the ballot box of life with conscious awareness and deliberate intent. Let us recognize the significance of each vote, each choice, and honor the opportunity to create ourselves anew every single day.

Day 233

Bias For Action

Having a bias for action is a powerful trait that sets those who thrive apart from those who merely survive. The most remarkable individuals, regardless of their field or background, share this common thread: They don't just dwell on ideas and aspirations, they put them into motion.

Imagine you're standing at the edge of a cliff, looking at the beautiful landscape you want to explore. You've planned, dreamed, and talked about it, but now it's time to jump. Of course, it's scary. What if you fall? But what if you fly?

People who act understand that the real value lies in taking tangible steps towards their goals. It's not about having all the answers or waiting for the perfect moment; it's about embracing the uncertainty and fear and taking that leap of faith.

In this exciting, sometimes terrifying leap, your dreams begin to take form. You'll make mistakes, stumble, and maybe fall. But you'll also learn, grow, and discover pathways that were invisible from the safety of the cliff's edge.

Action is the catalyst that turns dreams into reality, and those who are unafraid to venture into the unknown are the ones who leave a lasting impact on the world. Explorers, inventors, artists, and entrepreneurs all share this bias for action. It's a mindset that says, "I will do this," not just "I wish I could."

It's time to have a bias for action. Start small if you must, but start.

Day 234

The Balancing Act

I magine a tightrope walker balancing gracefully on a thin line, eyes fixed on the destination ahead but mindful of every immediate step. This delicate balance between the present moment and the future goal is a metaphor for how we can approach our life's pursuits.

The art of maintaining a balanced perspective between short-term actions and long-term visions is like that tightrope walker's grace. It requires awareness, precision, and a clear sense of direction.

Each step we take today is significant. It's a building block, a part of the journey. But these steps must align with our greater purpose, our grander vision. If we become mired in the minutiae, we risk losing direction and becoming trapped in a cycle of constant crises and setbacks. By recognizing the importance of both the immediate and the ultimate, we can move with intention, charting a deliberate and successful course toward lasting and meaningful accomplishments.

The wisdom lies in knowing when to take a step back and gaze at the horizon and when to zoom in and focus on the path beneath our feet. It's a dynamic interplay, an ever-shifting balance that leads us forward, one mindful step at a time, toward the life we envision.

So let's go after life with grace and purpose, fully engaging with the present moment while keeping our eyes on the prize. Let's build bridges between our daily endeavors and our lifelong dreams, understanding that the journey is as important as the destination and that each step we take shapes the trajectory of our future.

Day 235

Stop Settling for Mediocre

T ime is a finite resource, and if it is squandered on mediocre pursuits, there is little left for the truly exceptional ones. Let that sink in.

The danger isn't just in one poor decision, but in the pattern of settling for less, of accepting what's merely good enough, of letting the mediocre take up space in our lives that could be filled with something extraordinary.

Every hour spent on a job that drains your soul is an hour not spent pursuing your passion. Every book you read that leaves you unchanged is a missed opportunity to learn something that could transform your thinking. Every moment with a person who doesn't enrich your life is a moment not spent with someone who might inspire you to be better.

It's time to stop settling. The shift isn't about radical changes overnight but in deliberate, conscious choices daily. It's about recognizing where you're settling and taking small steps to change those patterns.

Take the time to assess and recognize where you might be settling. Then make the choice to pursue the extraordinary. Choose a career that aligns with your values, surround yourself with people who lift you higher, and invest in learning that propels you forward.

Life is too short and too rich with potential to settle for mediocrity.

Stop settling and start thriving. The extraordinary life you seek is within reach, and it begins with the choices you make today.

Day 236

Childhood Doesn't Get a Second Chance

A profound truth for parents: Childhood is fleeting, and it's never lived twice.

The years pass like shooting stars, and before we know it, our little ones have grown into young adults, leaving behind the carefree days of innocence. As parents, we hold the power to shape their early years and create memories that will be etched in their hearts forever.

So let us pause, take a breath, and remember that each moment spent with our children is an opportunity to make a lasting impact. Aligning our priorities, we must show up as the fully present and engaged parents they deserve — the ones who listen intently, play with abandon, and offer unconditional love and support.

Cherish every giggle, every story shared, and every moment of wonder in their eyes. Embrace the fleeting days with open arms, and make the conscious choice to be the parents they need — the ones who shape their world with love, guidance, and endless ambition.

The years may be fleeting, but the memories we create together will echo throughout their lives, reminding them they are cherished, valued, and celebrated every step of the way. The gift of being present for their childhood is an investment that yields a lifetime of returns.

Day 237

Living in Harmony

In the midst of our bustling lives, it's easy to lose sight of what truly matters to us. We might be achieving external success, but deep down, something feels off. That's because our daily actions should be a reflection of our core values, those guiding principles that define who we are and what we stand for.

Imagine your values as a magnet pulling you in the right direction. If your actions don't align with this pull, you'll constantly feel lost and unsatisfied. Take a moment to consider what truly matters to you. Is it family, growth, adventure, health, or something else? Now bridge the gap between values and actions.

Here are a handful of practical ways you can begin doing it. Don't feel like you need to adopt all of these strategies. Pick and choose what works best for you.

- **Define your values.** Start by identifying your top values — family, growth, health, adventure, whatever resonates. Write them down to visualize what truly matters.

- **Audit your schedule.** Examine your weekly routine. Do your actions align with your values? If not, pinpoint areas that can be adjusted.

- **Prioritize and plan.** Choose one value to focus on initially. Break it down into actionable steps. For instance, if health is a priority, plan regular workout times.

- **Set reminders.** Use technology to your advantage. Set alarms or calendar events to remind you to practice your chosen value-based activity.

- **Morning rituals.** Start your day with intention. Incorporate a value-aligned activity into your morning routine. It could be a mindfulness practice, exercise, or gratitude journaling.

- **Micro-moments.** Throughout the day, find micro-moments to live your values. If learning is crucial, listen to an educational podcast during your commute or lunch break.

- **Unplug time.** Dedicate specific periods to be device-free and focus on quality time with loved ones, fostering relationships if family is a core value.

- **Reflect at night.** Before sleep, reflect on how you embodied your chosen value that day. This reflection cultivates mindfulness and reinforces your commitment.

- **Weekly check-ins.** Set aside time each week to assess your progress. Celebrate successes and adjust strategies if needed.

- **Practice patience.** Remember, alignment takes time. Be patient with yourself as you make these adjustments.

Remember, this isn't about a major overhaul; it's about mindful adjustments. As you infuse your days with activities that echo your values, you'll experience a profound shift in your perspective. Life becomes more meaningful, success more satisfying, and happiness more genuine.

The Happiness Equation

If you want to be happier, do more of the things that make you happy. It sounds so obvious, doesn't it? Yet so often we find ourselves caught in a cycle of obligations, routines, and societal pressures that steer us away from what genuinely lights us up.

This is not about indulging in hedonistic pleasures or being irresponsible. It's about recognizing the activities, people, and experiences that genuinely nourish your soul and making a conscious effort to include them in your life.

Now, you may say, "But I have responsibilities, a job, a family to take care of!" Yes, those are important. But integrating what you love into your daily life doesn't mean abandoning your duties. It means enriching your life with what feeds your happiness.

Consider this approach.

- **Identify what makes you happy.** It might be painting, dancing, spending time with loved ones, hiking in nature, reading a good book, cooking, or anything else that brings joy to your life.

- **Make time for it.** Schedule it in your calendar. Even just an hour a week dedicated to something that fills you with joy can make a significant difference in your overall happiness.

- **Eliminate what doesn't serve you.** Sometimes happiness is about subtraction rather than addition. If there are activities or commitments that are draining you, consider whether they are necessary or if there's a way to reduce them.

- **Share it with others.** If possible, include your loved ones in what you love to do. Shared joy is doubled.

- **Reflect and adjust.** Regularly check in with yourself to see if you're following through and how it's impacting your life. Make adjustments as needed.

Remember, happiness is not a destination but a journey. It's a continuous practice of recognizing what lights us up and making space for it in our lives.

So why not take the simple yet profound step of doing more of what makes you happy? It might be the most significant investment you make in your own well-being and in creating a joyful and fulfilling life.

Day 239

A Last Time for Everything

It's a hard truth to swallow: There will be a last time for everything.

The last time we put our kids to bed as children before they grow into their independence.

The last time we hear our parents tell their cherished stories.

The last time we kiss our loved ones before the final day takes them away.

The realization that there will be a last time for everything isn't a morose thought but a call to mindfulness. It's an invitation to pause amidst the hustle and bustle and truly notice the simple joys around us — not to just go through the motions but to really be present in them.

Tonight, as I tuck my kids into bed, I won't do it mechanically. I'll take a moment to look into their eyes, feel their warmth, and listen to their laughter. I'll savor the routine, knowing that one day it will be a cherished memory.

As I exchange a loving kiss with my wife, I'll not let it be a fleeting act but a genuine connection, a moment in time when everything else fades away.

Because it's not the grand gestures that make life beautiful. It's the simple, ordinary acts performed with love and presence that truly matter.

So let's cherish these moments. Let's appreciate the beauty they hold while they're still with us. Let's not wait for the last times to notice the magic of now.

Day 240

The Author and the Critic

We all have a story — a narrative that we've crafted about who we are, what we've done, and where we're going. This story is constantly evolving, shaped by our experiences, choices, triumphs, and failures. But who gets to decide if this story is a success or a failure? Who is the ultimate judge of our life's narrative?

The answer is simple and profound: It's you.

Society has its criteria, friends and family have their opinions, and social media has its metrics. But none of those judgments matter as much as your own. You are both the author and the critic of your life story. You get to decide what's important, what's valuable, and what's meaningful.

This is not a passive process. Judging your own life story means actively engaging with it, reflecting on it, and learning from it. It means being both compassionate and critical, recognizing your growth and your mistakes, celebrating your strengths, and acknowledging your weaknesses.

By doing this, you create a narrative that's authentic and empowering. You craft a life story that resonates with your deepest values and aspirations. You become not just the author of your story but its most insightful and caring critic.

Your life is your story, and you are its ultimate judge.

Embrace that responsibility, engage with it fully, and write a story you'll be proud to call your own. No one else's judgment matters more than yours. No one else's approval is more valuable. In the end, it's you who must live with your story, so make it one you love.

Day 241

The Answer

L ife can feel like an unending quest for answers. We search for the perfect solution to our problems, the right path to happiness, or the secret to success. We often believe that somewhere out there is the magical formula that will fix everything.

But the truth is, the answer is rarely found in some external wisdom or universal solution. Instead, it's often found in a simple commitment: "In this moment, I'm going to do the very best I'm capable of."

This means letting go of the past with its regrets and mistakes and the future with its uncertainties and fears. It means focusing on the present — on what's right in front of you — and doing the best you can with what you have.

It's not about perfection or having all the answers. It's about effort, intention, and integrity. It's about showing up, being present, and giving your all, whatever that may be.

So next time you find yourself looking for the answer, remember this simple truth: "In this moment, I'm going to do the very best I'm capable of." That's an answer that always works, a solution that's always available, and a path that leads to fulfillment, growth, and joy. It's the answer that's always right there, waiting for you to embrace it.

Day 242

Sweeter After Difficulties

One of my favorite sayings is *Dulcius Ex Asperis*, or "sweeter after difficulties." This old but trusted saying urges us to embrace life's adversities as transformative opportunities. Just as gold is refined through fire, we find our true essence through navigating challenges.

Embracing *Dulcius Ex Asperis* means recognizing that adversity is not to be avoided but rather to be embraced as an integral part of the human experience.

When we accept and learn from difficulties, we grow in resilience and gratitude. This saying reminds us that strength and wisdom emerge from the depths of our struggles. By reframing our perspective, we recognize that even in the face of bitter experiences, life has a way of offering profound sweetness.

Go back and explore a difficulty you had to overcome. How has your life become better for it?

Day 243

In Transit

E ver pondered the depths of your potential — not just who you are at this moment, but the vast universe of what you might become? Here's the deal: It's not about lacking skills or not reaching our potential. We're in transit at a juncture between our present self and a future version gleaming with untapped promise.

The magic isn't outside. It's inside you. The path forward? It's laid with effort based on a dedication to evolve, driven by an indomitable spirit that keeps urging us on, drawing us closer to our best selves.

Daily choices and simple actions are your steps on this transformative journey. Each one is an opportunity, a moment to reach deep into ourselves and pull out something extraordinary.

Imagine a scene ten years from now. Close your eyes. You're gazing into a reflection, and the person staring back is you, shaped by the decisions you're making today.

Your life? It's the artwork of your thoughts and deeds. Intriguing, isn't it? Thoughts plant the seeds while actions nurture them. Dream big. Embrace love, innovation, and drive. But beyond just dreaming, act. Let your thoughts inspire tangible change.

Fast forward to when you see a self-assured individual in that reflection. Recognize that it's the version you sculpted through commitment.

The vision of your future isn't nebulous. It's palpable, reachable, and yearning for you to mold it. Go after it. Shape it. Your life, your masterpiece, is yearning for its creator's touch.

Day 244

The Power of Dark Reflections

In the midst of our busy lives, I've discovered a practice that might seem counterintuitive: deliberately taking my mind to dark places. Each day, I invest a few moments in contemplating scenarios that evoke fear and uncertainty. I envision the unthinkable—losing a loved one, facing wrongful accusations, or grappling with the aftermath of a natural disaster.

It might sound morbid, but this practice serves a profound purpose. It's not about dwelling in negativity but about shifting perspective. By momentarily stepping into the shoes of those facing life's harshest realities, I cultivate a deeper appreciation for the blessings in my own life.

These dark reflections are like a mirror that reveals the beauty of what surrounds me. They highlight the precious moments spent with family, the freedom I enjoy, and the shelter that shields me from the storm. As I ponder the fragility of life, I gain a fresh awareness of its value.

It's easy to take our blessings for granted until we're confronted with what life could be like without them. By willingly exploring these grim thoughts, I foster gratitude and empathy. I tap into a wellspring of compassion for those facing adversity, and it pushes me to make the most of my own situation.

So each day, I invite you to step into this practice. Allow your mind to journey to those dark places briefly — just enough to stir a shift in perspective. Let it ignite a greater appreciation for the good in your life. This isn't about dwelling in fear; it's about embracing the light that shines even brighter in contrast to the darkness.

Day 245

The Extraordinary Lens

Start with a simple but profound question any time you're starting something: What would an extraordinary outcome look like? It's a question that can apply to anything from a small task at hand to the grandest of our life missions.

The moment we engage with this question, our perspective shifts. We're no longer in the mundane. This question becomes our spark, lighting up the path ahead. Like the North Star, it doesn't waver. It provides consistent guidance, ensuring we don't veer off into the distractions of life.

Just by prompting ourselves with this question, we raise the standard we're accepting and going after in life. As we journey with this vision, there's a natural gravitation towards greatness, not just in the final outcome but in every step leading to it. This approach embraces both triumphs and challenges, viewing them as essential components of the journey.

If you let this question guide you, it becomes more than just a strategy for projects. It becomes a philosophy. A way of life. As you navigate each day, let this extraordinary lens reshape your reality not just to achieve greatness, but to live it.

So when starting that new project today, ask yourself, "What would an extraordinary outcome look like?"

Then make it happen.

Day 246

Sixty Seconds of Happiness

For each minute consumed by anger, sixty seconds of happiness slip away unnoticed. It's a peculiar thought, isn't it? A minute is just a minute, yet it's also an opportunity — a fork in the road where you can choose the direction of your happiness.

Imagine those seconds as gold coins. Would you throw them away carelessly? Probably not. But when we surrender to anger, that's exactly what we're doing.

We can't control everything that happens to us, but we can control how we react. It's a power we all possess but often overlook. Claim those sixty seconds back.

But how do you make that choice? It starts with awareness. Recognize when you're starting to feel angry. Notice it without judgment and then ask yourself that critical question: "Is this worth it?" If you're honest with yourself, you'll know that it's not.

Next, take a deep breath. Use the breath to slow down and get control. Breathe in the possibility of happiness, and breathe out the anger. It's not serving you.

Finally, make a conscious choice to move toward joy. It might be a small step, like smiling at a stranger or appreciating the beauty of the sky. It might be more significant, like letting go of a grudge or forgiving someone who's wronged you.

The path to happiness is not always easy, but it's always there, waiting for you to take that first step. The choice is yours, and it's a choice you make every minute of every day. Make it wisely.

Day 247

How We're Shaped

It's fascinating to look around and realize that people's lives often reflect the expectations of those around them. The people they surround themselves with all create a sort of gravitational pull that directs their lives.

It's not a judgment; it's an observation, an insight into how profoundly we are shaped by those we spend the most time with. What our friends expect from us and what we expect from them shapes our behavior, influences our thoughts, and even molds our destiny.

Here's the beautiful part: You have control over your peer group. You can choose to surround yourself with those who lift you up, challenge you, and push you toward your dreams. You can find communities, groups, and friends that align with your values, goals, and the person you want to be.

Or you can allow yourself to be influenced by those who don't align with your values and aspirations. But remember, that choice will have an impact on your life's direction.

Every relationship is like a two-way mirror, reflecting not just who we are but who we could be. The expectations of our peer group act like invisible guiding hands, leading us down a path for better or worse. Choose those guiding hands wisely. Surround yourself with people who inspire you, who make you want to be better, who expect the best from you.

Because in the end, those expectations can become self-fulfilling prophecies. What people expect from you and what you expect from yourself sets the stage for your life's play.

Day 248

Never Waste Suffering

D r. Dan Dworkis once imparted a line to me that remains etched in my thoughts: "Never waste suffering." He relayed a heart-wrenching moment when, despite all his efforts, a patient slipped away on the operating table. In the aftermath of that profound loss, another physician passed on this wisdom, urging him to draw lessons from the sorrow and utilize them for the next individual under his care.

It's human nature to retract and shield ourselves from pain. We often want to dodge suffering, to sidestep it like an obstacle on our path. What if we lean into it instead? What if we view suffering not as an impenetrable wall but as a teacher guiding us toward deeper understanding and empathy?

By confronting suffering head-on, it shifts from being a mere source of pain to a gift — a wellspring of invaluable insights. Suffering has things to teach us, and the only way to learn those lessons is by turning inward.

Just as Dr. Dworkis took his experiences and honed his skills, we too can transform our adversities. We can turn them into fuel, propelling us forward, and ensuring that the lessons etched in pain become the catalyst for positive change.

Day 249

The Overflowing Cup

Imagine a cup filled to the brim. If it's overflowing, the surplus liquid pours out beyond the cup itself. The same is true of us. When our inner cup is filled with passion, wisdom, love, and understanding, it naturally overflows, touching the lives of those around us.

The overflowing cup is a beautiful metaphor that illustrates an essential truth about our capacity to give. It reminds us that we can only share what we have within ourselves. To offer wisdom, compassion, and our unique gifts to the world, we must first cultivate and nourish these qualities within our own beings.

But here's the catch: If our cup is empty, or nearly so, there's nothing to overflow. We find ourselves depleted, unable to give to others or even to ourselves.

This principle calls us to prioritize our health, personal growth, and wisdom. It urges us to invest time and energy in our learning, well-being, and passions. By taking care of ourselves, we replenish our inner essence, ensuring that our cup is not just filled but overflowing.

The beautiful part of this practice is that it's not a selfish act. In filling our own cup, we're not hoarding goodness for ourselves. Instead, we're creating abundance that cascades outward like a benevolent fountain, enriching the lives of those we encounter. Our growth overflows and helps others reach a higher level of capacity.

So ask yourself: What fills your cup? What helps you grow? What ignites your passion and brings you joy? Seek those things. Embrace them. Make them a priority in your life. In doing so, you'll find that your cup overflows naturally as a genuine expression of who you are.

Day 250

The Joyful Wastes of Time

There's this funny notion floating around that if our time isn't stamped as productive, it's somehow wasted. It's as if every tick of the clock must contribute to a grander goal. But here's a rebellious thought: Time you relish squandering isn't squandered at all.

Imagine a day where you gaze at clouds, take a meandering walk without a destination, or laugh at silly videos online. By today's metrics, unproductive, right? But if it recharges your spirit, isn't that a profound product in itself?

The happiest people I've met have this uncanny knack. They can lounge on a grassy knoll, letting hours slip by simply watching the world, and feel utterly fulfilled. It's because they understand a truth many of us miss: Life's value isn't always in milestones achieved but also in moments cherished.

In this relentless chase for efficiency, we often forget to pause and simply be — but these "unproductive" moments can become the wellspring of our most creative ideas, our deepest reflections, and our fondest memories.

So the next time you find yourself losing track of time immersed in a seemingly pointless joy, don't chastise yourself. Celebrate! You're not just idling time away; you're living, cherishing, and recharging. Remember, a life richly lived isn't just about the tasks accomplished but also about the moments truly savored.

Ditch the guilt. Dive into the joy of the now. Because sometimes, the best use of time is to seemingly waste it.

Day 251

The Final Test of Wisdom

The final test of wisdom lies not in the accumulation of knowledge but in the way one chooses to live their life.

It is not enough to possess intellectual insights or philosophical ponderings; true wisdom is found in the actions we take, the decisions we make, and the way we interact with the world around us.

Wisdom is not a destination but a continuous journey of moral evolution, self-discovery, and growth. It is in the small, everyday choices we make that our wisdom is truly tested. How we treat others, how we respond to challenges, and how we navigate the complexities of life are all reflections of our inner wisdom.

Ultimately, our wisdom is not gauged by what we know, but by how we weave that knowledge into the fabric of our existence.

Are you living your wisdom?

Day 252

You Can't Build a Great Life by Denial

Lean in, because I'm about to share a little secret that often gets overshadowed by today's hustle mentality. Fulfillment doesn't stem from denial; it blossoms from positive intent.

Think about it. We often see life as a series of sacrifices. "Say no to this to get that," we say. But what if instead of pushing things away, we leaned into things that filled our hearts? Instead of focusing on what we shouldn't do, we zeroed in on what we should?

This shift from denial to intention is transformative. Denial is reactive. It's about barriers and restrictions. It tightens and narrows our journey. Positive intent, on the other hand, is proactive. It's expansive, enriching, and opens doors we didn't even know existed.

Consider an artist poised before a blank canvas. If they merely focus on what they shouldn't paint, they'll be paralyzed. But with a clear, positive intent, strokes become freer, colors brighter, and the masterpiece emerges.

The trick is to find what you love, what you believe in, and what aligns with your essence. Don't just resist what doesn't serve you; actively seek what does. Let your intentions guide your steps, making every move a stride toward a life of purpose and joy.

Day 253

A Critical Ingredient

Learning to take action when you don't feel like it is a crucial ingredient for long-term success. Motivation may wane and enthusiasm may dwindle, but discipline and consistency sustain you through the ups and downs of the journey.

The ability to push past resistance and act despite not being in the mood sets high achievers apart. It's in these moments of dwindling enthusiasm that the real magic happens. That's where discipline comes in. Discipline isn't glamorous. It doesn't come with the rush of excitement that motivation does. But it's reliable, consistent, and powerful.

Discipline is the quiet, steady force that keeps you moving forward even when you don't feel like it. It's what gets you out of bed for an early morning run when you'd rather sleep in or pushes you to write another page when you'd rather watch TV.

Those who achieve great things aren't necessarily more talented or more motivated than anyone else. They've just mastered the art of acting even when they don't feel like it. They've learned to push past resistance to do the work even when it's hard, boring, or inconvenient.

It's easy to work hard when you're inspired, but true growth happens when you continue to work hard even when you're not. Build that discipline. Cultivate that consistency. Recognize that these traits are muscles that can be strengthened over time with practice and perseverance.

Today, take small, steady steps. Commit to a routine. Hold yourself accountable and keep going, especially during those moments you don't feel like it.

Day 254

Nature's Never Complete

Nature never looks at itself and proclaims it is complete, so why do we place such expectations on ourselves?

Embrace the beauty of your own journey knowing that it is a lifelong process of learning, evolving, and discovering new aspects of yourself. Embrace the imperfections, fluctuations, and uncertainties, for they are the very essence of what makes you human.

It is far too easy to get entangled in the threads of complaints, fixating on the way things are and overlooking the boundless potential for change that lies within us. We become ensnared in the monotony of dissatisfaction and blind to the vast array of possibilities that await our grasp. But beneath the surface of our discontent lies a wellspring of power waiting to be tapped.

The truth is, we possess the ability to rewrite the script of our existence and to shape reality in the image of our dreams. In every moment, we hold the brush of transformation, capable of painting a brighter, more vibrant reality.

So let us unshackle ourselves from the chains of stagnation and embrace the profound truth that change is within our reach. With every decision we make and every action we take, let us follow nature and change with the seasons.

Day 255

Autotelic

A *utotelic*. Sounds like something straight out of a sci-fi novel, doesn't it? But it's not as complex as it might seem.

Autotelic comes from two Greek words: *auto*, meaning self, and *telos*, meaning goal. An autotelic activity is one done for its own sake because the doing itself is the reward. Think about that kid who gets lost in her drawings for hours or the musician who plays his guitar till his fingers are sore simply because they love what they do. That's autotelic.

In an autotelic state, you're not chasing after some external reward or recognition. You're in it for the sheer joy that comes from the activity itself. It's where passion meets presence, where the doer and the doing merge into one.

Our world often focuses on extrinsic rewards: money, fame, applause. And there's nothing wrong with those. But when your motivation is solely external, you can lose sight of the joy, the fulfillment in the activity itself. You become more concerned with the destination and forget to enjoy the journey.

That's why being autotelic is so powerful. It turns the journey into the destination. It makes the process its own reward. When you're autotelic, you're not just more engaged and fulfilled; you're also more resilient. Because your satisfaction comes from the doing and not the outcome, you can weather failures and setbacks without losing your enthusiasm. You can keep going not because of some distant prize but because you love what you're doing right here right now.

So think about what makes you lose track of time. What engages you so deeply that the world around you seems to fade away? That's your autotelic zone. Embrace it.

Day 256

The Measure of Courage

I had a revelation one morning: If we never really challenge our courage and strength, do we truly understand the depths of our fears?

Life has an uncanny way of placing obstacles on our paths. More often than not, these obstacles appear as fears — shadows of uncertainty that threaten to engulf our spirit. But what if these shadows are just figments that are more imagined than real?

We live in comfort zones cushioned by the familiar. This safety, while comforting, can also be limiting. When we tiptoe around our fears, never daring to confront them, they grow, casting larger shadows that darken more of our world.

It's akin to staring at a mountain from a distance, assuming its climb is insurmountable. But once you take those first steps navigating its terrain, the once daunting peak might just reveal itself to be a gentle slope.

This is why testing our courage is vital. It's not about seeking danger or being reckless. It's about understanding our limits, confronting our anxieties, and realizing that many of our fears stem from the unknown or the untried.

Each time we face a fear, measure our strength against it, and push past it, we not only debunk its myths but discover a version of ourselves that's braver, bolder, and boundlessly resilient.

So the next time fear whispers in your ear, don't just listen. Question it. Challenge it. See if its tales hold any water. For in understanding the true measure of our fears, we find the actual measure of our courage.

Creating and Controlling Energy for Optimal Living

Take a breath and consider this: Perhaps the most significant barrier to achieving your potential is the unconscious habit of letting external energy mold your internal rhythm.

Top performers, those who've touched the pinnacle of their craft, comprehend an essential reality: energy emerges from somewhere. It's either created internally or absorbed from the world around us. They opt to be the masters of their own energy, tailoring it to resonate with their ambitions.

Ever been with that person who, the moment they walk in, you can feel the room's energy deflate? Yeah, that energy vampire. But remember that one time when instead of letting them pull you into their storm, you stood strong as a beam of light? That moment showed you something vital: You can generate your own energy. Once you've done it once, you can do it anytime.

This realization changed everything for me. I grasped that I could be a self-sufficient powerhouse independent of discord from external forces. This isn't about shutting out the world but about deciding which frequencies you tune into.

Adopt the mindset of an energy creator. Mold environments, no matter the existing ambiance. This isn't the domain of the chosen few; it's a path open to everyone. It's crucial to underscore that every individual possesses this choice.

You're not just a reactor to energy; you're a generator.

Day 258

You're Not Lost

Y ou're not lost; you're just early in the process of figuring it out. And that's a beautiful place to be.

You see, being lost is often seen as something negative, something to be avoided. It's considered a place of confusion, a state of being off-track. But that's just a perspective, and not a particularly helpful one.

Consider that when you're lost, you're exploring. You're seeking. You're open to new experiences, new possibilities. You're questioning the path you're on and looking for something that resonates with you. You're willing to admit that you don't have all the answers, and that's a powerful realization. In fact, some of the most meaningful discoveries in life happen when you feel lost.

Think back to a time when you felt totally certain about something or completely sure of your path. That certainty can be comforting, but it can also be confining. It can keep you from seeing opportunities, growing, and changing.

Being lost means you're in a state of transformation. You're shedding the old, embracing the unknown, and allowing something new to take shape. It's easy to look at others who seem to have it all figured out and feel like you're falling behind. But their path is not your path. Your journey is unfolding exactly as it should.

If you find yourself feeling lost, instead of panicking or beating yourself up, try embracing it. Dive into the uncertainty. Ask yourself the big questions.

You're not lost; you're just early in the process. And that's a beautiful place to be.

Day 259

Life is a Verb

Imagine thinking of life as something static or unchanging, like a noun. It might lead you to believe that life is something that just happens to you — that you're handed a set of circumstances and that's it.

But that's not life. Life is a verb. It's active, dynamic, and ever-changing. It's not something you have; it's something you do.

Consider your daily routine. Every decision you make and every step you take is a part of living. It's action, it's movement, it's creation. Life doesn't just unfold in front of you; you're actively shaping it, constantly participating in it.

If you think of life as a verb, you recognize your role in it. You see that you're not just a spectator; you're a participant. You have the ability to act, to choose, and to change. Imagine if you approached each day with this mindset. How would that change your experience of life?

Now, this doesn't mean that life is entirely within your control. Of course there are external factors, unexpected events, and influences beyond your reach. But even in those situations, you still have choices. You choose how to react, how to adapt, and how to move forward.

Life as a verb means embracing the active role you play in your existence. It's about recognizing that life isn't something that's happening to you; it's something you're actively doing.

So live it. Engage with it. Play with it. Act on it.

Day 260

Becoming Friends with Discomfort

For today, refuse to shrink and hide from the feeling of discomfort. Become friends with discomfort and turn what used to be painful into what you seek out.

Discomfort serves as a powerful signpost on the road to who you can become. It's guiding us towards unexplored territories of the self.

When we encounter discomfort, we are faced with a pivotal choice: to lean into it and seize the opportunity for growth or to retreat and remain within the confines of our comfort zone. In this moment of choice, we find the true test of our resilience and determination. This moment becomes a mini moment for how we live our lives.

Ultimately, discomfort is an invitation to embrace change, resilience, and adaptability. It is the call to explore the uncharted territories within us, overcome obstacles, and discover the full extent of our potential.

The discomfort we encounter today becomes the stepping stone to the best version of ourselves tomorrow.

So let us not shrink away from discomfort, but rather embrace it as a guide on the path to unlocking our true potential.

Day 261

Default Responses

Our minds have become skilled architects of discontent, quick to construct walls of frustration when things don't go our way or when someone's actions challenge our patience. We have conditioned ourselves to react with frustration, anger, or disappointment when our expectations are not met, failing to realize that such reactions only serve to sow the seeds of negativity in our daily lives.

It's as if we have crafted a myriad of paths leading us to feel bad while leaving only a few narrow trails that lead to genuine feelings of joy and contentment.

It's time to evaluate the unwritten rules we've subconsciously accepted — particularly those that coax us into accepting distress as the default response to life's minor inconveniences. All too often we allow insignificant grievances to steal our joy, giving them undue influence over our emotional state.

What if we were to challenge this seemingly automatic response? What if we were to redefine our approach and instead infuse our daily lives with elements of delight, however small they may be?

In its simplest form, life is brimming with opportunities for joy. Let's seek to actively cultivate this joy and choose to focus on the good that exists around us. Rather than succumbing to minor frustrations, let's celebrate the opportunities for happiness within our reach.

By consciously shifting our focus and building these habits of gratitude, we create a reservoir of positivity, fundamentally altering our default responses and nurturing a more joyful, appreciative existence.

Day 262

Ready to Put Others First?

Relationships are a complex dance, aren't they? Two people, each with their own unique rhythms, attempt to synchronize in perfect harmony. It's a beautiful, challenging, and sometimes frustrating endeavor. But amidst the complexity, I've found that one fundamental question emerges as a beacon, guiding our connections: "Am I ready to put my ego aside and put the other person first?"

Imagine answering *yes* to that question wholeheartedly. It's not just a verbal agreement but a declaration of intent. You're saying, "I am here for you unconditionally." You embrace the commitment that true love demands. You're not just a partner; you become a supporter, a cheerleader, a confidant, a friend. The relationship doesn't just survive; it thrives.

This approach to relationships is transformative. I've seen it in my life, and I've seen it in others'. There's a strength that comes from putting another person's needs above your own; a richness that only selfless love can provide.

Now consider the alternative. When the answer to the question is *no*, the foundation of the relationship rests on shaky ground. Self-centeredness and ego creep in, bringing the seeds of discontent. You start to see the relationship as a transaction, a give-and-take where you're always calculating your return on investment. The challenges of life prove too much to bear, and the connection weakens.

The strength of a relationship is truly tested by our willingness to place the needs of our partner above our own, to sacrifice, and to show empathy. It's a journey worth taking, for it is this foundation that sustains and enriches us through the passage of time.

Day 263

Today's Transformative Choice

Isn't it fascinating — the idea that this very moment holds a pivot point that can redefine everything? Often, we await grand events to ignite change. But truthfully, the most profound shifts begin with a single choice, a deliberate decision.

Imagine standing at life's crossroads. Here, you have the power to declare with an unwavering voice, "I won't settle. Not anymore." This isn't about arrogance; it's about honoring your worth and vowing never to let mediocrity dull the luminous potential you possess.

Such a commitment is not a fleeting emotion. It's seismic. The day you decide to strive for nothing less than your best, you send ripples through the fabric of your life. This choice acts as a beacon to illuminate your path, guide every endeavor, and stoke fires of ambition.

Embracing this stance means no more 'what ifs' and no compromises on dreams. Instead, you've chosen a relentless pursuit, a dedicated chase setting your sights on your ultimate goal. This is your omega point.

With this newfound determination, challenges morph into stepping stones and doubts are mere reminders to push harder. The world might throw curveballs, but you've girded yourself with the armor of unwavering commitment.

So if you're waiting for a sign, this is it. Today, seize the opportunity. Make that transformative choice. Commit to your brilliance, your excellence. Dive deep, surge forth, and let the universe know you're here to play your best game. Mediocrity is no match for your boundless spirit. Today, you reshape your destiny.

Day 264

Stop Comparing

Comparing yourself to others seems to be a natural human tendency. We look at those around us, measure ourselves against them, and then make judgments about our worth based on those comparisons. It's as if we're in a never-ending race, constantly looking over our shoulder to see where we stand in relation to others.

But here's the problem: Comparing yourself to others is a path to disappointment. It's a game you can never win. When you compare yourself to someone else, you're taking a complex, unique individual (you) and reducing yourself to a set of comparisons against other complex, unique individuals (them). It's an oversimplification that leads to a distorted view of both yourself and others.

The truth is, no one on this planet has your unique combination of skills, experiences, values, and personality. That's your superpower, and it can't be compared.

Instead of looking to others and measuring yourself against them, turn your gaze inward. Focus on your own growth and progress. Are you better today than you were yesterday? Are you moving closer to your own goals and dreams? Those are the comparisons that matter.

Celebrate others' successes without seeing them as a reflection of your own worth. Be inspired by others without feeling the need to outdo them. Recognize that the only meaningful comparison is with your own yesterday.

You're not in a race against anyone else. You're on your own path, and it's a beautiful one. Enjoy the journey.

Day 265

Insights from Mortality

Years ago, amidst a whirlwind of activities and ideas, I stumbled upon a peculiar exercise: writing a letter as if it were your last. It may conjure a shiver of discomfort or seem darkly morbid, but bear with me. The revelations you unearth are not of death but of the richness of life.

The procedure is simple. Retreat to a quiet corner, shed the protective layers of daily hustle, and confront the hypothetical: If you were running out of time, what would be your parting words to your cherished ones?

In this raw, vulnerable state, the chatter of the world fades. The essence of relationships, the unspoken words, and the bottled emotions rise to the surface. You find yourself navigating a maze of regrets, unexpressed love, untapped potential, and the realization of unsung praises.

This isn't an exercise in morbidity. It's an introspective tool. It holds up a mirror juxtaposing our daily pursuits against what genuinely matters. More often than not, there's a gap — a divergence between the life we live daily and the depth of connection we truly yearn for.

Perhaps you'll find a gentle nudge to say "I love you" more often or a realization to prioritize family dinners over late office hours.

As you seal that letter, you're armed with a refreshed perspective. It's a reminder that life in its unpredictable splendor is a gift.

Day 266

Embracing the Rebound

Every legend — every great name in history — has faced setbacks: moments when they didn't shine their brightest or stand their tallest. For Steph Curry, the celebrated sharpshooter of the Golden State Warriors, one such moment arrived on November 4, 2016. The stadium watched in disbelief as he missed 10 three-point shots, ending an impressive 157-game streak that had become a part of NBA folklore.

But it's what came next that defines greatness.

No dwelling. No self-pity. One game later, Curry roared back with 46 points, sinking 13 three-pointers — a new NBA record. It wasn't just a comeback; it was a declaration.

It's not the fall that defines us, but the rise. Steph's story isn't just about basketball. It's a reminder for all of us that setbacks pave the way for comebacks. After the toughest times, there's a new beginning waiting to be seized.

What distinguishes the truly great from the merely good is not how they handle success but how they respond to adversity. This story is a narrative that underscores an invaluable lesson for all of us: setbacks, however disappointing, are merely setups for even bigger comebacks.

When adversity knocks on our door, we can either be overshadowed by it or learn from it and bounce back even stronger. The next time life challenges you, remember Curry's journey from setback to comeback. Let it serve as a beacon illuminating the path from momentary darkness to triumphant dawn.

There Are No Speed Limits to Personal Growth

There's a liberating realization awaiting all of us: There's no speed limit on personal growth.

Picture your life as an open highway. There are no road signs dictating how fast or slow you must go. An idea, a belief, or a dream can flash into existence in the blink of an eye, and you can allow it to alter your life's course instantly.

You can zoom down the road at your own pace, knowing that if you hit a plateau, it's only temporary.

Think of your potential as an endless tank of gas. That fuel source never runs out. You can step on the gas as hard as you want, break through plateaus, and reach new horizons.

The beauty of it? The road stretches out endlessly before you.

So why hold back? Go ahead, push the pedal, and see just how far and how fast you can go.

There are no limits unless you impose them on yourself.

Day 268

Step into the Spotlight

Authenticity is the vibrant energy that surges through our being when we shed the layers of masks and pretenses. It empowers us to step into the spotlight of our lives with unwavering confidence, embracing both our strengths and vulnerabilities.

When we choose authenticity, we unfurl our true selves before the world, daring to stand tall, unique, and grounded in our moral values and eccentricities. It is in this daring act of honesty that we find the courage to embrace our imperfections, realizing that they are the very threads that weave the tapestry of our humanity.

Authenticity is the gateway to liberation, freeing us from the shackles of seeking approval and validation.

Want help? Explore questions like these.

- What are the masks and pretenses I am currently wearing, and why do I choose to wear them?

- What steps can I take to liberate myself from the need for external validation and approval?

- Reflecting on my past, can I identify moments where I was authentic and how those moments positively impacted my life and relationships?

- What might change in my life if I choose to live more authentically?

In the sanctuary of authenticity, we find the strength to stand tall, unshaken by the winds of external judgment.

Day 269

The Music Only You Hear

I magine a person dancing to music only they can hear. To everyone else, their movements seem erratic, nonsensical, even insane. But in the ears of the dancer, there's a melody, a rhythm, and a flow that makes perfect sense.

Isn't this a beautiful illustration of how personal passion, belief, or vision can appear to others?

When you're following a dream that only you can see, guided by a vision that's uniquely yours, you're dancing to music that others may not hear. You may be judged, misunderstood, or dismissed by those who don't share your perspective. But that doesn't make your dance any less valid or beautiful.

When Steve Jobs envisioned a world where computers would become personal tools, many thought he was dancing to imaginary music. When Elon Musk dared to dream of commercial space travel, others scoffed at his fanciful approach.

But as they lived, they heard the music. They were guided by a vision, a purpose, and a passion that others couldn't perceive. And eventually, some of those who had laughed joined in the dance as they, too, began to hear the music.

Your vision, passion, and unique perspective are your music. Don't be discouraged if others don't hear it. Keep dancing. Embrace your unique expression even if it seems insane to others. It showcases your inventive nature, your one-of-a-kind character, and your authentic self.

And remember, those who are seen dancing may be thought insane only by those who can't hear the music. Someday, they may hear it too. So dance on.

Day 270

Malleable and Durable

S ifting through an old notebook amidst scribbles and thoughts, a handwritten note from my younger self caught my eye: "Live life like you're infinitely malleable yet extremely durable."

In that simple, unassuming sentence is profound wisdom.

Being malleable means remaining open to change. It's the willingness to adapt, reshape, and reinvent oneself in the face of life's myriad experiences. It's about being open-minded, flexible, and ready to embrace whatever comes your way. Imagine being like clay: receptive to the hands that shape it and willing to morph into any form.

Being durable is equally vital. It signifies resilience, strength, and tenacity. Life can toss storms our way, and in these tempests, it's our durability that lets us withstand, persevere, and emerge stronger. Think of it as being like a diamond: brilliant, tough, and unbreakable no matter the pressure.

This duality — malleability coupled with durability — is the essence of a fulfilling life. We need to be flexible enough to learn from our encounters yet resilient enough to bear the bruises and still march forward. We need to be supple to move with its rhythm and sturdy enough to stand our ground when necessary. It's a delicate balance but one worth mastering.

Today, as I pen these thoughts, I extend a message to you: Be like water, adapting to every vessel, yet be strong as rock, unyielding in your core convictions.

Day 271

This Is What Passion Is About

Passion. It's more than just a buzzword. It's a way of life. It's the energy that drives you out of bed in the morning, eager to face the day. It's the creative spark that turns an ordinary idea into something extraordinary.

Yet passion is not something that falls into your lap. It doesn't come knocking at your door. Passion is discovered, nurtured, and cultivated.

Think about what excites you. What makes your heart race? What do you lose yourself in, forgetting time and place? What would you do even if no one paid you for it? Your passion lies in those answers.

But recognizing your passion is only the first step. You must be willing to pursue it, to breathe life into it every day. Passion is not a stagnant thing. It evolves, grows, and sometimes even changes completely.

The word *passion* has a fascinating etymology. It comes from the Latin verb *pati*, which means to suffer or endure. This origin provides a profound insight into the nature of true passion. Your passion is something you're willing to suffer for, something that you endure challenges and setbacks for because it means that much to you. It's not just a fleeting interest or a hobby but a commitment, a calling that resonates with the deepest part of you.

So ignite that inner fire. Let it burn brightly. Don't hide it, don't minimize it, and don't let it be extinguished by doubts or fears. Your passion is your gift to the world. It's your unique voice, your unique contribution. Share it. Live it. Revel in it.

Day 272

Hope

We often think of hope as a fragile, fleeting thing. But in my experience, it's a lot more than that. It's a way of seeing, a lens through which we can choose to view our lives.

Hope is a *choice*. A choice to see the potential instead of the limitations, the opportunities instead of the obstacles, the growth instead of the failure.

I remember times when I faced seemingly insurmountable obstacles and everything seemed to be conspiring against me. Yet when I looked through the lens of hope, I was able to see not just the barriers but the pathways around them.

Through the lens of hope, I've seen that even in our darkest moments, there's always a glimmer of light. It's not about denying reality or ignoring the challenges; it's about choosing to see them in a different way.

Hope is the sun that pierces through the clouds of despair, illuminating a path of possibilities even in the darkest of times.

The lens of hope doesn't just show us the silver linings; it helps us create them. It reminds us that we have the power to shape our own destiny, turn challenges into opportunities, and transform our dreams into realities.

So next time you face a situation that seems hopeless, remember to look through the lens of hope. Look for the silver linings, the hidden opportunities, and the strength within yourself. You might just find that hope is not just a fleeting feeling but a powerful force that can illuminate your path and guide you to greatness.

Day 273

One Conversation Can Change Everything

Isn't it remarkable how a single conversation can change everything? I'm not talking about a casual chat about the weather or the latest news. I mean a deep, meaningful conversation that reaches into the core of your being and turns the key, unlocking something you didn't even know was there.

You meet someone — it might be a stranger, mentor, or friend — and something about the exchange stirs you. They say something, ask something, or share something that resonates with you. It's like they've reached into your soul and flicked a switch, illuminating a path you hadn't seen before.

I've had those conversations. You probably have, too. A casual talk suddenly dives deep, and you walk away feeling inspired, challenged, or even a bit shaken. Suddenly, your dreams seem attainable, your potential limitless, and the world a place filled with possibilities.

But here's the thing: These conversations don't just happen by accident. You have to seek them out. You have to be willing to engage, ask questions, listen, and share your thoughts and feelings. Look for people who think differently, see the world through a unique lens, and challenge conventional wisdom.

Life is filled with opportunities for connection and growth. And just one conversation can change everything. All it takes is the courage to start it and the openness to see where it leads.

The Illusion of Only One Path

L ife is not a straight line. But oh, how we wish it were. We adore simplicity. One way, one answer, one secret formula. Like there's this singular golden path everyone else has missed, but if we're attentive enough, we might just find it. This sentiment gets drummed into us early on. "Follow these steps. Avoid those mistakes."

Yet, as I delve into experiences and stories, I find a truth resembling a sprawling map more than a narrow corridor. Every path is unique and every journey distinct, but they all have one thing in common: none strictly adheres to a "one-size-fits-all" route.

I've met folks who've stumbled into success by accident and others who meticulously planned every inch of their journey. Some chose a scenic route, drinking in life's varied flavors, while others sprinted straight ahead, eyes locked on the horizon. All different, yet all right in their own way.

The pressure to pick the "perfect path" can be paralyzing. But here's a little revelation I stumbled upon: there isn't just one. Every turn you take and choice you make crafts a path that's uniquely yours. Life isn't a standardized test with predetermined answers. It's an open essay question waiting for your original response. Sure, there are guidelines, but they're just that — lines that guide, not bind.

So next time you find yourself at a crossroads, remember this: There's no single right turn. And what may look like a detour to others might just be your personal highway to wonder. Embrace the possibilities, cherish the detours, and remember that while there may be a common destination, the routes are countless.

Day 275

The Triad for Positive Transformation

A rut: It's a place we'll dwell many times during our lives. A rut can feel like a trench with steep walls trapping us in a habitual cycle of negative thinking. But there is a potent technique to climb out of this trench and change your trajectory. This technique I call the triad of Awareness, Aim, Action.

When you're stuck in a rut, this is how you get yourself out.

- **Awareness.** It all starts here. This is where you halt the mind's automatic pilot. You notice the negativity, the self-doubt, or the procrastination. You don't judge it; you just acknowledge it. This awareness is the first step out of the rut. It's like switching on a light in a dark room.

- **Aim.** Next, align yourself with your higher self. Aim at the person you're striving to become. Visualize it. Feel it. This isn't about aiming for perfection but aiming for alignment with your values, dreams, and potential. This is your North Star.

- **Action.** Finally, translate that vision into immediate action. Even a small step can shift your entire day when taken decisively. It's the action that proves to yourself that you're not just dreaming but doing.

Remember, change isn't always a giant leap; often it's a series of small, consistent steps. The Awareness-Aim-Action cycle isn't a one-time fix; it's a tool you can use again and again. Like turning the steering wheel of a car, these small adjustments keep you on the road headed in the direction you choose.

Day 276

Seeking Depth over Comfort

Life is filled with bandages: Temporary solutions that provide instant comfort and a fleeting sense of relief. It's easy, right? A quick fix for that nagging problem. Most people lean into these because they're convenient. They provide immediate gratification.

However, merely patching things up on the surface can do more harm than good. It's like silencing an alarm instead of putting out the fire. The issue remains, festering beneath, waiting for another moment to resurface.

Those committed to genuine growth, however, take a different route. They're not seduced by the allure of the immediate. They dive deeper, searching for the root, the real cause. It's not about merely feeling better for them; it's about *being* better fundamentally and wholly. Choosing a cure over relief might be the tougher, less traveled path, but it's where genuine transformation happens.

So next time you're faced with a challenge, ask yourself: "Do I want a moment's peace or a lifetime's worth of growth?" Your answer will shape the trajectory of your journey.

Getting to the root cause of things requires a deliberate, methodical approach. An approach you are ready for; an approach that's been waiting for you.

Day 277

The Fire Within

It's easy to look at people and assume they're lazy if they aren't leaping out of bed excited for the day. It may not be a matter of laziness but rather the lack of compelling goals that leaves many adrift in the currents of life.

In a society so often obsessed with instant gratification and quick fixes, the pursuit of gripping, life-defining goals can be overshadowed by the allure of convenience and comfort. That's understandable. It's hard work to dig deep and find those truly compelling visions that inspire us.

But without them, we may find ourselves wandering aimlessly, our potential untapped, our energy scattered, our fire unlit.

What's needed is a profound exploration of what makes us come alive. When we do this—when we unearth the dreams that resonate with our soul—we unlock the floodgates of motivation and drive. These aren't just goals; they become a calling. They fuel our actions and energize our every step, transcending mere obligation and transforming into a genuine, thrilling passion.

So let's not settle for the shallow waters of convenience. Let's dive deep, find those goals that truly ignite our hearts, and chart our course towards a life that unleashes us.

It's not a path of least resistance; it's a path of most aliveness. That's where the real adventure begins.

Day 278

Emotional Agility

Life is a constant flux of emotions, a dance where feelings play the tune. Sometimes the music is uplifting and joyous; other times, it can be somber and heavy. It's a rhythm we all participate in whether we like it or not.

The key to living a fulfilling life doesn't lie in avoiding or suppressing these emotions but in learning to move with them gracefully. This is what emotional agility is all about.

Imagine emotions as different dance partners, each with their own style and tempo. Anger may be a fast and intense tango, while joy might be a lively jive. Sadness could be a slow waltz and anxiety a complex foxtrot. Each emotion, each dance, brings its own unique challenge and beauty.

Emotional agility is the ability to follow the rhythm without being overwhelmed. It doesn't mean you won't stumble or make mistakes. What it means is that you recognize the music, acknowledge your partner, and engage in the dance without losing yourself.

To build emotional agility in your life, you must tune into your emotions. Listen to the music your emotions are playing. Recognize what you're feeling without judgment. Labeling and understanding your emotions allows you to respond rather than react.

Accepting and embracing what you're feeling, even if it's uncomfortable, is essential. Emotions are not right or wrong; they simply are. Embracing them gives you the power to navigate them.

You must recognize that you have a choice in how you respond. You can choose to dance gracefully or stumble through the motions. This choice allows you to align your actions with your values.

Emotional agility is not a one-time achievement but a continuous practice. Like any dance, it requires practice, patience, and perseverance.

Sometimes the dance can be overwhelming, and that's okay. Seek support from friends, family, or professionals when you need it. We all need a dance partner now and then.

After the dance, take a moment to reflect. What went well? What could you do differently next time? Learning from each dance helps you become more agile for the next one.

Emotional agility turns the unpredictable dance of life into an art form. It allows you to move with grace through joy and sorrow, anger and love, fear and excitement.

The dance floor of life is always open. Will you step in with agility, or will you watch from the sidelines?

Ten Minutes to Transformation

If someone told you that you could change your life, broaden your perspective, and cultivate a deeper understanding of the world in just ten minutes a day, would you believe them? It may seem like an extravagant claim, but the simple act of daily reading holds the key to this transformation.

Ten minutes is a modest investment of time, yet the return is extraordinary. This daily practice is more than a leisure activity. It's a ritual of growth, a deliberate choice to expand your mind and enrich your life. As you turn the pages every day, you're not just absorbing information; you're engaging with thoughts and perspectives that challenge and inspire you. You're planting seeds that will flourish into insights and wisdom.

But the true magic lies in the consistency of this practice. Ten minutes a day may not seem like much, but it adds up. The average number of words in a typical non-fiction book can be 50,000 to 60,000 words, so if you were to read for just 10 minutes a day at an average adult reading speed, you could complete around 15 books in a year. In a decade, that's 150 books that could change your life.

The power of this habit is cumulative. It builds on itself, gradually shaping your understanding, sharpening your intellect, and deepening your empathy. It equips you with the tools to approach life's challenges with a nuanced perspective and the resilience to adapt and thrive.

So let's make a pact. Commit to those ten minutes a day. Open the door to the vast library of human knowledge and wisdom, and step into a world of endless possibilities.

Day 280

Not Deciding Is a Decision

L ife has a funny way of sneaking up on us. Often we're so preoccupied with analyzing the array of options that we forget something vital: Inaction is its own form of action. By hesitating at the crossroads, we may think we're buying time. But really, the world just keeps moving.

Every time you stall, mull over, or procrastinate, it's a decision, albeit a silent one. And these silent decisions? They're quite chatty. They whisper, "Maybe later." But *later* often translates to *never*. And these "nevers"? They accumulate. Before you know it, they're a heap of missed opportunities, lost connections, and "what could've been."

Sometimes the loudest echoes in our lives are the spaces where we opted to do nothing — those moments of indecision where we hoped that fate would intervene or someone else would choose for us. Yet the universe in its vastness doesn't micromanage our lives. We must.

Life is too short for could've, would've, should've. Dive in. Embrace the beautiful messiness of active choice. Even if it's wrong, it's a step. And steps, even backward, keep you moving and learning.

Life is moving. Don't be caught standing still. In doing nothing, you're making the loudest decision of all. Don't let the silence deafen you.

Day 281

The Art of Selecting What Shapes Us

In our digital age, we stand at the mouth of a river, a constant flow of information rushing towards us. Every day, we're pelted with news, advertisements, social media updates, and countless bytes of data. It's easy to get swept away.

But what if we approached this not as consumers but as curators? What if we saw ourselves as gallery keepers carefully selecting what deserves our attention and shapes our inner world?

We have control over what we let into our minds. We can choose to shut out the noise and fill our minds with meaningful content that resonates with our values and goals.

Let's fill our minds with things that are going to get us to where we want to go.

In being a curator, we become more intentional with our time and attention. We nurture our minds with wisdom, creativity, and substance rather than letting them be a dumping ground for everything that demands our gaze. Being a curator means taking responsibility for our mental environment.

So let us approach our daily information diet with discernment and choose what nourishes our intellect and soul.

Day 282

The Pull of Curiosity

C uriosity is often thought of as a childlike wonder, a fleeting desire to know why the sky is blue or how a bird can fly. But what if we saw curiosity as something more profound: A force that could guide us through life, opening doors and illuminating paths we never knew existed?

Let your curiosity lead. Instead of pushing it aside or drowning it in daily distractions, nurture it. Listen to its whispers and follow its nudges. Allow it to pull you towards books, conversations, experiences, and ideas that resonate with something deep within.

In doing this, you become an explorer of your own life, a seeker of wisdom driven by a need to know and understand. You don't just accumulate knowledge; you integrate it, letting it shape you and deepen your connection to the world around you.

Your curiosity becomes a magnet pulling you towards growth and fulfillment. It urges you to ask questions, delve deeper, and see the world from new perspectives. It's a relentless pursuit of understanding that never gets old because the landscape of knowledge is boundless.

The spirit of inquiry leads you to unexpected places, revealing layers of yourself and the world that you never knew were there.

So cultivate curiosity. Feed it, listen to it, and let it guide you.

Day 283

Just Keep Going

In the face of adversity and uncertainty when the road seems long and the challenges overwhelming, remember these three simple words: Just keep going.

These three words can be a rallying cry when you think you can't go on.

The journey may be arduous, and at times you may stumble and fall. But in those moments of doubt and fatigue, summon the courage to keep going, for it is in the act of perseverance that you find your true strength.

Let every setback become a stepping stone and every obstacle a chance to grow. Trust in the path you've chosen, and trust in yourself.

Embrace the power of resilience, for it is the beacon that guides you through the darkest of nights towards the light of your dreams. Embrace the grit and tenacity that lie within you, for they are the driving force that propels you forward step by determined step.

In times of struggle and uncertainty, remember these three powerful words: Just keep going.

Day 284

The Courage to Ask

Often we stand at the precipice of our desires. We stare out but never make the leap — not because we can't, but because we don't ask.

Here's a thought: How many doors remain closed simply because we didn't knock?

It's staggering when you think about it. Opportunities untapped, relationships unformed, adventures unexplored. That promotion, that connection with someone you admire, that intimate chat with a loved one — they all rest on the other side of a question. A simple ask.

Fear, uncertainty, or even complacency might hold us back. But remember: *A no* might sting, but the ambiguity of not knowing gnaws far longer.

So consider this: What's burning in you right now? What yearning tugs at your heart? Identify it. Then muster the courage to ask for it. Because life is far too short for what-ifs.

You've got this. Go get what you want.

Day 285

Inner Growth, Outer Service

Inner growth, outer service: an elegant pairing of concepts that merge together in beautiful symmetry.

The first half of this dance is about personal cultivation. Inner growth is not about seeking external validation or conforming to societal expectations. It's about aligning with your true self and understanding what resonates with your core. This is the journey inward, filled with introspection, self-awareness, and self-love. It's about finding that still point inside — the essence of who you are — and nurturing it.

But what's truly wonderful is how this process doesn't end with oneself. Once you've fostered that inner growth, it starts to radiate outward. It leads to the other half of the dance: outer service.

Service to others is not merely an obligation or a duty. It becomes a natural expression of your gifts and of the love, compassion, and understanding you've cultivated within yourself. Your personal growth begins to align with a higher purpose, one that connects you with others. You start to see opportunities to make a positive difference, uplift, and contribute.

It's a feedback loop of sorts. Your inner growth fuels your ability to serve others, and in turn, that service nourishes your soul, leading to further growth.

So don't stop. Keep evolving, keep growing, keep serving.

Day 286

Stop Trying to Figure It All Out on Your Own

I 've been guilty countless times of stumbling through life trying to find my own way and being unwilling to look up for help. But here's something to consider: Rather than trying to figure out life all on your own, find guidance from those who have already mastered the art of living a fulfilling life.

Seek out those mentors and heroes. Discover the people who have achieved your wildest dreams. Look to those who radiate contentment and joy and observe them. What choices do they make? What values do they uphold? What actions do they take?

It's like they've left behind a map for us to follow. By starting with this living model, we can uncover insights that resonate with our own path. It's not copying; it's learning from the best.

But you can't learn from them if you're unaware of them. Find them. Learn everything you can about them, and allow their lessons to become your guide.

Day 287

Transitions

Transitions. Oh, how they can shape us.

Life seems to have a way of never staying still. Just when we think we've found our footing, something shifts, and we're called to adapt, change, and grow.

It can be a new job starting, a relationship ending, moving to a new city, or even something as subtle as a change in perspective. These transitions weave intricate patterns, often demanding we leave behind the well-trodden paths of safety and familiarity.

What I've found is that these shifts call for a particular kind of courage. It's the courage to step into the unknown. It's the willingness to relinquish the comfort of what we know and embark on a journey of transformation.

Sounds scary? It can be.

But here's the beauty of it: In the midst of these transitions, I have learned that when you trust yourself more profoundly than ever before, you become your own greatest guide to an incredible life you could never have imagined.

It's as if the very act of stepping into uncertainty amplifies our internal intelligence. We learn to listen more closely to that little voice inside us that knows what's right. We learn to lean into our intuition and trust that somehow, we're on the right path.

It's not always easy. Venturing into uncharted territory means that the landscape is uncertain and the destination may not be crystal clear. Doubts can creep in. Fears can take hold. But in those moments of uncertainty, growth happens.

In those spaces where we feel lost, we find new parts of ourselves. We discover strengths we didn't know we had. We learn to be resilient, adaptable, and open to what comes next.

What's essential is to recognize that transitions aren't something to be feared but embraced. They're opportunities. They're invitations to a richer, more meaningful life.

So if you find yourself at the cusp of a transition, take a deep breath and step forward. Trust yourself. Trust the process. And remember, in the words of Joseph Campbell, "The cave you fear to enter holds the treasure you seek."

Transitions are not just changes; they're gateways to growth. They might demand that we leave behind what's comfortable, but what lies on the other side is often more valuable than we could ever have imagined. It's a lesson I've learned time and again, and one I'm grateful for.

Embrace the transitions. Trust the journey. Trust yourself. You know the way.

Day 288

The Timeless Treasure of Old Friends

There's a Japanese concept called *kintsugi* where broken pottery is repaired with gold. The idea? Embrace flaws, making them more beautiful than the original. Friendships that span decades are like *kintsugi*. Time-tested, occasionally fractured, but mended with golden memories, lessons, and shared experiences.

Old friends aren't just a comfort; they're a mirror to our past, reflecting our evolution. With new friends, there's always a phase of introduction, a need to catch up on years lived separately. With long-standing friends, there's a shared history. There's mutual understanding. There's the skipping of formalities. They've seen your highs and lows, been part of your stories, and vice versa.

In an era where digital interactions often replace face-to-face ones, it's easy to forget the depth of connections that have withstood the test of time. These relationships aren't just for reminiscing about the old days; they provide perspective. They remind you of your roots: of who you were and who you've become.

Cultivate these relationships like a gardener tends to ancient trees. While planting new seeds is essential, it's also vital to nourish the roots that run deep. The value isn't just in a shared past, but in witnessing each other's growth and changes.

Challenge yourself: In the next month, reach out to an old friend. Not a casual "Hi," but a genuine conversation. Dive deep. Remember, relive, reconnect. The golden bonds of time-tested friendship aren't just about the past. They're foundational for our present and inspirational for our future.

Day 289

The Advice You've Been Waiting For

Imagine meeting a mirror image of yourself: someone with the same experiences, resources, and problems. What advice would you give this person? What words of wisdom or encouragement would you offer? What paths are obvious to you that you would tell them to take? What relationships would you tell them to end? Which dreams would you tell them to pursue?

Take a moment to really think about it. Write down what you'd say if you could.

The advice you'd give to this mirror image of yourself is likely the very advice you need to hear. It's what you need to act on right now. It's a rare glimpse into your own wisdom unclouded by the usual self-doubt or hesitation.

The beauty of this mental exercise is that it cuts through our usual excuses and blind spots. We're able to see the situation from a different perspective and give the kind of advice we might be hesitant to apply to ourselves.

So take that advice. Apply it to your own life. Recognize that you do know what to do. You have the insights, the wisdom, and the capability to make positive changes. It's there within you, waiting to be acknowledged and acted upon.

Don't ignore this inner wisdom. Embrace it. Live it. Your mirror self has shown you the way. Now it's up to you to walk the path.

Jumping Off Cliffs Is How You Discover Wings

We often fear our edges and stretch points, those boundaries of comfort and familiarity. They seem like barriers keeping us safely ensconced in the known. But the truth is, our edges are where growth happens. They're the endless abyss off the cliff, daring us to leap into the unknown.

When you challenge your edges and leap off that cliff, something magical happens: You discover you were meant to fly. The wings you never knew you had unfurl, and suddenly the leap is not a fall but a soaring.

It's not about recklessness, but about embracing the possibilities that lie beyond what you thought were your limits.

You see, it's only at the edges where you can truly test your wings. In the comfortable center, you never know what you're capable of.

So run towards your edges, leap, and discover that you were always meant to fly.

Day 291

Make Yourself Proud

Every decision we make is a cornerstone that sets the foundation for the stories we'll someday tell. Life frequently presents us with forks in the road, each path leading to a distinct destination. The uncertainty can be overwhelming, with each option holding its own set of promises and perils.

But in those moments of indecision, rather than getting swayed by the myriad of external voices or fleeting emotions, ask yourself a straightforward, yet profound question: "Which of these choices will make me the most proud?"

This isn't about seeking validation or applause. It's about resonating with your core values, aligning with what truly matters to you. It's about the kind of stories you want to share, the memories you wish to cherish, and the legacy you aim to create.

By anchoring our decisions in what makes us proud — not the arrogant type of pride, but the kind that stems from integrity, authenticity, and purpose — we ensure that our choices resonate with our true selves.

So the next time you find yourself deciding, ask: "Which of these choices will make me the most proud?"

It Doesn't Always Turn Out Right

L ife is quirky, unpredictable, and delightfully unscripted. You can meticulously follow the "right" path, do everything according to plan, and still end up somewhere unexpected — maybe even somewhere you perceive as wrong. Conversely, you can blunder and fumble your way through, do everything "wrong," and still stumble upon something brilliant and right.

But here's the key: The unpredictability of outcomes shouldn't deter you from giving it your best. The quality of your effort matters even if it doesn't always directly translate into the expected results. Your best effort is the compass that guides you, the driving force behind your actions.

So what if you've done everything "right" and it turns out "wrong"? Or everything "wrong" and it turns out "right"? These are labels we attach to the unpredictable twists and turns of life. The real magic lies in your dedication to giving it your best regardless of the outcome.

Your best effort isn't just an action; it's an attitude, a philosophy, a commitment to yourself. It's a promise to engage with life fully with all its ups and downs. It's about realizing that success isn't only defined by the final destination but by the richness of the journey and the integrity of your approach.

Give it your best, always. That's where true fulfillment is found.

Day 293

Every Step Was Critical

Want to know something? Every step, every stumble, and every triumph on your journey was indispensable in shaping the person you have become today.

The pain you endured and the failures you encountered were not in vain; they were transformative forces that fortified your spirit and honed your resilience. Recognize that each twist and turn of your path was part of a magnificent creating process whose work of art is the person you are today.

Your past has been a gateway to transformation, arming you for the inevitable challenges that await you.

While life's unpredictability remains a constant, your proven ability to adapt and progress stands as a testament to your innate resilience. The mere fact that you've reached this point signifies the tenacity and the strength within you.

Step into the future with confidence, knowing that every challenge you've faced and surmounted is evidence of your readiness for the journey ahead.

Day 294

The Darkest Hour

I t's easy to be gracious, generous, and principled when the sun is shining and the path is clear. But what happens when the clouds roll in and the path becomes dark and treacherous? That's the real test of character.

Your darkest hours — those challenging times filled with uncertainty, failure, or pain — are your crucible. Their heat and pressure reveal your true essence. It's in these moments that you discover what you're really made of: infinite potential.

When everything is going wrong and you're facing insurmountable odds, what do you do? Do you bend your principles? Do you abandon your values? Or do you stand firm, holding tight to what you believe in even if it's the harder path?

Your actions in those dark times — those decisions made when no one is watching — define your character more than any success or accomplishment ever will. It's the integrity, resilience, and unwavering commitment to your true self that matters.

So when you find yourself in those dark hours, remember they are not just an obstacle; they are an opportunity to show who you really are and prove to yourself what you're capable of. It's your chance to shine even when there's no light.

Day 295

The Natural Rhythm of Life

T he natural rhythm of life is oscillation. Stress + Rest = Growth.

It's a universal law that guides life and growth.

Consider the process of building strength in our bodies. Stress in the form of exercise breaks down muscle fibers. But then comes rest, and with it, recovery. During recovery, the body rebuilds those fibers stronger than before. Without the stress, there would be no stimulus for growth. Without the rest, there would be no recovery, no growth.

This principle isn't just about physical fitness. It's a metaphor for life itself.

Stress isn't necessarily bad. It can be a challenge, a push to grow, a motivation to improve. Whether it's a demanding project, a learning opportunity, or a personal goal, stress can be a powerful catalyst for growth.

But without rest, stress becomes only strain. Without recovery, it leads to burnout, fatigue, and breakdown. That's why rest is not just a break from stress; it's an essential part of the process. It's where the growth happens.

Rest isn't just sleep or relaxation. It's reflection, connection, enjoyment; it's the time spent doing what feeds your soul. It's the pause that lets you assimilate what you've learned, heal from what you've endured, and rejuvenate for what's to come.

So remember, life works in oscillation. Stress + rest = growth.

Day 296

Our Influence on the Future

It's a humbling thought to consider how our lives are intricately woven into the fabric of history, stitched together by the actions, dreams, and sacrifices of those who came before us. The roads we travel, freedoms we enjoy, and technologies we use all have their roots in the efforts and vision of previous generations.

But this flow of progress and influence doesn't stop with us. We are part of a continuum, a grand relay race of humanity. The choices we make, values we uphold, and innovations we create today will resonate into the future and shape the lives of generations yet unborn.

So what are we doing with this precious gift of influence? Are we squandering it in pursuits that will vanish with the wind, or are we investing it in something that will endure — something a future generation will thank us for?

You don't have to be a world leader or a billionaire to make a lasting impact. Your kindness, wisdom, encouragement, and pursuit of excellence can ripple out in ways you may never see, touching lives in the future as others have touched yours.

In our everyday choices, we compose a symphony that will continue to play long after we have left the stage. Our actions are seeds. We may never see the trees that grow from them, but future generations will sit in their shade.

So let's be intentional. Let's consider not just the immediate impact of our choices but the echoes they will send into the future. We are part of a grand story, and our chapter matters.

Day 297

Finding Depth in the Daily

Life rarely hands us profound moments with flashing lights saying, "Here's your purpose!" Usually, it's in the humdrum daily routines that our mindset and intentions find fertile ground. Why? Because these are the moments we get to revisit every day.

Imagine making your toothbrushing ritual into something more: A moment not just about dental hygiene but self-vision. Standing there, you're not just doing an obligatory task. You're meeting your eyes, seeing beyond today's imperfections. You see a trajectory, hints of who you can become and what you might achieve.

It's a two-minute act, but in those minutes, you align with your goals, remind yourself of your passions, and mentally prep for your day. You do this not just in thought but in feeling — embodying that ambition with each brush stroke.

This mindset needn't be limited to the bathroom mirror. It can infuse how you greet the day, eat your meals, or choose your outfit. These aren't mundane tasks but daily affirmations.

So next time you stand in front of that mirror, know that it's not just a reflection staring back. It's potential. And with each small daily act, you're stepping into it.

Your ordinary moments are quietly extraordinary. Embrace them.

Day 298

I'd Rather Be Spent Than Saved

In life, it's easy to cling to caution: to withhold a part of ourselves, saving our energies, passions, or resources for a tomorrow that may never come. It's a seductive trap, this idea of waiting for the "right" moment, and it can keep us on the sidelines as spectators of life instead of active participants.

But I've come to realize that I'd rather be fully spent than saved. This doesn't mean throwing caution to the wind and acting irresponsibly. It doesn't mean ignoring the needs of tomorrow. But it does mean embracing today with intention, vigor, and whole-hearted engagement.

Every day is an opportunity to pour ourselves into what we love, what inspires us, and what calls to us.

Fully engaging with life means living without the lingering "what ifs" that haunt those who always keep something in reserve. It's to know that we've lived, loved, and worked with all we have. It's to feel the gratification of complete investment in the present moment, knowing that this is all we have and it's more than enough.

Being fully spent is about committing to a life where we don't let fear or hesitation rob us of our joy and our purpose. It's about finding that delicate balance where we honor our responsibilities while still seizing the opportunities of today.

I choose to live fully, to be spent, to engage with this wild and wonderful life with everything I've got.

It's a choice that transforms existence into living, and it's a choice available to us all. Why wait?

Day 299

The Familiar Good or the Remarkable Great

The familiar good is like a warm blanket, comforting and safe. It's the well-trodden path where success is predictable and risks are minimal. There's an undeniable appeal to this route, as it offers stability, reassurance, and the satisfaction of competence. It's easy to settle here and decide that good is good enough.

But then there's the remarkable great. It's the path less traveled, fraught with uncertainties, challenges, and demands that stretch us beyond our comfort zone. Pursuing the great is not about mere improvement; it's about transformation. It's a calling to rise above the ordinary, venture into the unknown, and strive not just for awesome but extraordinary.

This choice between the familiar good and the demanding great is a recurring theme in our lives, and it's a decision that shapes our destiny. Each time we encounter this junction, we are offered a new opportunity to reflect, reassess, and realign our paths. The pursuit of the great is not a one-time decision but a daily choice, a conscious determination to live not just a good life but a truly remarkable one.

Are we content with the comfort of the good, or are we willing to brave the challenges of the great? Will we settle for competence or strive for excellence?

This choice becomes a defining thread coloring our lives with the hues of our decisions, our courage, and our aspirations. Choose wisely, for in that choice lies the essence of our true selves.

Pause to Ask the Big Questions

Today, right now, let's take a pause — a vital and profound pause. Let's step back from the hustle and hurry of daily life, away from the noise and rush, and give ourselves the gift of contemplation. The space and time to ask the important questions worth answering.

Am I living in alignment with my values and beliefs? This isn't just a question; it's a mirror reflecting our deepest selves.

What people, places, and activities allow me to feel naturally myself and most fully alive? Again, not just a question but an exploration of who and what nourishes our soul.

Starting today, what is one thing I could stop doing, start doing, or do differently that would most improve the quality of my life? This is the action step, the challenge, the commitment to tangible change. This question is an invitation to take immediate control of your life's path.

These aren't casual, offhand questions to be answered hastily and then forgotten. They are deep, probing inquiries that require honest, thoughtful reflection. They might unsettle you, surprise you, or even transform you. The answers may lay the groundwork for a life more in tune with your truest self.

So today, grant yourself the time and space to ponder these big questions. Listen to your inner wisdom and your authentic voice, and see where these questions lead you.

Day 301

Noli Timere

Imagine standing on the edge of something new. You're filled with excitement, yes, but also fear. That nagging voice inside tells you all the reasons why you might fail. It paints vivid pictures of all the things that could go wrong. That's when you need to hear those two powerful words: *Noli Timere*. Don't be afraid.

Now, don't get me wrong: Fear itself is not the enemy. In many ways, it's a helpful guide, a signal pointing us towards areas where we might need to grow or change. It can also protect us from real danger. But all too often, fear becomes a wall, an insurmountable barrier that keeps us from moving forward.

What if we used fear not as a stop sign but as a starting point? What if instead of running away from fear, we lean into it, explore it, and understand what it's trying to teach us?

When we say *Noli Timere*, we're not just dismissing our fears; we're choosing to face them with courage and determination. We're choosing to believe in ourselves, in our abilities, and in our dreams. But how do we actually live *Noli Timere*? How do we transform this phrase from a mere saying into a lived philosophy?

Notice when fear creeps in, and rather than pushing it away, invite it in. Ask yourself, "What am I afraid of? What is this fear trying to teach me? How can I grow from this experience?" Then take action. Make a commitment to take one step, no matter how small, in the direction of your dreams.

Noli Timere is not about never feeling fear; it's about not letting fear dictate our lives. It's about having the courage to move forward even when the path is uncertain, trusting that we have the strength and resilience to handle whatever comes our way.

Light Beam of Focus

Imagine your focus as a beam of light. When hitting a prism, it becomes scattered, diffusing its power, illuminating many things but revealing the detail of none. However, when you fine-tune that focus through a magnifying glass, it becomes a laser, piercing through the noise to highlight what matters most.

Both the prism and magnifying glass can be powerful instruments, but both serve vastly different purposes.

Starting something new? Pause. Breathe. Consider the type of focus you need to cultivate to excel. Is it a broad, exploratory focus, casting a wide net to capture many possibilities? Or is it a sharp, concentrated focus, zeroing in on the precise details and techniques that will allow you to master your craft?

This intentionality in your focus can become a superpower. It's a tool you can wield to cut through distractions, deepen your understanding, and build mastery in your pursuits.

Remember, life is a series of moments, and where you direct your focus in each of those moments shapes your journey. Consciously choosing what type of focus and where to aim it is a tool in defining your life.

It Doesn't Cost a Dime

As we reflect on our lives, we notice that some of the most priceless treasures are available to us free of charge. Love, friendship, laughter, a breathtaking sunset, or the simple pleasure of a heartfelt conversation—these gems sparkle with a value that transcends monetary worth, yet they aren't handed to us on a silver platter.

You see, the best things in life might come without a price tag, but they require something far more precious: our time, attention, effort, and often our sacrifice.

Falling in love is free, but maintaining a loving relationship requires continuous effort, understanding, and sometimes giving up our own desires for the sake of our loved ones.

Friendship doesn't cost a dime, but it calls for our presence, empathy, and willingness to stand by a friend even when it's inconvenient.

The beauty of nature is there for all to enjoy, but it demands our respect, care, and commitment to preserving it for future generations.

These beautiful aspects of life are not commodities to be purchased but experiences to be nurtured. They call us to pour our hearts into them and recognize that their true value lies not in their availability but in the depth and quality of our engagement with them.

So let's celebrate these incredible gifts. Let's cherish them, cultivate them, and recognize that while they might be free of charge, they are far from cheap.

Day 304

Between Stimulus & Response

Life is filled with stimuli that provoke reactions from us. Sometimes these stimuli are pleasant and bring joy, but at other times, they present challenges, hurdles, and adversity. Here's where a hidden treasure lies, an uncharted territory that we often overlook: the space between stimulus and response. The space that allows us to choose how we respond.

That brief moment, that pause, is where our real power resides. It's the crucible of choice. We may not have control over what happens to us, but we certainly have control over how we respond to it if we notice the space between.

Catch yourself on the verge of a knee-jerk reaction or when you see a tidal wave of emotion racing towards you. In that instant, detach; take a figurative step back. Breathe in deeply. This deliberate breath is your secret weapon, giving your mind the clarity and time it needs. As you breathe out, create spaciousness in your body and feel your stomach softening. As the air exhales out, visualize the chaos receding.

Then think about the person you want to be in this moment. Ponder, "Do I want this to define my day?" You're at a crossroads: act on impulse or act with intention. Finally, respond in the way that is aligned with who you want to be.

Yes, mastering this is hard, and no one's asking for perfection. But getting better at it? Absolutely doable. Perfection isn't the aim. Progress is.

Because in the end, it's not just about what happens to you — it's about what you do with what happens to you.

Day 305

Sparks of Serendipity

Isn't life a fascinating interplay of unexpected twists and turns? As we glance back over the arc of our existence, the realization begins to emerge that some of our most defining and extraordinary moments are not crafted by careful planning but are instead borne out of serendipity: those unpredictable occurrences that fall into place in the most wonderful way.

Like when you walked into the coffee shop at the exact same moment as the woman you married. You missed your flight, and while waiting in the airport you met your business partner. You were strolling down the street after losing a loved one and someone walks by with a shirt that reads, "They're still with you," and that gives you the strength to go on.

These are not mere coincidences. They're magical alignments, windows of opportunity that open at just the right moment. They remind us that life's tapestry is rich with unexpected beauty and meaning, woven together by the threads of chance and synchronicity.

Embracing serendipity means trusting the process of life even when we can't see where the road is leading. It's about remaining open to the surprises and accepting that sometimes the best things happen when we're not looking for them.

As we move forward, let's not become so fixed on our plans and goals that we miss these sparks of serendipity.

Day 306

Bright Lines

You know those moments when you're on the edge of making a decision, teetering between commitment and compromise? It's in those times that we must summon the concept of "bright lines." This isn't about giving 99%. This is about giving it all, making full commitments, and setting clear and unwavering boundaries.

Imagine bright lines as laser-sharp, resolute markers in the sand. They're not vague or wobbly. They're not negotiable. They're definite lines that we draw to solidify our intentions and goals. They delineate the path of unwavering dedication to a cause.

Why are bright lines so powerful? Because they cut through the murkiness of half-hearted commitment. They eliminate the exhausting cognitive load of "Should I? Shouldn't I?" By drawing bright lines, we free our minds from constant negotiations and dedicate our energy to action, clarity, and determination.

If your goal is to exercise daily, make it a bright line. No excuses, no negotiations, no wavering. That's your line, clear and bold, and you don't cross it.

Remember, it's easy to be swayed and distracted. It's easy to waver and drift. But bright lines keep us anchored. They're our lighthouse, illuminating the way even when the journey gets tough. Draw your bright lines, and let them light the way.

Day 307

The Hidden Cost of Doing Nothing

In our intricate calculations of life, we often dwell on the price tag attached to our actions. A choice made in haste could result in a costly mistake. It's a common narrative we're all familiar with. Yet in the symphony of consequences, there's a less-discussed but equally significant note: the price of inaction.

While the aftermath of our actions is easily seen and felt, the invisible cost of not acting can weave a web of consequences just as intricate and far-reaching. Think of the opportunities left untapped, the moments left unseized, and the dreams deferred. This is where the often-muted toll of inaction chimes in. It's the story of the relationship not pursued, the adventure not embarked upon, the venture not initiated.

While it might not manifest in immediate loss, the accumulation of unseized moments can leave us with a sense of yearning, a lingering what-if echoing in our thoughts. The price of inaction isn't just the absence of results; it's the potential unrealized, the growth stunted, and the roads not taken. Inaction can silently erode our confidence, our sense of agency, and our zest for life.

Acknowledging the price of inaction is not a call to impulsiveness, nor does it diminish the weight of considering our actions carefully. Instead, it's a reminder to recalibrate our perspective; to evaluate not only the cost of action but also the potential toll of not acting.

So as we navigate our choices, let's remember that inaction, too, carries a cost.

Day 308

You Might be Wrong

It's a humbling and perhaps disconcerting realization to recognize that much of what we think in life is untrue. Think back to the many times you were absolutely certain about something only to discover later that you were wrong. Those instances weren't anomalies; they were potent lessons in the fallibility of our own judgments.

In recognizing that we can be wrong even when we think we are right, a door opens. It's a doorway to humility, curiosity, and empathy. We begin to see that our beliefs, as strongly held as they may be, are not infallible truths but rather our interpretations of reality. Embracing this perspective invites us to approach life with an openness, a willingness to listen, question, and learn. It helps us see differing opinions not as threats to our worldview but as opportunities to expand it.

The recognition that we might be wrong doesn't diminish our convictions; it enhances them. It invites us to investigate our beliefs and test them against new information and perspectives. It encourages us to be deliberate in our thinking, open to the possibility of change, and grow from the rich diversity of human experience. This perspective is not just about accepting that we may be wrong. It's about embracing a way of living that prioritizes learning over being right.

So the next time you find yourself in unwavering certainty, remember those moments from the past when you were wrong. Let that memory be a gentle reminder that certainty is not always truth and that wisdom lies in the willingness to question, listen, and grow. After all, it's in the spaces of uncertainty where the greatest learning often resides.

Day 309

Building The Bridge

Friedrich Nietzsche wrote, "No one can construct for you the bridge upon which precisely you must cross the stream of life, no one but you yourself alone." Let that sink in.

Are you looking for a bridge across the roaring chasm of life? You think someone's just going to hand it to you all neat and pre-made? Think again.

You've got your own storms to weather, your own battles to fight, your own demons to conquer. No one else's path is going to match yours. Stop searching for an easy route. Stop hoping for someone to build the bridge for you. Want to do something meaningful? Pick up hammer and nails and start building that bridge.

Your bridge won't look like anyone else's, and it shouldn't. It's *yours*. Your fears, passions, and dreams make up the blueprint. Your failures, triumphs, and sacrifices are the bricks and mortar.

Forget the naysayers, the doubters, the voices that whisper, "You can't." They don't know you. They don't know what you're capable of. And frankly, they don't matter. What matters is you. What are you willing to fight for? What are you willing to bleed for? How far are you willing to go to make your unique mark on this world?

So build that bridge. Make it wild, make it fierce, make it uniquely yours. And when you've crossed to the other side, take a look back and marvel at what you've created.

Because that bridge, with all its flaws and all its beauty, is you. And no one can take that away from you. No one.

Day 310

Choosing Your Perspective

Two people stand side by side gazing at the same sunset. One sees a glorious end to a beautiful day filled with hope and tranquility. The other sees a somber closing, a melancholy reminder of time slipping away. Same sunset, two entirely different experiences.

Life is like that.

We often think our circumstances define us. We believe that the places we visit, the events we encounter, and the things we possess offer us a true reflection of our position in the world. But it's not external factors that truly define our experience; it's the perspective we choose to adopt.

You can be in the most beautiful place on earth and feel miserable, or in the simplest setting and feel pure ecstasy. It's not about where you are; it's about how you see.

This understanding liberates you. It tells you that your happiness, fulfillment, and sense of meaning don't have to hinge on circumstances outside your control. It's rooted in your perspective, attitude, and mindset.

So next time you find yourself facing a metaphorical sunset, remember that you have the power to choose what you see. You can decide your experience. It's a choice, a conscious perspective, and it's entirely in your hands.

See the world not just as it is, but as you choose it to be. That's the real reflection of your position in the world. That's the real power of perspective.

Day 311

What Game Are You Playing?

What game are you playing? It's a question that doesn't often get the attention it deserves. But think about it for a moment. Are you playing a finite or an infinite game?

In the finite game, the rules are clear. It's about winning or losing. There are boundaries, and it's zero-sum. If I win, you lose. It's a game with an endpoint driven by competition and often fueled by ego.

Then there's the infinite game. This one is expansive, without clear winners or losers. It's open-ended; the rules might evolve as the game goes on. The goal isn't to win but to keep playing, growing, learning, and evolving. It's a positive-sum game where my gain doesn't have to mean your loss.

Understanding which type of game you're playing can change everything. If you're locked into a finite-game mindset, you might miss the joy of growth and the fulfillment of contributing to something larger than yourself. You might overlook the profound connections that come from collaboration rather than competition.

But if you choose the infinite game, you open up a world of possibilities. You free yourself from the constraints of win/lose and embrace a perspective that's about continuous development and shared success.

So take a moment to reflect on the game you're playing. If it's finite, ask yourself if it's truly satisfying. If it's infinite, cherish the journey and the ever-evolving nature of the game.

Your life, your rules. Play wisely.

Day 312

Where Dreams Die

At some point, we need to understand that the divide between thinking and doing is where dreams perish.

There's a certain comfort in contemplation, in living within the cozy confines of your plans and visions. But life isn't built in the comfort of our thoughts. Life is out there in the arena, where the action is.

Sure, planning is an important aspect of any endeavor, but there's such a thing as over-planning. Each moment we spend in this state of perpetual planning is a moment lost in actual doing. Each second spent in contemplation is a second not spent in action.

And here's the hard truth: Action is where it happens. Action is where dreams become reality. Action is where ideas become tangible. Action is where plans become accomplishments. There's a magic in the doing, a thrill in the execution, and joy in the realization. It's messy, it's uncertain, and it's risky, but it's also alive, real, and rewarding.

So what's your dream? What's your plan? What's your vision?

Now, what's your action? What's your step? What's your move?

Don't let your goals and dreams perish in the divide between thinking and doing. Don't let them languish in the comfort of contemplation. Take them out into the arena. Take them into the world of action. Take them into the realm of reality. Because that's where they come to life. That's where you come to life.

Day 313

The Proving Ground of Character

Beautifully crafted speeches and ambitious declarations hold little weight without the grinding force of action to solidify them. Words are shadows while actions are substance, casting their undeniable light into the world. Action, not rhetoric, is the proving ground of our character.

Don't merely announce your intent to change or grow — lean into the grueling, raw labor it demands. Recognize that each decision, action, and habit is a chisel striking the stone of your life. Each swing shapes your path and defines your character.

So be relentless in your actions — not just in the grandiose feats but also in the small, daily tasks. Embrace the reality that your actions, not your words, etch the narrative of your life.

What is one action you've been putting off that will get you closer to the life you want to live?

Day 314

You Are a Leader to Someone

True leadership lies not in coercing others to walk in your footsteps but in illuminating a path that empowers them to discover their own way forward. Like a beacon of light, a leader guides with wisdom and inspiration, illuminating the possibilities and potentials that lie ahead.

Instead of imposing their will, they nurture the seeds of individuality and foster growth in others. A genuine leader understands that greatness is not in leading from the front but in empowering others to rise and lead from within. They recognize that true leadership lies not in controlling others but in unleashing their hidden potential. They inspire by example, encouraging those around them to explore, innovate, and chart their unique course towards success and fulfillment.

Always remember you are a leader to someone. Whether it's a colleague, a friend, or a child looking up to you, your influence can spark a flame of confidence that burns brightly not just for a moment but throughout a lifetime.

So be that beacon. Illuminate the path not by dictating the way but by encouraging others to find their unique journey towards success and fulfillment. The path you light today may be the road someone else bravely travels tomorrow.

Day 315

Opportunities

In every moment, life presents us with possibilities that may never reappear. As a mentor once said to me, "Life is full of fleeting opportunities. Are you willing to catch them while they're in front of you?"

Sometimes these opportunities are glaringly obvious, and other times they're subtle, almost hidden. But they're invisible to the person not even looking.

Are your eyes open to the fleeting opportunities in front of you? What possibilities are presenting themselves to you right now? What doors are open at this very moment that may soon close? They're questions worth taking the time to deeply consider.

I discovered that often it's not about finding a definitive answer but more about adopting a mindset: a mindset that's open, looking, curious, and ready to seize opportunities even if they feel a little risky or uncomfortable.

So bring that mindset into your life. Open your eyes. Explore the fleeting opportunities and see what they offer.

Remember, every choice you make shapes your journey. The paths not taken fade into the distance and are replaced by new possibilities and choices. So pay attention to the here and now. Tune into your intuition. Listen to that inner voice that nudges you towards one path or another.

Depersonalizing Challenges and Decisions

Amid the labyrinth of life's challenges and the intricate dance of decision-making, there's a remarkably effective tool that many astute minds wield: the art of depersonalization. It's like putting on a different pair of glasses that allows us to see things from a detached perspective. When we're caught up in the whirlwind of our emotions and thoughts, depersonalization is the lens that brings clarity to the chaos.

Imagine a problem that seems to be closing in on you like a tightening knot. Often, our first instinct is to feel overwhelmed, as if the issue is a part of us. But what if we step back, view it as an outsider might, and break it down objectively? Depersonalization enables this shift. It's realizing that the knot isn't our identity; it's a puzzle to be solved. This approach doesn't diminish the significance of the challenge. It enhances our ability to approach it with a clear mind and a steady heart.

Similarly, when faced with decisions that feel like forks in the road, depersonalization can be a trusted tool. Instead of feeling the weight of every potential outcome, we distance ourselves from the emotional entanglement. We envision ourselves as advisors to our own lives, offering counsel to a dear friend. This distancing offers a broader perspective that enables us to evaluate choices with more clarity and neutrality.

Depersonalization isn't detachment; it's a way of transcending the immediate emotional storm to see the bigger picture. It's about understanding that challenges and decisions are experiences we encounter, but they don't define us. In those moments when dilemmas feel all-consuming, depersonalization offers a lifeline to perspective.

Picture a wise mentor who calmly assesses a situation free from emotional biases. This is the gift we bestow upon ourselves through depersonalization. It's a tool that whispers, "You're not just the challenge, and you're not merely the decision. You're the observer, the navigator, and the sculptor of your journey."

So in the throes of life's complexities, remember the power of depersonalization. Embrace it as a tool that enables you to stand back, see clearly, and make choices with a wisdom beyond the immediacy of the moment.

The Invisible Sign Around Our Necks

M ary Kay Ash, founder of the cosmetics empire, once articulated a profound insight into human nature: "Everyone has an invisible sign hanging from their neck saying, 'Make me feel important.'" It captures an essential yearning we all share — a desire for recognition, validation, and a sense of significance.

It's intriguing how something so apparent can be so easily overlooked. Mary Kay Ash's observation speaks volumes about our shared human experience. We all, in our core, have this quiet plea: "Acknowledge me. See me. Make me feel important."

In navigating the complexities of our daily interactions, imagine if we kept this quote at the forefront of our minds. Every conversation, meeting, and casual encounter becomes an opportunity to make someone feel seen, valued, and significant.

Now, it's not about flattery or inauthentic praise. It's about genuine recognition. Listening a bit more attentively, showing genuine interest in someone's story, or simply being present can make all the difference. They are small gestures that resonate deeply.

As you go about your day, try to read those invisible signs around people's necks. Respond to their silent pleas.

Day 318

Your Word

One word. That's all it takes to set the tone for your day. Imagine waking up each morning and picking one word that will guide you through the next 24 hours. This simple act is more than just an exercise in vocabulary; it's a declaration of intent, a calibration for your day.

Why just one word? Because in simplicity, there is power. In a world filled with noise, distractions, and constant demands on our attention, it's easy to lose sight of what truly matters. By choosing one word, we cut through all the chaos and focus our energy on what's most important.

Think of your word as a guiding light that aligns your thoughts and actions. Let's say you choose the word *momentum*. Throughout the day, you'll find yourself driven to keep moving forward, to build upon the small victories, to keep the energy flowing. Each task completed adds to the momentum, propelling you toward your goals.

And the beauty of this practice? It's fluid. Each day is an opportunity to choose a new word that reflects your current state, goals, challenges, and aspirations. Today, you might need *courage*. Tomorrow, *compassion* might be calling to you. The next day, *creativity* might be your guiding star.

The words change, but the practice remains the same: one word chosen with intention to guide your day. Try it. Tomorrow morning, take a moment to reflect on the day ahead and choose your word. Write it down, make it your phone's wallpaper, or simply hold it in your mind.

Your word is waiting. What will it be?

Day 319

Rise Above

As you step out into the world today, you will undoubtedly encounter individuals whose attitudes are less than savory. They may be rude, disrespectful, or self-centered. However, remember that their behavior is a reflection of their internal struggles, not a judgment of your worth.

Instead of allowing their negativity to affect you, rise above the darkness and be a beacon of light for others. Your strength lies in your ability to remain composed even in the face of adversity.

When the moment arrives — and trust me, it will — that you face someone trying to burden you with their anger, just repeat to yourself: *rise above*.

Rise above anger, hatred, anxiety, stress, tension, fear, and doubt.

These two words become your mantra and guiding light in the face of the inevitable muck that life will throw at you.

In a world filled with shadows, be the one who shines brightly, illuminating the way for those in need.

Day 320

Everything Flows

When I feel the whirlwind of life, I think about the ancient concept of *Panta rhei* — "everything flows." Even in today's complex world, this concept still rings deeply.

The world doesn't pause or wait. Trees grow, tides shift, days turn into nights, and we age. This incessant motion can be beautiful, but it can also feel overwhelming.

In the chaos and flux of life, finding stillness might seem impossible. Yet the key to navigating this ever-changing world lies in something timeless and internal: equanimity.

Equanimity isn't about being emotionless or indifferent. It's about grounding ourselves, finding that inner balance that allows us to see things as they are without being swayed by external forces. It's being centered in ourselves not because the world around us is stable but because we've found stability within.

This doesn't mean we ignore changes or retreat from life. On the contrary, equanimity allows us to fully engage with life — to ebb and flow without being swept away. It empowers us to act with wisdom and clarity no matter what comes our way.

We stay grounded when we are guided by our principles, rooted in our truth, and move ever upward with courage.

Remember, the world will keep moving whether we want it to or not. By finding our calm center, we can move with it, appreciating the beauty of the flow without losing ourselves in the storm.

We All Become Fatigued

E ven the strongest amongst us have moments of fatigue. It's a universal human experience that doesn't discriminate. It's a sign that we are human.

But fatigue doesn't have to be a failure or a finality. It's a gentle nudge from our bodies and minds that we need to pause. It's about recognizing that we need to reset, recover, and renew our energy.

In a culture that often glorifies constant hustle and ceaseless striving, it's easy to overlook the importance of rest. We can get caught up in the race and forget that even the most well-tuned engines need downtime for maintenance.

When we honor our fatigue and give ourselves the necessary time to recuperate, we're not quitting or admitting defeat. We're practicing wisdom. We're acknowledging our human limitations and aligning ourselves with the natural rhythms of life. We're respecting our need for balance and understanding that sustainable success isn't built on burnout.

So if you find yourself feeling fatigued and on the verge of breaking, don't chastise yourself or push through the exhaustion with sheer willpower. Listen to what your body and mind are telling you. Take the time to rest, refuel, and rejuvenate. Embrace the power of pause. And then get back to it even better than before.

Day 322

You Might Fail

You can play it safe. You can stick to the well-trodden path, doing what you're "supposed" to do, even if you hate it. But here's the kicker: You can still fail at that. Even in the realm of the safe and predictable, failure is not just a possibility; it's a fact of life.

So if failure is a given, why not take a chance on something you love? Why not pursue that passion, that dream, that thing that makes your heart sing?

It's a simple yet profound shift in thinking. Instead of avoiding failure, embrace the pursuit of fulfillment. Recognize that if failure is going to happen either way, it might as well be in the service of something that matters to you.

Doing what you love is not a guarantee of success. But it's a guarantee of engagement, meaning, and joy in the process. And isn't that success in itself?

When you pursue what you love, even the failures become part of a beautiful journey — stepping stones on the path to something true and fulfilling. The setbacks aren't just obstacles; they're lessons and experiences, part of the rich tapestry of a life well-lived.

So take that chance. Do what you love. Embrace the possibility of failure not as a deterrent but as a sign that you're on a path worth traveling.

Remember, you're going to spend your life doing something. Why not spend it on something that resonates with your soul? Even if you fail, you'll have lived authentically, passionately, and with purpose. That's not failure; that's success redefined.

Day 323

Navigating Life's Eternal Classroom

It's tempting to think that there's a point in life when you'll have all the answers. We often look at those folks a few steps ahead and think, "They've got it figured out." But here's a little secret: They're probably looking at someone else and thinking the exact same thing.

Life isn't a puzzle to be solved where once all pieces fit, clarity emerges. Instead, it's more like an ever-evolving mosaic.

Each of us is in a perpetual state of learning, unlearning, and relearning. That uncertainty you feel? It's universal. That sense of being lost at times? Everyone feels it, no matter how outwardly confident or accomplished they may seem.

Embracing this truth is liberating. It means it's okay to ask questions and not have all the answers. It's okay to change your mind, to grow, to evolve. It's the natural state of being human. It's what makes each of us unique as we carve our own paths, guided by our own internal compass, learning with each step.

So next time you feel overwhelmed by not having everything figured out, remember you're in good company. Every person you meet is on their journey of discovery, grappling with their questions and seeking their answers.

Let's approach life with the curiosity of a child and the wisdom of an elder, understanding that we're all students in this vast classroom called life. Perhaps the beauty lies not in having all the answers but in the pursuit of the questions.

Day 324

The Power of Patience and Decisiveness

In the realm of extraordinary accomplishments, there's a vital, often overlooked dynamic: the relationship between patience and decisiveness. Together, they form a potent combination.

Patience is not about simply waiting; it's about understanding the value of time. It's a conscious acknowledgment that meaningful progress requires persistence and that good things often need time to unfold. It's the ability to stay committed and unwavering even when the path seems slow or uncertain.

Decisiveness, on the other hand, is about swift and confident action. In a world filled with endless possibilities and distractions, the ability to make decisions quickly and with conviction is invaluable. It's the catalyst that turns opportunities into realities, ensuring we're moving forward even in the face of adversity.

Balancing these two is key. Excessive patience can lead to missed chances while unchecked decisiveness might see us acting rashly without adequate thought. The journey to unparalleled results doesn't rely solely on continuous action or perpetual waiting. Instead, it's about discerning when to reflect, plan, and be patient, and when to act with purpose and determination.

So as you strive for your goals, remember to let patience give depth to your aspirations, offering them stability and endurance. Simultaneously harness the power of decisiveness to fuel your actions, making sure every step you take is meaningful.

Day 325

We All Have Something

We've all been in those moments when it feels like our abilities are outmatched by the circumstance — where we feel we have nothing to offer, nothing to contribute, or nothing to add.

But what I've seen countless times is that this is never really the case. We all always have something.

That "something" is your unique strength, your individual gift, your special talent. And sure, at times it's hidden or seemingly unavailable, but it's always there.

Maybe the situation seems too big or the people far outmatch our abilities. The situation may be big and the people may have abilities that exceed yours, but the truth is that you still have something to contribute.

Maybe it's your ability to connect with others, or perhaps it's a creative skill, passion, or even a perspective that only you hold. Whatever it may be, this "something" is valuable. It's authentically yours.

Your "something" isn't just a part of you. It's a part of the world's tapestry, waiting for your attention, ready to be woven into something bigger. So focus on your something. Cultivate it, treasure it, share it. It's where your true wealth lies.

When the world is wearing you down and you feel you have nothing to add, remember that you always do.

Day 326

Walking the Right Path

Sometimes we find ourselves on a path we never intended to walk down. Whether through societal expectations, pressure from others, or simply a wrong turn, we may continue down this path out of fear, commitment, or confusion. But deep down, something gnaws at us, whispering that this is not the way.

It's hard to stop walking, especially if we've been on this path for a long time. Admitting that we've been going in the wrong direction can feel like failure or defeat. But sometimes, the most courageous step we can take is not another step forward but the step of stopping altogether.

Stopping doesn't mean failure; it means wisdom. It means listening to that inner voice that's been trying to get our attention to tell us that something isn't right. It means honoring ourselves enough to say, "This path isn't for me," and having the courage to turn around.

It can feel like starting over, unsure and inexperienced. But when we are climbing the right mountain, the entire journey feels different. It's not just about reaching the summit but enjoying the views along the way, relishing each step because we know it's where we're meant to be.

Listen to your inner wisdom. Feel if your steps are in alignment with your heart's true desire. If they're not, have the courage to stop and reassess. You're not lost; you're just on the way to finding the right path. And remember, it's not about how fast you get there but the authenticity and joy with which you travel.

Day 327

Living on Borrowed Time, Learning for Eternity

I found a quote from Gandhi tucked in one of my old journals: "Live as if you were to die tomorrow. Learn as if you were to live forever." It's powerful, isn't it?

Imagine waking up and truly absorbing the weight of those words. The immediacy, the urgency of "live for today" paired with the infinite curiosity of "learn for a lifetime." It's a contrasting philosophy, yet it feels so harmonious.

To live as if today were your last isn't about recklessness but rather richness. It's the vibrant colors, the loud laughs, the deep connections. It's about not letting fear dictate your steps. Live fully, embracing every moment and holding nothing back.

Then there's learning as if you were to live forever. The world is vast, filled with infinite wonders, cultures, perspectives, and lessons. Dive deep into the rabbit hole of knowledge. Chase the thrill of not knowing, the joy of discovery, and the humbling moments when you realize how much more there is to grasp.

This dual approach means you're not just amassing facts; you're absorbing life. Every interaction is a lesson. Every moment is an opportunity.

So let's take Gandhi's words to heart. Live passionately today, and stay endlessly curious for all your tomorrows.

Day 328

Today I Will

There's an incredible power that resides in the words "Today, I will." They're not just words; they're a pledge, a commitment to oneself. They represent a declaration to the universe that today, you're taking the reins.

You're saying, "Here I am, world. Ready and unwavering."

Today I will:

- Stand tall.

- Speak my truth.

- Show humility.

- Share my gifts.

- Shine bright.

- Strengthen others.

I'm going to make today a great day.

Remember, making today a great day isn't a chance event; it's a choice. Embrace that choice, seize the moment, and shape your destiny with intention. Today, you've decided that greatness is your only option.

Day 329

Your Thoughts Are Self-Fulfilling Prophecies

Your mind's a trickster, you know. It whispers things about you, shaping your reality in subtle ways. "I'm not good enough," "I can't do this," "I'm destined to fail." These thoughts, like tiny architects, build the foundations of your reality.

But here's where it gets interesting: those whispers? They're not truths; they're choices. They're self-fulfilling prophecies.

You tell yourself you can't, so you don't. You say you'll fail, so you do. Like planting a seed and watching it grow, the thoughts you cultivate determine the harvest of your life.

But flip it around, and the power's just as potent. Believe you can, and you're halfway there. Trust in your talent and your worth and watch as doors swing open and opportunities unfold.

Your thoughts about yourself are like a mirror reflecting your potential back to you. If it's clouded by doubt, all you'll see is obscurity. But polish it with belief, and the view is breathtaking.

Choose your thoughts wisely. Let them be a guiding light, not a shadow of doubt. Because in the end, you become what you think, and that's a prophecy worth fulfilling.

Day 330

The Genius Within

We often associate the word *genius* with extraordinary talents, intellectual feats, or prodigious abilities. We point to the mathematicians, the chess masters, the musical savants, and exclaim, "There's a genius!" And yes, those are forms of genius, incredible manifestations of human capability.

But let's take a moment to delve into the very essence of the word. The origin of *genius* comes from Latin, referring to an "attendant spirit present from one's birth." It's a beautiful notion that shifts our perspective on what genius truly means.

This inner genius isn't about performing an intellectual feat or demonstrating unparalleled skill in a specific field. It's about listening, recognizing, and embracing that inner spirit that resides within us. It's a form of knowing: an innate wisdom and a connection to our authentic selves. This genius is universal, and it's accessible to all of us.

Think about those times when you've had a sudden insight, a moment of clarity, or a burst of creativity. That's your inner genius speaking, the guidance that's been with you since birth, nudging you in the right direction.

When you tap into this inner genius, you're not trying to be the best in the world; you're trying to be your best *for* the world, contributing your unique voice.

So don't be daunted by thinking that the traditional notion of genius is reserved for the elite few. Embrace your inner genius, the wisdom and intuition that's been with you all along. Listen to it, honor it, and let it guide you. Genius merely articulates what your heart already knows. Trust in that, and you'll find the path that's uniquely yours.

Day 331

Individuality & Connectedness

The interplay between individuality and connectedness defines our human experience. Our individuality gives us a unique voice, empowering us to contribute our distinctive strengths, thoughts, and ideas. It's what sets us apart, fuels our creativity, and drives our passion.

Connectedness, on the other hand, ties us to the greater community of humanity. It's the recognition that we are part of something bigger, something beyond ourselves. It's the understanding that our actions, no matter how small, have an impact on others, shaping the world in which we live.

Striking the right balance between these two forces is like walking a tightrope. Lean too far toward individuality and we risk becoming isolated, losing touch with the very relationships that give life meaning. Lean too far toward connectedness and we risk losing ourselves, our voice drowned out by the cacophony of the crowd.

To walk this tightrope with grace, we must first recognize the value of both our individuality and our connectedness. Our individuality is our strength, our spark, our essence. It's what makes us who we are, and it's what allows us to contribute something unique to the world. Our connectedness is our anchor, our grounding force. It's what reminds us that we are not alone, that we are part of a group, a family, a community. It's what binds us together, creating a sense of belonging, of unity.

It's about knowing who we are and what we stand for while also recognizing the needs and desires of others. It's about speaking our truth while also listening with empathy and compassion. It's a delicate balance, but it's one that we can achieve. And when we do, we find our place in the world.

Day 332

Your Self-Concept

Your self-concept is like the central character in the story of your life. It's your internal answer to the question, "Who am I?" and it informs your every thought, decision, and interaction. Your self-concept guides how you do everything in life.

What's fascinating is that you can choose the character traits and values you want to embody, but often people don't consciously choose. They let their past experiences or other people's opinions define who they are. Then they wonder why they feel stuck, frustrated, or unfulfilled.

So how do you take control of your self-concept? How do you shape it into something empowering that aligns with who you truly want to be?

Start by taking an honest look at how you currently perceive yourself. Do you see yourself as confident or timid? Creative or unoriginal? Compassionate or indifferent? Recognize that these are not fixed truths but choices you are making.

Then ask yourself, "Who do I want to be? What qualities do I want to embody?" List the traits that resonate with your highest self. Don't be shy. This is your chance to define your own character in the story of your life.

Now here comes the transformational part: Start acting like the person you want to become. Embody those chosen traits in your daily life. Speak, think, and act as if you are already that person. This isn't faking it. It's consciously choosing who you are and bringing that choice to life.

The more you align your thoughts, words, and actions with this chosen self-concept, the more it becomes your reality. The world responds to you differently. Opportunities align with your new identity. Your relationships reflect the person you've chosen to become.

Your self-concept is not a static thing. It's dynamic, evolving, and entirely in your control. The key lies in recognizing the power of this guiding concept and taking the reins to shape it consciously.

Day 333

Long-Term Games With Long-Term People

Life is filled with opportunities to play games. I'm not talking about board games or sports, but the strategic games we play in life, business, and relationships. Many people approach these games with a short-term mentality. They're looking to win now no matter the cost. But there's a different way to play, a more rewarding and fulfilling approach: Play long-term games with long-term people.

A long-term game isn't about immediate victory or instant gratification. It's about building something that lasts, something that grows and evolves over time. It's about planting seeds and nurturing them, trusting that they will eventually blossom into something beautiful. This kind of game requires patience, commitment, and a willingness to put in the work even when the rewards are far off in the distance.

To play a long-term game, you need long-term people. These are the people who share your vision and values, who are willing to invest in something that may not pay off for years or even decades. They're people who are trustworthy and reliable and will stick with you through the ups and downs, the triumphs and failures.

Playing long-term games with long-term people isn't easy. It requires a different kind of mindset. You have to be willing to sacrifice short-term gains for long-term rewards. You have to be patient and persistent even when progress is slow.

So as you navigate the games of life, consider the long-term approach. Look for opportunities to invest in something that will last. Because in the end, the most rewarding games are the ones that take time to play, and the most valuable players are the ones who are in it for the long run.

Day 334

The Sisyphean Task

There's a fruitless endeavor that many of us engage in, sometimes without even realizing it: trying to shape-shift into the constantly shifting image others have of us. It's like trying to hit a moving target while blindfolded.

Consider this: Every individual you encounter comes with their own set of beliefs, biases, and baggage. Their opinions, judgments, and expectations are fluid and influenced by countless factors, many of which are fleeting or superficial. If you try to mold yourself to meet each of these standards, you're setting yourself up for a dizzying dance — one where you're always one step behind.

The irony? Even if you manage to contort yourself perfectly into someone's vision of you today, tomorrow brings a new perspective and a different opinion. This Sisyphean effort not only drains you but disconnects you from your true self.

The real tragedy unfolds when you start mirroring these external judgments internally. In trying to appease every external voice, you might begin to berate your own for not measuring up. This internal discord can lead you down a path where you no longer recognize or like the person staring back in the mirror.

The antidote is simple, though not always easy: Ground yourself in your own values, your own beliefs, and your own vision of who you want to be. It's okay to listen, understand, and even consider others' opinions. But let these be inputs, not impositions. At the end of the day, the only standards you need to live up to are your own.

Day 335

The Power of Focus

One evening, amidst gleaming chandeliers and an aroma of delectable cuisine, Bill Gates Sr. played host to a congregation of the world's finest minds. As conversation flowed, he posed an intriguing question, curious about the secret elixir of their towering success. "What single factor," he asked, "do you attribute your achievements to?"

There was a split second of contemplative silence, and then in harmonious synchrony, both Bill Gates and Warren Buffett exclaimed, "Focus!"

That word, so simple and yet so potent, holds within it the crux of unparalleled success. In our journey, we often find ourselves ensnared in the vastness of possibility, scattering our energies like rays of the early morning sun, diffused and widespread.

What if instead of being the sun, we chose to be the magnifying glass, concentrating those rays into a singular, powerful beam? That's what focus is. It's not just about paying attention but about aligning every ounce of our being — every thought and every action — toward our ultimate goal.

No matter how grand, dreams can be elusive phantoms if we allow our pursuit of them to branch out aimlessly. To capture them and turn them from wisps of imagination into tangible reality requires the art of focused determination.

Like Gates and Buffett, whose success stories resonate across the globe, let us embrace this powerful mantra. Let's narrow our gaze, channel our energies, and set our sights unflinchingly on our ambitions. Because when focus becomes our ally, the extraordinary becomes our reality.

Day 336

Infuse Meaning into Work

I was sitting across from a mentor of mine, and I could sense another one of his profound insights brewing. He leaned in, narrowing his gaze, and said, "Give meaning to the work people are doing because if work has meaning, it is never trivial."

The weight of that statement settled in, echoing with truth. Most of us have felt the twinge of monotony in our jobs — moments when tasks feel redundant or when the purpose behind an assignment seems elusive.

Yet what my mentor illuminated is the intrinsic value hidden in every task and role. It's not always about the physical output but the deeper significance behind it.

Think of it this way: A painter isn't just adding colors to a canvas. They're capturing a moment, evoking emotions, and sharing a perspective. Similarly, a janitor isn't merely cleaning; they're creating a safe, welcoming space for others.

As leaders, it's our role to help individuals connect with this deeper purpose. It's about shifting the focus from the task itself to its impact, its larger contribution to the whole. When people understand the *why* behind their work, they don't just complete tasks; they contribute to a vision.

So whether you're leading a team, guiding a mentee, or finding your own place in the world, remember: Work, in its truest essence, is never just about the job at hand. It's about understanding, appreciating, and communicating the greater meaning behind every effort. Then work becomes an act of purpose and an expression of passion. And with meaning, nothing is ever trivial.

Bad Things Happen Fast, Good Things Happen Slow

L ife has a funny way of catching us off guard. Bad things can happen fast. A sudden turn of events can change everything in an instant. Setbacks, failure, or loss can hit us like a storm, leaving us to grapple with their aftermath.

But when you turn your attention to the good things in life, you'll notice a different pattern. Almost all good things happen slowly. They require time, patience, effort, and persistence. Whether it's building a meaningful relationship, growing a business, mastering a skill, or any other worthwhile pursuit, good things don't happen overnight.

Why is that? Perhaps it's because good things often require us to grow, to stretch beyond our current abilities, to learn and adapt. Growth takes time. It requires a steady, consistent effort.

If you're feeling frustrated because success is taking longer than you'd like, remember that you're in good company. Every meaningful achievement takes time to develop. It's the gradual stacking of effort upon effort that leads to something beautiful and lasting. These things cannot be rushed. They unfold in their own time with a grace and a pace that can't be forced.

So don't be disheartened by the slow pace of progress. Embrace it. Recognize that the journey itself is where the real magic happens. Keep your eyes on the long game, keep nurturing the good, and trust that the best things in life are worth the time they take to blossom.

No One Owes You Anything

In life, it's easy to fall into the trap of feeling entitled, as though the world owes us something. We might think that others should treat us a certain way or that success should come more easily. But embracing a sense of entitlement can lead to disappointment and frustration.

A more empowering approach is to recognize that no one owes you anything. When you take full responsibility for your own life and stop expecting others to give you what you want, something remarkable happens. You become the driving force of your own destiny. You act with purpose and determination, knowing that it's up to you to make things happen.

This doesn't mean you shouldn't ask for help or collaborate with others. It means approaching relationships with an attitude of mutual respect and contribution rather than demand or expectation.

When you operate from a place of self-reliance and personal responsibility, you tap into a profound source of strength and autonomy. You recognize that your success, happiness, and fulfillment are in your hands. You approach others with gratitude rather than expectation and engage with life as an active participant rather than a passive recipient.

By acknowledging that no one owes you anything, you free yourself from dependence on external validation or assistance. You empower yourself to pursue your goals with tenacity and resilience.

Stop holding others accountable to give you what only you can earn. Don't wait for others to give you what you want. Go out there and make it happen for yourself.

Day 339

Want to Grow? It Starts With This

P rogress is a compelling force in our lives. It's what drives us to learn, grow, and strive for something better. But at the heart of progress lies a fundamental truth: Progress is impossible without change.

We often think of change as something external that happens to us or around us. But the most profound change, the one that leads to real progress, starts within. It starts with changing our minds. Those who cannot change their minds cannot change anything.

If you cling to a belief, a method, or a way of seeing the world, you create a barrier to growth. You lock yourself into a fixed position, unable to move forward. But when you open your mind, allowing new information and new perspectives to shape your thinking, you unlock a pathway to progress.

The ability to change your mind is a skill, and like any skill, it can be developed. It requires curiosity, humility, and courage: curiosity to explore new ideas, humility to recognize that you don't have all the answers, and courage to admit when you're wrong or when you need to shift your thinking.

So embrace change not just as something that happens in the world around you but as a vital part of your own growth and development.

Progress is impossible without change. And the most powerful change starts with you.

Day 340

Their Dying Words

You go to the hospital to sit by the bed of a dying loved one, someone who's lived a long life. But what hits you is what comes out of their mouth. Their voice trembles as they tell you about the aspirations they never chased, the chances they never took, and the life they never lived. They speak of the what-ifs and if-onlys that now plague their thoughts, lamenting opportunities lost to complacency and conformity. The pain in their eyes is unmistakable, a tangible testament to the tragedy of a life lived in the shadows of unfulfilled potential.

As you sit there absorbing their story, something profound shifts within you. You begin to see your own life through a different lens. Their regrets become a mirror reflecting your own choices, dreams, and hesitations. You realize that their story could be your story if you allow fear and doubt to guide your path.

But then, with newfound clarity and determination, you make a silent vow to yourself. You decide that you will not let their regrets become your destiny. You will pursue your dreams with relentless passion and unwavering conviction. You will take risks, embrace challenges, and honor the calling that stirs your soul.

This one conversation becomes a turning point, a moment of awakening that forever changes how you think about your life. It serves as a poignant reminder that life is fleeting and that dreams deferred can become dreams denied.

You walk away from that conversation with a fire ignited within you, a fire fueled by the wisdom of someone who knows the true cost of not living fully. You now know that to honor your life means to honor your dreams.

Day 341

How Are You Spending Your Time?

Time is our most precious resource. It's the currency we spend on our lives and the investment that shapes our experiences, relationships, skills, and legacy. Everything we have, everything we know, and everything we are is a result of how we've chosen to spend our time.

But unlike money, fame, or possessions, time is finite. We can't earn more of it no matter how hard we try. What we can do, however, is spend our time better.

We often protect our material possessions with great care. We secure our money, our homes, and our gadgets, thinking they are vital to our well-being. But the truth is, we can figure out how to get more of everything we protect so dearly just by spending our time better.

Think about it: By investing time in learning, you gain knowledge and skills that lead to better opportunities. By dedicating time to relationships, you nurture connections that enrich your life. By focusing on what truly matters, you can create more value, more joy, and more meaning.

Remember, you have the power to shape your life by the way you spend your time. Use it wisely, invest it in what truly matters, and watch how everything else falls into place.

So the question is: How are you spending your time? Are you investing it in what truly matters to you, or are you letting it slip away on things that won't serve you in the long run?

Day 342

A Haunting Loss

Imagine waking up tomorrow to find that the person you love most in the world is no longer there for you. Feel that emptiness, that gaping void where warmth and connection once thrived. It's a thought that can pierce your heart, taking your breath away.

But instead of shying away from this gut-wrenching idea, let it serve as a poignant reminder. Let it bring into sharp focus the value of the present moment and the people we hold dear.

We often get caught up in the hustle and grind of daily life. We take for granted the smiles, the touch, the shared laughter, and the simple presence of those we love. But life's fragile nature reminds us that every moment is precious and every interaction a treasure. Every moment in the future isn't guaranteed.

So today and every day, let's make a conscious effort to cherish those we love. Let's not wait for birthdays, anniversaries, or special occasions to express our feelings. Let's make love a daily practice.

Look into their eyes a little longer. Hold their hand a little tighter. Speak words that uplift, encourage, and celebrate them. Make the time to be truly present with them. Show them through every word and action how much they mean to you.

And if you're holding on to any grudges or misunderstandings, let them go. Life is too short and too unpredictable to let petty differences stand in the way of love.

Day 343

When You're Going Through Hell

S ometimes life throws you into situations so difficult that they feel like a metaphorical hell. Whether it's a gut-wrenching diagnosis, a professional setback, or an emotional hardship, these moments can test your strength, resolve, and character.

But here's the thing: If you find yourself walking through hell, walk through it like you own the place.

What does that mean? It means to embody a sense of authority, confidence, and command even in the midst of adversity. It's about recognizing that you have the inner power to navigate the flames and come out on the other side stronger, wiser, and more resilient.

It's about standing tall, looking the challenge in the eye, and declaring, "I've got this." It's about refusing to be a victim and choosing instead to be the hero of your own story.

Adopt a mindset that says, "I'm not just surviving this; I'm thriving through it." And do it with grace, poise, and unshakable self-belief.

So if you find yourself in a tough spot, remember that you have a choice in how you approach it. You can cower and complain, or you can stride forward with the assuredness of someone who knows they can handle whatever comes their way.

If you're going to walk through hell, do it with the conviction and courage that leaves no doubt that you're not just passing through; you own the place.

Day 344

Calm is Contagious

Imagine walking into a room filled with chaos, noise, and confusion. People are arguing, phones are ringing, and there's an unsettling feeling of tension in the air. Then someone enters the room exuding a sense of calm. They speak softly, move gracefully, and carry a sense of peace. Slowly, the room starts to change. Voices lower, movements slow, and the chaos begins to subside.

Calm is contagious.

It's not just a nice saying. It's a truth that you can observe in families, workplaces, and even in yourself. When you interact with someone who is truly calm, you can feel your own heart rate slowing down, your thoughts becoming clearer, and your emotions settling.

Why is this? Calm communicates control not in a domineering way but in a reassuring one. It says, "I've got this." It communicates confidence, not arrogance, and a quiet assurance that everything will be all right.

Being calm doesn't mean you're indifferent or disconnected. It means you're present, focused, and in control of your emotions. It means you're responsive, not reactive. Calm isn't just a state of mind; it's a skill, a practice, and a choice. It's something you can cultivate in yourself and spread to others.

So the next time you find yourself in the midst of chaos, remember: Calm is contagious. You can be the calm in the storm and the beacon in the fog.

And who knows? You might just change the room.

Day 345

The You You've Been Ignoring

Who is the you inside you that's been yearning to be seen? That authentic self is not just a whisper or a fleeting thought; it's the core of your being. It's the unbridled passion, the untamed curiosity, and the unquenchable longing for something more.

Why do we ignore this authentic self? It's often because we're afraid. We fear what others might think or how they might react. We worry that we're not enough and we might fail or be judged. So we build walls and wear masks, losing touch with the very essence that makes us unique.

But consider this: What if you embraced that authentic self? What if you started listening to that inner voice, honoring its wisdom and taking its guidance seriously?

Imagine living a life that resonates with your deepest truths. Imagine pursuing dreams that fill you with purpose and joy. Imagine relationships that are authentic, nurturing, and fulfilling. All of this becomes possible when you reconnect with the you inside you that you've been ignoring.

Start by listening. What does that inner voice have to say? What passions has it been urging you to explore? What truths has it been begging you to embrace? Next, take action. Align your life with those inner whispers. Dare to take the steps your authentic self has been guiding you toward. Take the plunge.

Remember, the you inside you isn't a stranger. It's the purest, most genuine version of you. So don't ignore it any longer. It's time to live your truth.

What Matters is How Much You Love Doing It

People often ask, "What's the secret to becoming the best?" Scan through the greats in any domain, and you'll find a common thread. It's not always raw talent or even sheer willpower. It's love. They're utterly enamored with what they do.

You see, it's easy to assume it's all about discipline or grit, and sure, those play a part. But at the heart of true mastery lies a deep-seated love for the craft. It's that quiet joy that keeps them practicing when others might quit. It's the genuine curiosity that drives them to dig deeper long after others are satisfied.

Loving the process is the real game-changer. When you love it, 10,000 hours don't feel like a grind; they're just the playground. And in that playground, amidst trials, errors, and small wins, greatness takes root.

The world's best aren't just working. They're playing, exploring, and delighting in every nuance.

So if you're chasing mastery, ask yourself: "Do I love this?" Because in that love lies the difference between the good and the truly great.

Day 347

The Jungle

You're standing there facing a daunting jungle, feeling the call of something wild and unknown. It's a metaphorical crossroad, but it feels real enough to touch. In your gut, it resonates, doesn't it?

To one side, the known: predictable, comfortable, safe. It's the path of least resistance, a well-trodden trail where most linger, never knowing what lies beyond the lush trees.

But then there's the other side. The wild terrain of possibility. That's where the magic happens: where ordinary is shed like a second skin and extraordinary is embraced.

That jungle, with all its unknowns and possibilities, is calling to you, and it doesn't just call once. It's a persistent whisper in the quiet moments, an echoing roar in the triumphs and failures. The question keeps coming back: Will you take the risk? Will you journey into the wilds of possibility?

It's more than a whimsical choice. It's about recognizing that within you is a force, a burning passion, and a desire for something more. It's about not settling for less than you are capable of, even when the well-worn path seems easier or more secure. It's about understanding that the uncertainty of the unknown is where growth happens and transformation occurs.

As you stand on that precipice, you're not alone. Your dreams and aspirations, the very core of who you are, stand with you. They know the potential within, and they cry out for you to embrace it. They know that within that jungle lie treasures of experience, wisdom, and self-discovery.

But they also know the price.

To venture into that jungle requires courage, determination, and resilience. There will be moments of doubt and fear. There will be obstacles and setbacks. You will face your own demons and confront your own limitations. But that's where the alchemy of self-transformation occurs.

By daring to step into the unknown, forge your path, and embrace both the triumphs and the struggles, you become something more. You shed the constraints of mediocrity and allow yourself to become the person you were meant to be.

So as you stand there with the world's possibilities laid out before you, listen to that call. Feel it in your bones. Understand that this is your life, your story, and you are the author.

Are you ready to write something breathtaking?

The jungle awaits. Your adventure begins now. Will you venture forth?

How Life's Defeats Can Shape a Positive Future

We've all felt it: the gut-wrenching agony of defeat, the stinging bitterness of a missed opportunity, or the overwhelming despair that follows a great loss. These feelings are intense and consuming, sometimes feeling like they'll never fade.

But here's a perspective that might help you see these moments differently: What if these painful experiences are not merely setbacks or failures? What if they are the seeds of a profound transformation and the soil necessary for personal growth and evolution?

When we are in the midst of suffering, it's hard to imagine that anything positive could come from it. But life has a peculiar way of turning our most agonizing experiences into our most enlightening lessons.

I'm not trying to romanticize pain or minimize its impact. The suffering is real, and it can be all-consuming. However, if we can step back and view these moments not as the end of a journey but as a turning point, we may find hidden treasures within them.

Think back to a time in your life when you faced significant adversity, a moment that felt unbearable. Now, with the benefit of hindsight, can you see how that moment might have shaped you? Did it teach you resilience, empathy, or a new understanding of yourself? Did it force you to reevaluate your values, redirect your path, or connect with others in a more meaningful way?

These painful experiences often compel us to ask deeper questions — to dig into the core of who we are and what we want from life. They push us out of our comfort zones and challenge our preconceived notions. They force us to grow in ways we might never have imagined.

And while the transformation may not be immediate, over time these defeats or missed opportunities can become the catalysts for significant change. They can lead to new careers, relationships, or personal revelations that shape our lives in extraordinary ways.

This is not to say that we should seek out suffering or relish our pain. Rather, it's about recognizing the potential for growth within our most challenging experiences and being open to the lessons they may offer.

It's about cultivating a mindset that sees adversity not as a dead end but as a detour that might lead us to a more fulfilling and purpose-driven path.

If you find yourself in a place of pain or defeat right now, know that you are not alone. Also know that this moment could be a pivotal one, a turning point that may someday be seen as the catalyst for something beautiful in your life.

Allow yourself to grieve, to feel, and to heal. But also hold space for the possibility that this experience might be more than just suffering. It could be the beginning of something new, something meaningful, something that will change you for the better.

Remember, today's defeat may be tomorrow's triumph.

Day 349

A Life Without Fear

Close your eyes and envision the life you would lead if fear didn't hold you back. What action would you take today? What dreams would you have? What mindsets would you embrace?

Feel the exhilaration and sense of freedom that surges through your veins. Embrace that version of yourself: the one unbound by limitations and hesitations.

Today, take a step towards that fearless vision. Allow your heart's desires to guide you. Let go of the doubts that have held you captive for too long. Be courageous, be bold, and take that step towards your unbounded potential.

Remember, fear is merely an illusion that can be conquered with a single act of bravery.

Each day, commit to taking one more action step without fear.

As you consistently push through the barriers of fear, you will witness a profound shift within yourself. With each step, you become a person who fearlessly pursues their dreams, unyielding in the face of obstacles.

The journey towards fearlessness is not about eliminating fear entirely, but rather about mastering the art of moving forward despite its presence.

Commit to taking daily action steps, and soon you'll look back and marvel at how far you've come on your way toward becoming a fearless soul.

When you put down this book today, immediately do one thing that you would do in a world where you're not held back by fear.

Day 350

Deflating the Stress Balloon

We've all been there: the weight of the world seemingly on our shoulders and stress piling up, looming like an ever-expanding balloon ready to burst. But what if there was a simple method to release that pressure slowly and steadily?

Enter the stress balloon technique. Picture a balloon bloated with every ounce of your stress. Each worry, tension, and challenge inflates it. Daunting, isn't it? But here's the beauty: You hold the power to release that air.

With every inhale, imagine drawing in clarity, calmness, and resilience. Feel the air nurturing you. With each exhale, envision a stream of air leaving the balloon, making it smaller and more manageable. As you release your breath, release your stress into the universe, letting it dissipate.

In, out. Draw in calmness, let out tension. Slowly, the balloon deflates, and so does the weight on your heart and mind.

This isn't just an exercise in visualization. It's a lesson in self-regulation, a realization of your inherent strength. It's a reminder that no matter the weight of your burdens, you have the capacity to let them go — not by ignoring them, but by addressing them, managing them, and keeping them in perspective.

The next time the world feels heavy, remember your stress balloon. Acknowledge it, face it, and take control. Breathe in, breathe out, and watch as you deflate the challenges before you, reclaiming your peace and your power.

Day 351

Your Future is Calling

Today, zoom out and take some time to ponder. Look around at your daily routine, habits, relationships, work, passions, and dreams. Now project that image 20 years into the future.

If you continue living in the same way, what does that future look like? Are you excited by what you see? Is there a sense of fulfillment, joy, and alignment with your deepest values? Do you see yourself thriving, growing, and contributing to something larger than yourself? If so, you're on a path that resonates with who you want to be. Keep going!

But if that future vision feels stagnant, uninspiring, or misaligned with your core values, don't ignore it. It's a signal, a gentle nudge to reassess your direction.

It's easy to get caught up in the inertia of life, letting days turn into months and months into years without ever stopping to question if we're on the path that's truly meant for us. But your future is not set in stone. It's constantly evolving and being woven together by the choices you make today.

So if that 20-year vision doesn't excite you, ask yourself what needs to change. What can you do differently? What small steps can you take today that will steer your life toward a future that feels alive, purposeful, and true to who you are?

The power to shape that future lies within you. Reflect on your path, trust your intuition, and don't be afraid to make the choices that align with your true self.

Your future is calling. How will you answer?

Which Wolf Will You Feed?

There's an old story called The Tale of Two Wolves. An old Cherokee chief was teaching his grandson about life. "A fight is going on inside me," he said to the boy. "It is a terrible fight between two wolves. One is evil — he is anger, envy, sorrow, regret, greed, arrogance, self-pity, guilt, resentment, inferiority, lies, false pride, superiority, and ego."

He continued, "The other is good. He is joy, peace, love, hope, serenity, humility, kindness, benevolence, empathy, generosity, truth, compassion, and faith. The same fight is going on inside you and inside every other person, too."

The grandson thought about it for a minute and then asked his grandfather, "Which wolf will win?"

The old chief replied, "The one you feed."

This lesson is a stark reminder of the duality present within each of us and the power of our choices. Every day, we're presented with countless decisions, thoughts, and actions that can feed either the good wolf or the bad one.

It's easy to be swayed by our emotions, act out of impulse, or be influenced by external pressures. But this tale brings to the forefront a fundamental truth: The essence of our character is shaped by the deliberate choices we make daily.

Thinking about the two wolves isn't just about recognizing this inner struggle; it's a call to mindful action. Each morning as we embark on a new day, we should ask ourselves: "Which wolf will I choose to feed today?"

Day 353

Living With Full Aliveness

What would you have to do in order to feel greater aliveness today?

It's a deceptively simple question, yet one that can guide you to the core of what it means to be truly alive.

Aliveness isn't about grand gestures or extraordinary achievements. It's found in the essence of living authentically, engaging with life wholeheartedly, and embracing the present moment. It's the spark that lights up your eyes, the passion that stirs your soul, and the joy that fills your heart.

The pursuit of aliveness isn't a one-time event. It's an ongoing exploration, a conscious choice to engage with life in a way that resonates with your unique being. It's a commitment to listen to the inner voice that knows what makes you feel most alive and honor it with action.

So ask yourself, today and every day, "What would I have to do to feel greater aliveness today?" Then follow the answer with curiosity, courage, and an open heart, and watch as your life transforms into a vibrant tapestry of experiences filled with the richness of being fully alive.

Day 354

Tombstone

Here's an intriguing thought experiment that can deeply influence the trajectory of your life. Imagine your tombstone standing firm against the test of time. If it could only have one line to capture the essence of your life, what would that line be?

A tombstone, in its quiet and unassuming way, tells a story. It marks the existence of someone who once laughed, cried, loved, and lived. In just one line, it communicates the legacy of a lifetime. What do you want yours to say?

"Devoted mother and selfless friend"? "A catalyst for change"? "Lived with fearless authenticity"?

This isn't about crafting a catchy phrase or being remembered by the masses. It's a deeply personal reflection on the life you wish to lead and the life you will lead.

So take a moment. Sit in silence. Listen to that inner voice, and ask yourself: What one line would genuinely encapsulate the essence of who I am and aspire to be?

Now, here's the important bit: Don't wait for the end to let that line define you. Start today. Let that one line be your North Star, guiding every choice, action, and interaction. Shape your days, mold your relationships, and influence your decisions with that guiding principle.

Remember, it's not about predicting the future; it's about crafting the present. Live that one line every day.

Day 355

The Big Five

L ife is vast, chaotic, and full of options. With infinite choices before us, how do we prioritize our time and energy? Enter what I like to call the Big Five: The five things I'm committed to spend my life enriching.

The Big Five isn't about hobbies or short-lived passions. It's about those few pursuits that resonate with your soul and make the world blur into the background because of their significance. These are the pursuits that, if ignored, would leave a void in your life's narrative. They might be dreams you've held since childhood, missions that give you a purpose, or the people whose well-being is intertwined with your own heart.

But here's the magic: Once you identify your Big Five, life's fog of uncertainty starts to clear. Suddenly, decisions have a measure, a litmus test. Does this align with my Big Five? If not, maybe it doesn't deserve my precious time. Such clarity transforms not just the big choices but the daily ones, giving every action purpose and direction.

Perhaps your Big Five includes your children, creating art, physical wellness, spiritual growth, and philanthropy. Or maybe it's entrepreneurship, adventure, lifelong learning, storytelling, and community-building. The specifics of your Big Five aren't for anyone else to dictate; they're uniquely calibrated to your journey.

So dare to define them. In doing so, you create a life filter that refines choices and focuses your path. The Big Five isn't a limit but a liberation, freeing you to live with unmatched purpose and joy.

So what are your Big Five?

The Mirage of Downward Comparison

There's a peculiar trap many of us fall into —a distortion in our perception of success. It's the whisper in our ears that says, "If they have it, it means there's less for me." This is the realm of downward comparison, a silent saboteur of contentment.

We see someone achieving, be it in career, love, or life in general, and an instinctual pang of envy or inadequacy emerges. But why? Does their accomplishment truly deplete our own potential? No. The world isn't a zero-sum game. One person's success doesn't vacuum away our opportunities.

Here's a fresh perspective. When you admire something in another, it often resonates because it's a reflection of something you value, something that exists within you. That talent, that skill, that joy —if you can see it and appreciate it in another, it means you already possess a kernel of it in yourself.

Think of admiration as a compass. It's pointing you towards what you desire, what you could potentially nurture in your own life. Instead of envying the entrepreneur, perhaps there's a business in you waiting to come to life. Instead of being jealous of a writer, perhaps there's a story within you yearning to be told. Every quality you admire in another is a silent testament to your own potential. Don't let downward comparison blind you to your brilliance.

Next time you feel the sting of comparison, try this: Celebrate their achievement and then dive deep within and ask, "Why does this resonate with me?" The answer will be enlightening.

The Upper Limit Problem

Gay Hendricks introduced a fascinating concept in his groundbreaking book, *The Big Leap*. He coined it as the "upper limit problem," and it refers to the psychological or emotional barriers and self-imposed ceilings that prevent us from fully embracing positive feelings or greater levels of success and happiness. It's the invisible ceiling we set for ourselves.

Why is it that just when things seem to be going wonderfully, we self-sabotage? Why, after a streak of productivity or a surge of creativity, do we suddenly freeze? Hendricks argues that we hit our upper limit, a deep-seated belief that we've reached the peak of what we're worth.

Recognizing you're facing an upper limit problem can be transformational. Here are some signs to help you determine if you're grappling with a ULP.

- **Self-sabotage**. Just as everything seems to be going smoothly in your life, whether in relationships, work, or personal achievements, you suddenly make a mistake or create a drama that undermines your success.

- **Downplaying success**. You deflect compliments or downplay achievements, finding it challenging to accept and internalize your successes.

- **Procrastination.** When on the verge of a significant breakthrough or decision that could elevate your situation, you start to procrastinate or become indecisive.

- **Distraction with minor issues**. Rather than focusing on significant growth opportunities or joyous experiences, you become preoccupied with trivial problems or get bogged down in minutiae.

- **Reverting to old, unhelpful patterns.** Even after making progress, you find yourself slipping back into outdated habits or mindsets that don't serve your best interests.

- **Feeling out of sorts after good news.** Instead of feeling elated after receiving good news or achieving something significant, you feel off-balance, sad, or even depressed.

So how do we transcend this ceiling?

- **Awareness**. Recognize the pattern. Start by tuning into moments when you're feeling out of sorts after a victory. Ask, "Is this my upper limit showing its face?"

- **Question the limiting belief.** Dig deep. What narratives are playing on repeat in the back of your mind? Maybe it's "I don't deserve this," or "This is too good to last." Identify them. Write them out.

- **Reframe and rebuild.** Once you've pinpointed those stories, rewrite them. If the old narrative was "I'm not good enough," pen a new story: "I am continually evolving and I embrace the abundance that comes my way."

- **Celebrate the small wins.** Instead of downplaying your successes, celebrate them. Let the joy sink in. This recalibrates your emotional setpoint and stretches your upper limit.

- **Stay committed to growth.** Committing to lifelong growth means accepting that expansion sometimes comes with discomfort. Embrace it.

By recognizing and actively working against your self-imposed ceilings, you grant yourself the freedom to leap into broader horizons. So today, break through your ceiling and expand your limits.

Day 358

Actions Express Priorities

Intentions can be seductive, can't they? They paint pictures of possibility, articulate our dreams, and express our deepest values. Yet they remain in the realm of thought until propelled into the world of action.

It's like the difference between reading a recipe and tasting a meal. One is an idea; the other is an experience. The real substance, the true flavor of our lives, is found not in what we say we value but in what we demonstrate through our actions.

Our actions are not just external behaviors; they are profound expressions of our innermost priorities. They reveal what truly matters to us more honestly than words can convey. They are our values made visible.

What do your actions say about your priorities? If you say you value health but never make time for exercise or good nutrition, what's the truth? If you say you value relationships but spend no quality time with loved ones, what's the reality?

We often think our intentions are enough — that wanting or meaning to do something is the same as doing it. But intentions without actions are like unopened gifts: their value remains locked inside.

So let's embrace the honest mirror of our actions. Let's align our behaviors with our beliefs, knowing that through this alignment we genuinely live our values, not just speak them.

Day 359

Reframing the Story

Many of us go through life like directors of a play, waving our arms frantically to position the actors just so. We hope that if we can get everyone in their right places, the story will fall into harmony. There's a fundamental flaw in this approach: You can't control the other actors, and often they don't even know they're in your play.

Your mother with her set ways, your best friend with their quirks, or even your children with their budding personalities — none of them are puppets on your stage. To expect them to transform based on your script is to set yourself up for a life of frustration and resentment. They have their own plays in which they, too, are trying to be the directors.

But here's the liberating truth: In the grand theater of your life, there's one character over whom you have absolute control: yourself.

Imagine if, instead of trying to rearrange the stage, you focus on developing the protagonist — you. What if you cultivate resilience, understanding, flexibility, or any other trait that helps you navigate the dynamic play of life?

Suddenly, you're not burdened by the need for others to change. You adapt, you grow, and your story shifts not because the world bent to your will but because you chose to rewrite your role in it.

In this evolution, you discover the potent magic of personal transformation. Your world changes not by external reconfiguration but by the profound shift within the main character. The true power lies in rewriting yourself.

Day 360

What I'm Trying to Teach My Kids

In the beautiful journey of raising my kids amid the whirlwind of life's demands, there are two core values that I hold dear and return to time and time again: courage and compassion. These are the bedrock we're trying to build our family values on.

I strive to instill in my children the courage to face their fears, to step outside their comfort zones, and to embrace uncertainty with open hearts. Courage is not the absence of fear but the strength to take action despite it. I want my children to understand that through facing challenges, they will grow and discover their true potential.

Equally important is the value of compassion. In a world that often seems harsh and divided, I want my children to learn the power of empathy and kindness. I encourage them to see the beauty in others, recognize that we all carry our own struggles and vulnerabilities, and remember that a kind word or gesture can make all the difference in someone's day.

Teaching these values is not just about words but about embodying them in my own actions and interactions. The most influential lessons aren't those spelled out loud but those lived out. So what values are you living?

Living one's values isn't just a personal commitment; it's a promise to everyone we influence. It's a silent but powerful message that says, "This is what I believe in, and this is how I show it." The real question is: Are the values we preach aligned with the values we practice?

Day 361

The Flow of Influence

The root of the word *influence* comes from the Latin *influere*, which means "to flow in." Like a river. A current. An endless cycle of giving and receiving, flowing and moving.

What's remarkable is that this influence isn't one-directional. It doesn't just flow from you to others. It also flows from others to you. Ideas, inspiration, and wisdom flow in and out, circulating, shaping, and reshaping.

You can see this in the people who have shaped your life: the mentors who guided you, the authors who inspired you, and the friends who supported you. Their influence flowed into you, shaping your thoughts, your character, and your path.

And now that influence flows from you. Perhaps to a colleague you advise, a child you nurture, or even a stranger you assist in a small, seemingly inconsequential way. It doesn't have to be grand or dramatic. Influence is often subtle, quiet, but powerful. You can decide to let the best of what flows into you flow out of you again.

As you go through your day, week, and life, think about this flow of influence. Recognize it. Respect it. Nurture it.

What will you do with your influence today? What will you allow to flow into you? And where will you direct that flow as it moves on from you, continuing its journey through the landscape of humanity?

Day 362

Beyond Identities

There's an allure to labels that neatly package ourselves into categories and roles. "I'm an entrepreneur," "I'm a vegan," "I'm an introvert." These identities provide a sense of belonging, understanding, and, to some degree, a roadmap for behavior. But what if the very act of defining is, in essence, confining?

Every identity we attach to ourselves is a limitation. It's a self-imposed boundary that dictates how we should act, react, and even think. But what lies beyond these boundaries?

Authenticity. It's the state of simply being without layers, without masks, without the weight of expectations. It's the space where you don't react based on what a particular identity would do; you act based on the pure, unfiltered essence of the moment.

Letting go of identities doesn't mean rejecting all roles or responsibilities. Instead, it's an invitation to interact with the world without a pre-defined script; to be curious, open, and spontaneous.

In shedding these carefully curated identities, you might find something profound: a freedom, a lightness, an authenticity that's more genuine than any role you could play. It's in this space, unburdened by labels, that you truly meet yourself.

Day 363

How Escaping Entraps Us

We've all felt it: the instinctual pull to avoid discomfort, pain, or confusion. It's human nature to seek the path of least resistance. At a glance, this might seem like a formula for a peaceful life; avoid the challenges, and surely tranquility will follow.

But there's a deeper truth at play that's somewhat counterintuitive: Sidestepping discomfort often leads to a self-made prison where we become trapped in a loop of evasion.

Think of discomfort as a signal. It might indicate a lesson to be learned, a fear to be confronted, or a change awaiting embrace. When we consistently sidestep these signals, we're not merely delaying a moment of discomfort; we're setting up barriers around ourselves. Each evasion becomes a brick in a wall that over time encircles us, leaving us confined within our own created limitations.

In our quest for immediate comfort, we build our own long-term prison. By running from challenges, we restrict our growth, limit our experiences, and stifle our potential. The very act of escaping becomes the chain that binds us.

Breaking free demands confronting the issues we want to flee from. By facing these discomforts we resolve them, but we also dismantle the walls brick by brick, allowing ourselves space to grow, learn, and thrive.

So when challenges emerge, as they inevitably will, it's worth pausing to ask: "By avoiding this, am I building another wall around me?" The path to true freedom isn't found in evasion but in facing challenges head-on. In confronting discomfort, we liberate ourselves from the self-imposed constraints that running away creates.

Day 364

The Ultimate Investment

There's a wealth that outshines any bank balance or gold reserve. It's not measured in dollars or precious gems, but in seconds, experiences, and choices. This currency? Your life. Every decision and every moment contributes to the narrative you're crafting.

Think of life as your portfolio. Just as in finance, we juggle risk and reward. Yet here, the stakes are moments, memories, relationships, dreams, and purpose. We're not just managing money; we're curating a lifetime.

Here's the heart of this book: Your life, every single day, is the most significant investment you'll ever invest in.

There's no stock tip or insider trading advice that can rival the returns of investing in your own growth, deepening your relationships, and pursuing what sets your soul on fire. These returns are measured not in dividends but in joy, contribution, and fulfillment.

Now imagine if we approached our days with the same meticulous care we give to our financial investments. What if we studied our choices not for monetary gains but for gains in happiness, knowledge, and love?

That's the invitation of this book: to shift your focus, reallocate your life's resources, and see every day as an opportunity to invest in the boundless potential of your own journey. In the market of life, you're both the investor and the investment. Make it count.

Day 365

New Page

A year. It sounds like a long stretch of time when it begins, doesn't it? But looking back, it seems to have flown by in the blink of an eye. This past year? Just another chapter in the constantly evolving storybook of your life. It was brimming with highs and lows, unexpected twists, surprise turns, moments of elation, and deep lessons.

Yet if there's one thing I've realized, it's this: Our life's story is never stagnant. The end of a chapter only marks the beginning of another. And as the calendar pages turn to reveal a brand-new year, we're presented with a blank slate, a fresh page. It's not just a change in date; it's an opportunity to reimagine, redefine, and reignite our passions.

Now here's the most powerful part: You're the storyteller. This tale? It's yours to write. With every thought, decision, and action, you craft the narrative. So as you stare at that fresh page, I urge you to write with conviction, clarity, and purpose.

Reflect on the journey you've had, but don't anchor yourself to it. The horizon is vast, beckoning with untapped potential and adventures you haven't even conceived. Stay fervent in your pursuits. Remain inquisitive. And even when the path gets hazy, maintain a laser-like focus on your direction.

Keep pushing boundaries, expanding horizons, and always, always believing in the remarkable entity that is you. You've got what it takes and then some. Remember, every chapter you've lived has shaped you, but it's the unwritten ones that hold the magic. Embrace them.

Acknowledgments

Kelsey, from the depths of my heart, I owe so much of this journey to you. Your unwavering support and the inspiration you've ignited within me have been the foundation upon which this book was built. Every word and idea that flowed from my pen was influenced by your presence in my life. Without you as my steadfast rock and ever-present muse, this accomplishment would remain a distant dream. I am eternally grateful.

To Daxton and Donovan, my dynamic duo: You are the radiant beams of light in my universe, revealing a dimension of love within me that's far grander than I ever imagined possible. Every day, I strive, learn, and grow in my journey as a father, aiming to match the magnitude of love and joy you both bring into my life. You inspire me to be better, to do better, and to love without boundaries. Thank you for being the compass of my heart. Your presence is my greatest joy.

Mom and Dad, in every line of this book, I see the foundation of the roots you set for me and the wings you gave me, constantly encouraging me to see how high I could fly. This book and my life have been fueled by your infinite love and my wish to make you proud. With each passing day, the gift of you as my parents becomes even more precious.

Tommy Cassel, for a quarter of a century you've been my unwavering companion, sharing every step and every milestone. The path to this achievement would have been incomplete without your enduring presence and support. It's an immense privilege to journey through life with you and wear the badge of 'old friend' with immense pride and gratitude.

Yen Liow, as both a cherished friend and a guiding mentor you've illuminated my path, revealing clarity even in the darkest of times. Your wisdom and insight not only showed me the way but truly unlocked the potential within me. I am eternally grateful for the light you've been and the laughter you've brought into my life.

Bob Turco, as a coach, mentor, and friend, you imparted to me the invaluable lesson that I am my only limit. Your belief in me and that powerful advice, "The only person who can stop Sean DeLaney is Sean DeLaney," has been a guiding star in every challenge I've faced. My journey is richer and brighter because of the potential you recognized and nurtured within me, and I will forever carry a deep sense of gratitude for the gifts you've bestowed upon me.

Mary Beth, I am deeply grateful for your commitment and for the pivotal role you've played in bringing this vision to life.

To everyone who has paved the way before me so I could walk this path, thank you.

About the Author

For over a decade, Sean DeLaney has been an empowering force, masterfully navigating the territories of peak performance, innovative entrepreneurship, and impactful personal development. Transitioning from a career as a professional athlete, Sean now shines as a top-tier executive life coach and the driving force of the What Got You There Podcast. Through his coaching, Sean has influenced a myriad of CEOs, executives, and athletes, fostering their growth and success. His unwavering mission is to enable individuals to discover and leverage their boundless potential, guiding them to a life of deeper meaning and fulfillment.

To learn more about how Sean can help you on your journey, check out

Whatgotyouthere.com